An Introduction to Japanese Phonology

SUNY Series in Linguistics
Mark R. Aronoff, Editor

AN INTRODUCTION TO JAPANESE PHONOLOGY

Timothy J. Vance

State University Of New York Press

Published by
State University of New York Press, Albany

© 1987 State University of New York

For information, address State University of New York
Press, State University Plaza, Albany, N.Y., 12246

Library of Congress Cataloging-in-Publication Data

Vance, Timothy J.
   An introduction to Japanese phonology.

   (SUNY series in linguistics)
   Bibliography: p.
   Includes index.
   1. Japanese language—Phonology. I. Title.
II. Series.
PL540.V36   1986   495.6′15   86-5800
ISBN 0-88706-360-8
ISBN 0-88706-361-6 (pbk.)

10   9   8   7   6   5   4   3   2   1

For Kishiko and Karen

CONTENTS

PREFACE

This book represents my attempt to provide a broad survey of interesting topics and important issues in Japanese phonology. Faced with the prospect of teaching a course on the structure of Japanese for linguistics students, I found myself at a loss for an appropriate phonology text, and colleagues teaching similar courses at other universities expressed the same feeling. I am certain that no one will be entirely satisfied with my choice of topics, but I think the coverage is reasonably comprehensive. The almost total lack of material on intonation is a glaring omission, but unfortunately I have nothing worthwhile to contribute at present. It goes without saying that I have no definitive answers to any of the questions I raise, and my hope is that the discussion will stimulate readers to pursue those questions further.

I have tried to appeal to a broad range of readers by not presupposing a great deal of background in linguistics, but I assume familiarity with the basic concepts, terminology, and notation in four areas. The first of these is articulatory phonetics, including IPA transcription and rudimentary vocal tract anatomy. The second is traditional phonemic analysis, which involves such notions as contrast, complementary distribution, and free variation. The third is traditional morphophonemic analysis, including allomorphy and alternation. The last is generative phonology, which involves distinctive features, underlying forms, phonological rules, and derivations.

When I use a less familiar term, I capitalize its first occurrence. I explain some of these terms in the text, but in most cases I simply provide a reference. As far as possible, these references are to introductory textbooks or other readily available sources; I do not attempt to cite original sources for well-established jargon. My purpose is simply to make it possible for a reader who is unfamiliar with a particular term to find an explanation, and I hope these references will not prove too distracting for readers who do not need them.

In spite of this effort to serve a wide audience, some sections of the book touch on theoretical questions that are not likely to be of much interest to non-linguists. Readers with only minimal background will probably have difficulty with sections 5.3, 8.5, 9.6, 9.7, 12.4, and 12.5.

Other readers will be disturbed to find so little discussion of recent "three-dimensional" theories. My decision to exclude such discussion was motivated primarily by the desire to keep the book within the reach of as many readers as possible.

A number of people contributed directly to my writing, and I would like to thank all of them here. Shōko Hamano, Samuel E. Martin, James D. McCawley, Katsuhiko Momoi, and S. Robert Ramsey read the entire manuscript and provided many helpful suggestions. Alice Faber, Yoshiko Higurashi, and D. Gary Miller all read and commented on individual chapters. Some thoughtful criticisms from Gerald B. Mathias on a paper I presented improved Chapter 3. Shigeyuki Kuroda corresponded with me for several years about the material in Chapter 9, and I owe much of the data there to him. Conversations with Kunihiko Imai, Alexis Manaster-Ramer, and Richard Rhodes also contributed to Chapter 9, as did an unpublished review by David Johns. Cynthia Chennault helped me with some of the etymologies in Chapter 11, and Pierre Ramond calculated the probabilities I cite in Chapter 12. Hiroko Itō and Kōzaburō Kurokawa administered the questionnaire described in Chapter 12 to their students at Sagami Joshi Daigaku, and Shōko Hamano helped with the pilot study. Rosalie M. Robertson, Marilyn Semerad, and the people at the State University of New York Press put the manuscript into production. My wife, Kishiko Hayashi, put up with incessant requests to say idiotic things. The defects that remain are, of course, entirely my own responsibility.

Chapter *1*

INTRODUCTION

1.1 MODERN STANDARD JAPANESE

I will use the term MODERN STANDARD JAPANESE to mean a variety of the Tokyo dialect typical of educated, middle-class natives of the YAMANOTE ('uptown') region. This region comprises roughly the western half of Tokyo proper and the western suburbs. This variety is more prestigious than that of the older, eastern part of the city known as SHITAMACHI ('downtown'). The normative standard language (**hyōjungo**) is based on the Yamanote variety (Nakamura and Kindaichi 1955).

This book is a synchronic account of the phonology of modern standard Japanese, but I will consider historical developments whenever I can to provide some background for the present situation. I will use the term OLD JAPANESE to refer to the language of the oldest existing written records. These texts data from the eighth century and presumably reflect the spoken language of the aristocracy in Nara, the capital city at that time.

1.2 VOCABULARY STRATA

It is convenient to divide Japanese morphemes into four groups on the basis of differences in phonological characteristics (McCawley 1968:62–75). These differences include the inventory of phonemes that occur, the range of phoneme sequences that occur, and the morphophonemic alternations that affect the morphemes. NATIVE JAPANESE morphemes are generally the modern descendants of morphemes that were part of the Japanese vocabulary before heavy borrowing from Chinese occurred. SINO-JAPANESE morphemes are typically the modern descendants of morphemes that entered Japanese in several waves of borrowing from Chinese that began about 400 (see section 11.4.1). RECENT BORROWINGS have entered Japanese from languages other than Chinese, mostly European languages. MIMETIC morphemes are involved in an elaborate system of SOUND SYMBOLISM (Lyons 1977:104) and occur almost exclusively in a class of manner adverbs that I will call MIMETIC ADVERBS. Such adverbs are commonly called ONOMATOPOETIC (McClain 1981:202).

Many of the morphemes in the native Japanese group were undoubtedly borrowed long ago, some even from Chinese (Miller 1967:237), but they are so thoroughly assimilated that there is no point in treating them as a separate class. Some Sino-Japanese morphemes were coined by Japanese as Sino-Japanese pronunciations for Chinese characters invented in Japan (Tsukishima 1964:63). The great bulk of recent borrowings have entered Japanese in this century from English, although a few European loans date back as far as the sixteenth century. Some of these older loans behave like native or Sino-Japanese morphemes (see sections 1.3 and 10.2.3). Mimetic morphemes are just as native as those in the native Japanese group but show several phonological differences (see sections 5.3, 9.4.5, 10.2.3, and 10.4).

1.3 ORTHOGRAPHY

The Japanese struggled for centuries to adapt the Chinese writing system to their needs (Miller 1967:90–140), and the modern system that has evolved is undoubtedly the world's most complicated orthography. For the most part, each character in the Chinese system represents a morpheme, and in general, this is how the modern Japanese system represents Sino-Japanese morphemes. Chinese characters are called KANJI ('Han(-Chinese) letters'), and each morpheme in a Sino-Japanese word is written with a single kanji.

In many cases, kanji have come to be used for native Japanese morphemes with similar meanings. For example, the same kanji is used to write the Sino-Japanese morpheme **ken** 'dog' and the native Japanese monomorphemic word **inu** 'dog'. The Sino-Japanese morphemes associated with a kanji are known as its ON-YOMI (literally, 'sound readings'), and the native Japanese morphemes as its KUN-YOMI (literally, 'meaning readings').

The Japanese also developed a syllabic system called KANA, in which a small set of simplified kanji were used for their sound values alone. Since the Chinese writing system uses one character for each syllable, kana made it possible to write any Japanese word by spelling it out syllable by syllable. Subsequent phonological changes in Japanese have altered the syllable structure, and single kana letters represent moras rather than syllables in modern standard Japanese. (I will treat the distinction between moras and syllables in sections 7.1–7.3.) There are also some digraphs, but I will still refer to this system as the "kana syllabary." There are two varieties of kana, the cursive HIRAGANA and the squarish KATAKANA. Each has the same number of letters corresponding to the same set of sounds.

Chinese differs radically from Japanese in grammatical structure, and one of the problems in adapting Chinese writing was that there were no Chinese morphemes (and therefore no kanji) corresponding to many of the grammatical endings and particles that play such an important role in Japanese. In modern Japanese orthography, these endings and particles are spelled out in hiragana, while noun, verb, and adjective stems are generally written in kanji. For example, **nobore**, the imperative of a verb meaning 'climb', is written by using a kanji for **nobo** and a hiragana letter for **re**. The polite past of the same verb, **noborimashita**, is written with the same kanji followed by four hiragana letters, one each for the four syllables **ri-ma-shi-ta**. Native and Sino-Japanese morphemes for which kanji are no longer in general use are also commonly written in hiragana. Children's books ordinarily use hiragana to write native and Sino-Japanese morphemes for which the readers are not likely to know the kanji.

Recent borrowings are generally written in katakana, but some old and well-assimilated loans from European languages are commonly written in kanji or in hiragana. For example, the noun **tabako** 'tobacco' was borrowed from Portuguese in the sixteenth century (Umegaki 1966). It is sometimes written in hiragana, and there is no phonological reason why it could not be a native Japanese morpheme. It can also be written with two kanji meaning 'smoke grass', but this spelling is an example of a special use of kanji. The morphemes ordinarily associated with these two kanji are Sino-Japanese **en** 'smoke' and **sō** 'grass' and native Japanese **kemuri** 'smoke' and **kusa** 'grass', but clearly none of these is involved in **tabako**, which is monomorphemic. The kanji are used for their semantic values alone, disembodied from any morphological structure. This practice is something like using +% to write the English noun *interest* (on a loan).

The noun **kappa** 'rain cape', another sixteenth-century Portuguese loan (Umegaki 1966), is often written with two kanji meaning 'fitting feather'. This spelling originated as another kind of special kanji use that we might call a "rebus." In other words, the kanji were chosen primarily for their sound values. In particular, there is a Sino-Japanese morpheme associated with the first kanji and a native Japanese morpheme associated with the second that could give the pronunciation **kappa** in combination. It is possible, though perhaps not very likely, that some modern speakers interpret this word as an idiomatic combination of two morphemes meaning 'fitting' and 'feather', and presumably semantic considerations played some role in the original choice of this spelling over other possibilities that would be even more farfetched.

In addition to recent borrowings, katakana spellings are often used to indicate emphasis. Mimetic adverbs frequently appear in katakana, since they are often emphatic.

I transliterate most Japanese words and names in the modified Hepburn romanization used, for example, in Masuda (1974), but I depart from this practice in two ways. First, for the sake of convenience, I omit the macrons from the place names **Tōkyō** and **Kyōto**. Second, in references to English language publications by Japanese authors, I retain whatever spellings those authors use for their own names. I give Japanese personal names in the English order, that is, given name first and surname second.

Chapter 2

ARTICULATORY SETTING

.

2.1 DEFINITION

Abercrombie (1967:91–93) defines VOICE QUALITY as "those characteristics which are present more or less all the time that a person is talking: it is a quasi-permanent quality running through all the sound that issues from his [or her] mouth." This definition differs from common usage in that it excludes temporary qualities used for specific purposes or in specific situations. For example, Japanese women typically use BREATHY VOICE (Laver 1980:132–135) when being very polite, and this voice quality is characteristic of the young women who work as elevator operators in Japanese department stores (McCawley, personal communication, 1984). Work on transient voice qualities of this kind would surely prove interesting, but I will not pursue this topic here.

Laver (1978:1) divides voice quality into intrinsic features and extrinsic features. Intrinsic features are never under the speaker's control; they simply reflect the anatomy of the speech organs. As Abercrombie (1967:91–93) notes, intrinsic features cannot be learned and therefore serve only to identify speakers as individuals or as members of some group of people with certain physical characteristics in common. Extrinsic features, on the other hand, reflect what Laver calls "long-term muscular adjustments of the intrinsic vocal apparatus, which were once acquired by social imitation or individual idiosyncrasy and have become habitual." Speakers are generally not aware of these muscular adjustments or their auditory effects. Although they must be learned in some sense, Abercrombie points out that "the habit of such muscular tensions can, once acquired, be so deeply rooted as to seem as much an unalterable part of a person as his [or her] anatomical characteristics."

I am concerned here with the extrinsic features of voice quality that are acquired by social imitation and not those that are idiosyncratic. Voice qualities can be characteristic of particular languages or dialects (Abercrombie 1967:94), and this chapter treats the extrinsic features characteristic of modern standard Japanese.

Honikman (1964) introduces the term ARTICULATORY SETTING to refer to the extrinsic muscular adjustments involved in voice quality. Laver (1978:1) points out that "while the term itself is new, the general concept is not." Laver surveys the historical development of the concept of articulatory setting and notes that the more familiar term BASIS OF ARTICULATION has been in use since the late nineteenth century.

Laver (1980:3–4) describes a rather wide variety of phenomena as articulatory settings, but Honikman (1964) restricts her attention to the articulatory settings of particular languages, that is, to features of the kind that are relevant here. Laver (1980:9–10) interprets Honikman's characterization as involving two essential aspects. The first is the notion of features common to the individual segments of a language. Honikman (1964:73) says, "Articulatory setting does not imply simply the particular articulations of the individual speech sounds of a language, but is rather the nexus of these isolated facts and their assemblage, based on their common, rather than their distinguishing, components." Laver describes this notion as "the highest common factor in the various segmental articulations of a language."

The second aspect of Honikman's characterization is the idea that segments contribute to the setting in proportion to their frequency. Honikman (1964:76) says, "The internal articulatory setting of a language is determined, to a great extent, by the most frequently occurring sounds and sound combinations in that language." Laver describes this as giving "a statistical weighting to the contribution of individual segments on the basis of their frequency in the spoken language."

Laver (1978:11) suggests a refinement involving the relationship between segments and settings. He says that "no articulatory setting normally applies to every single segment a speaker utters." For example, as Laver points out, a speaker with a nasal voice quality still produces oral stops. On the other hand, when such a speaker produces distinctively nasal segments, the contribution of the setting is redundant. Laver proposes a distinction between segments that are SUSCEPTIBLE to the influence of a setting and those that are not. A setting would then apply only to susceptible segments. Keeping this important reservation in mind, I will now turn to descriptions of the articulatory settings of English and Japanese.

2.2   THE SETTINGS FOR ENGLISH AND JAPANESE

Honikman (1964) gives a quite detailed account of the articulatory setting for standard British English, although she does not consider all the parameters listed by Laver (1980:14–15). The description covers lip, jaw, and tongue activity, and I will consider each of these in turn. Someda (1966) takes Honikman's work on English as a point of departure and compares the articulatory setting for standard Japanese.

Honikman (1964:74–75) says that in English, "on the whole the lips neither round vigorously nor spread very much but mostly remain rather 'neutral' — slightly and loosely apart, slightly cornered and with only moderate mobility." Honikman compares this characteristic with French, in which she says there is much greater lip activity and frequent energetic rounding. In Russian, on the other hand, she says the lips are generally spread, with only intermittent rounding. Someda (1966:331) cites Hattori (1951:89) and says that in Japanese the lips play almost no active role in pronunciation; they are neither rounded nor spread, but neutral. Someda goes on to claim that although lip rounding is relatively weak in English, it is even weaker in Japanese. My impression is that my own midwestern American English has the same kind of moderate lip activity that Honikman describes for British English. I also agree with Someda that lip activity in Japanese is weaker.

As for jaw activity, Honikman (1964:80–81) says that in English there is almost no movement and that the jaws are held "loosely together," whereas in French the average position is "slightly open." Someda (1966:330) interprets Honikman's description of French to mean that the degree of jaw opening is large, and he says that Japanese is between English and French. My impression is that Honikman's characterization of English fits midwestern American English quite well, and I agree with Someda that the average position in Japanese is distinctly more open.

Honikman (1964:80) mentions that the most frequent vowels in English seem to be [ɪ] and [ə], whereas the low vowel [a] is relatively more frequent in French. It is not necessary to open the jaws to pronounce [ɪ] or [ə], but it is to pronounce [a]. Someda (1966:331) investigated the ratio of low to high vowels in several languages, and the figures of interest here are as follows: English, 0.41, Japanese, 0.78, and French, 1.68. Someda does not explain how he arrived at these figures, but presumably he divided the number of low vowels in some text by the number of high vowels. The results appear to support the claim that Japanese is intermediate between English and French in terms of average jaw opening, but the low vowels in one language may differ considerably in jaw opening from the low vowels in another. It is therefore not clear what these figures really mean.

Tongue activity is the most complicated aspect of articulatory setting that I will consider. Honikman (1964:76–77) says that in English "the tongue is tethered laterally to the roof of the mouth by allowing the sides to rest along the inner surfaces of the upper lateral gums and teeth." She refers to this tethering as the ANCHORAGE of the tongue, and in English it leaves the tip free to move. Honikman claims that alveolar consonants are more frequent than any others in English, and she takes this fact as indicative of the anchorage she describes. She says that during alveolar articulation, the tip of the tongue is tapered and the body of the tongue is somewhat concave to the roof of the mouth.

Someda (1966:334–335) says that the anchorage in Japanese is lightly and centrally on the floor of the mouth, and he describes the average position of the tongue as that for the low back vowel [ɑ]. The tip of the tongue is not tapered, and the body of the tongue is convex to the roof of the mouth, with the dorsum slightly raised and the tip behind the lower front teeth. This anchorage makes it very easy to move to the other back vowels and to the velar consonants, and Someda gives figures on frequencies to support the claim that such back articulations are characteristic of Japanese. He reports that the ratio of back to front vowels is 0.36 in French, 0.50 in English, and 2.12 in Japanese. One problem with these figures is that Someda counts Japanese /a/ as a back vowel. We will see in section 3.1.1 that this is the only low vowel in modern standard Japanese, and for some speakers it is probably more central than back. Someda also reports that 27 percent of all consonants in Japanese are velar, and he says that this percentage makes velars the most frequent consonants in Japanese and much more frequent than in English or French.

It should be clear even from this cursory survey that articulatory setting is an important topic. In discussing the relationship between articulatory setting and ordinary phonetic segments, Laver (1980:3) argues that the two are not complementary. A segment-by-segment analysis should, he says, describe the phonetic quality exhaustively. The description of an articulatory setting is then a second-order analysis in which certain features are abstracted out of a complete segmental description. The segmental descriptions we ordinarily encounter, however, are not exhaustive, and Laver concedes that it is convenient to discuss an articulatory setting as if it had some independent existence. Honikman (1964:74) says, "Where two languages are disparate in articulatory setting, it is not possible completely to master the pronunciation of one whilst maintaining the articulatory setting of the other."

Chapter *3*

VOWELS

3.1 SHORT VOWELS

3.1.1 Phonetic Description

Japanese has five phonemically distinct short vowels, as illustrated by **ki** 'tree', **ke** 'hair', **ka** 'mosquito', **ko** 'child', and **ku** 'phrase'. Nihon Onsei Gakkai (1976:735) compares the Japanese vowels to the so-called CARDINAL VOWELS of Daniel Jones (Abercrombie 1967:151–162). The traditional description of a vowel articulation involves specifying the highest point of the tongue, with lip activity as an independent variable. Ladefoged (1971:67–75) and others have argued persuasively that vowels involve acoustic targets and cannot be specified in articulatory terms, but I will retain the familiar articulatory terminology for the sake of convenience. The entire range of possible positions of the highest point of the tongue is called the VOWEL AREA, and the cardinal vowels are points on the periphery of the vowel area that serve to mark its perimeter.

If an x-ray photograph is taken from the left side of a person's head, the lips will be at the left, and the back of the head will be at the right. The highest point of the tongue will also be visible, and viewed from this angle, we can represent the vowel area with a diagram, as in [1]. The locations of the highest point of the tongue for the eight "primary" cardinal vowels are connected with solid lines. Nihon Onsei Gakkai (1976:735) cites an unidentified x-ray experiment and superimposes the articulations for the five Japanese vowels on the vowel area. The locations of the highest point of the tongue for the Japanese vowels are connected with broken lines. Although the description does not say so, the Japanese vowels were probably pronounced in isolation, that is, with no preceding or following sounds.

Sakuma (1973:32) says that the phonetic symbol generally used for the Japanese high front vowel is [i], and the diagram in [1] shows this vowel with the same tongue position as cardinal [i]. Kawakami (1977:21) agrees that the Japanese vowel is essentially cardinal [i], and he equates it with French [i] (as in **qui** 'who'). Sakuma, however, claims that it is different from the high front unrounded vowel in French or German, and his description indicates that the difference is a lack of lip spreading in Japanese. This description is in keeping with the lack of lip activity in the articulatory setting for Japanese (section 2.2). I will transcribe this vowel phonemically as /i/.

Sakuma (1973:32) says that for most Tokyo speakers, the mid front vowel is between the qualities ordinarily represented by [e] (as in French **état** 'state') and [ɛ] (as in English *set*), and the diagram in [1] supports this description. Kawakami (1977:21–22) gives a similar description, but he says that the Japanese vowel is closer to the English vowel in *set*. This may be because the standard British pronunciation of words like *set* has a slightly higher vowel than the standard American pronunciation. Sakuma uses British *air*, which he transcribes [ɛɑ], to illustrate [ɛ], and this vowel is certainly lower than the one in British *set*. I will transcribe the Japanese vowel phonemically as /e/.

Sakuma (1973:33–34) describes the Japanese low vowel as between French [a] (as in **pas** 'not') and (British) English [ɑ] (as in *father*), and the diagram in [1] indicates that this description is accurate. Kawakami (1977:22) says that the range of individual variation for the Japanese vowel is rather wide and includes cardinal [a] and [ɑ]. This variation may account for the quite front character of the Japanese vowel that Homma (1973:353) reports, using spectrograms of her own pronunciation. I will transcribe this vowel phonemically as /a/.

Sakuma's (1973:34) description of the Japanese mid back vowel puts it between the qualities ordinarily represented by [o] (as in French **beau** 'beautiful') and [ɔ] (as in English *saw*), and here again the diagram in [1] agrees. Kawakami (1977:23) describes this vowel as the only one in Japanese that involves active lip rounding. Sakuma says that although the lips are pursed, the rounding is weak, and this weakness is in accord with the lack of lip activity in the articulatory setting for Japanese (section 2.2). I will transcribe this vowel phonemically as /o/.

Sakuma (1973:34) characterizes the Japanese high back vowel as conspicuously different from the French [u] (as in **nous** 'we'). For one thing, he says, the place of articulation is quite different. The diagram in [1] shows the highest point of the tongue rather far forward of cardinal [u], and this position agrees with Kawakami's (1977:23) description. More salient, however, is the difference in lip activity. The Japanese vowel is commonly described as unrounded, and it is often transcribed [ɯ]. It certainly does not involve the vigorous lip rounding of

[1]

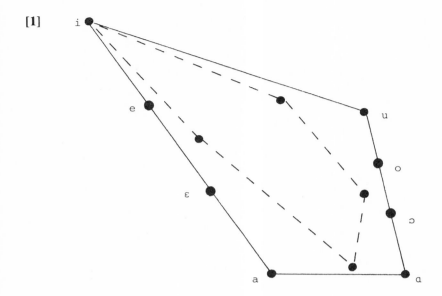

French [u]; nonetheless, there is obvious lip activity for the Tokyo speakers I have observed closely.

To describe the Japanese high back vowel accurately, we need to distinguish two different kinds of lip activity. Ladefoged (1971:62) suggests the terms LIP ROUNDING and LIP COMPRESSION. In rounding, the corners of the mouth are brought forward and the lips are protruded. In compression, the jaws are closed, bringing the lips together vertically so that the side portions are in contact. The Tokyo speakers I have observed closely pronounce the high back vowel with clear lip compression in very careful speech. My impression is that this compression is substantially weaker, and sometimes totally absent, in connected speech at normal conversational tempo. This observation suggests that although the compression overrides the articulatory setting (section 2.2) in careful speech, the setting begins to dominate in more rapid speech. I will transcribe this vowel phonemically as /u/.

The only one of the Japanese vowels commonly described as having positional allophones is /u/. Sakuma (1973:35) says that after [s] and [z], /u/ is farther front than in other contexts, and Kawakami (1977:24) agrees. Homma's (1973:352–353) measurements indicate a fronted /u/ not only after alveolar fricatives and affricates (sections 4.3.1 and 4.4.1) but also after the alveolar nasal /n/ (section 4.5) and the high front glide /y/ (section 4.6.2).

In connected speech, of course, all vowels are influenced to some extent by the vowels in neighboring syllables. Acoustic measurements show such influence clearly (Hattori et al. 1957:90), but the perceptual effects seem to be minimal in Japanese. Arisaka (1940:13) mentions allophones of /a/ that depend in part on nearby vowels, but he says the differences disappear in careful speech.

3.1.2 Utterance-Final [ʔ]

Bloch (1950:130) says that a glottal stop occurs after a short vowel and before a pause, but only in a few expressions, most of which are interjections. His examples are **to** [toʔ] 'so saying', **che** [cçeʔ] 'ugh!', and **kora** [koɾɑʔ] 'hey!'. Martin (1952:13) gives a similar account, and both he and Bloch (1950:141) assign this glottal stop to an independent phoneme. I will argue, however, that examples of this kind do not warrant a separate glottal stop phoneme.

My impression is that a short vowel before a pause is always followed by a rapid closing of the glottis. When a word like **ko** 'child' is pronounced in isolation, this abrupt offset makes it easy to tell that the vowel is short. When a word like **kō** 'thus' is pronounced in isolation, the long vowel fades away more gradually. Not surprisingly, the glottal stop after a short vowel is more salient when a speaker is excited and emphatic. My claim is that this glottal stop is present after any utterance-final short vowel, and the reason Bloch and Martin recognize it only in interjections and particles is simply that these are the words most likely to end emphatic utterances.

There is an orthographic convention by which this final glottal stop in emphatic utterances is represented with the kana letter for the syllable **tsu** reduced in size. (This same device is used for the mora obstruent; see section 5.2.2.1.) A well-known Japanese-English dictionary (Masuda 1974) lists several words with final glottal stops, and in the romanization a vowel followed by a glottal stop is marked with a breve (˘), a convention I will follow here. Comic books with dialogue involving a lot of shouting are good sources of examples, and those in [2] are all from Fujikawa and Hio (1974).

[2] a. Kōgeki shirŏ! 'Attack!' (page 9)
   b. Yoshi, utĕ! 'OK, fire!' (page 9)
   c. Kusŏ 'Shit!' (page 96)
   d. Yamato ga kieta zŏ!
      'The Yamato's disappeared!' (page 113)
   e. Kanzen ni Mokusei no inryoku ni tsukamarimashită!
      'We're completely trapped by Jupiter's gravity!' (page 128)
   f. Kono kosumogan wa nīsan no aiyō shite ita mono dă!
      'This cosmo-gun's the one my brother used to use all the time!'
      (page 147)

Examples [2a] and [2b] end with imperative verb forms, which are usually spoken emphatically. Example [2c], like the English translation, is a noun used as an expletive, and example [2d] ends with the emphatic particle **zo**. Example [2e] ends with a polite verb form and is shouted out in fear, while example [2f] ends with the copula.

Since Japanese is a rigid verb-final language, verb forms and sentence particles naturally predominate in utterance-final position, but any word can be shouted in exasperation or anger and can thus constitute an emphatic utterance. The orthographic practice in comic books is probably not very consistent, but the examples in [2] suggest that any short vowel before a pause in an emphatic utterance can be spelled with a following glottal stop. Bloch's (1950) examples would support a separate phoneme if a word like **to** 'door' could never occur with a following glottal stop, since this would differentiate it from **to** 'so saying'. But although **to** 'door' is not particularly likely to occur at the end of an emphatic utterance, if it did, the final glottal stop would become salient and the pronunciation would be no different from that of an emphatic **to** 'so saying'.

To do a thorough treatment of glottal stops in Japanese, I will have to consider additional data, and I will return to the problem in sections 3.2.2, 4.10, and 5.2.4. My tentative conclusion in this section is simply that there is always a nondistinctive glottal stop after a short vowel and before a pause. Kawakami (1977:40) adopts the same position.

The short high vowels /i u/ are regularly devoiced under certain circumstances, and the other short vowels are occasionally devoiced as well. I will treat this topic in detail in Chapter 6.

3.2 LONG VOWELS

3.2.1 Phonetic Description

Each of the five short vowel qualities also occurs long, as illustrated by **onīsan** 'older brother', **onēsan** 'older sister', **okāsan** 'mother', **otōsan** 'father', and **kūki** 'air'. There are no striking quality differences between long and short vowels in Japanese as there are, for example, in German. Long [e:], however, does present a problem.

Many Sino-Japanese morphemes originally had [ei] and are still spelled **ei** in kana orthography. According to Inoue (1977), /ei/ had already become [e:] in the late eighteenth century, and modern Tokyo speakers generally pronounce orthographic **ei** as [e:]. As Kawakami (1977:77−79) points out, however, some morphemes ordinarily pronounced with [e:] can have [ei] under certain circumstances. For example, Sino-Japanese **kei + ki** 'the times' is usually [ke:ki] but sometimes [keiki]. The English loan **kēki** 'cake', on the other hand, can only be [ke:ki]. I have heard Tokyo speakers pronounce orthographic **ei** as [ei] when teaching new words to young children and in songs when the [e] and the [i] are on separate notes. Kawakami says that some words with orthographic **ei** are less likely than others to be pronounced with [ei], and he also says that **hē** 'No kidding!' can be [hei]. In general, however, orthographic **ei** is pronounced [ei] in very careful pronunciation, while orthographic **ee** is not.

Long [o:] is also spelled two different ways, **ou** and **oo**, but there is no contrast in pronunciation. Kawakami (1977:79) claims that no one would ever pronounce **ou** as [ou], and I know of no reason to doubt this statement.

The vowel sequences /e + i/ and /o + u/, with a morpheme boundary intervening, are not uncommon. Typical examples are compounds such as **ke + iro** 'hair color' (from **ke** 'hair' and **iro** 'color') and **ko + ushi** 'calf' (from **ko** 'child' and **ushi** 'cow'), and nonpolite nonpast verb forms such as **araso + u** 'fight'. In recent borrowings, /ei/ and /ou/ can even occur within morphemes, as in **Supein** 'Spain' and **Souru** 'Seoul'. The vowel sequences in these cases are ordinarily pronounced [ei] and [ou], and Maeda (1971:172) claims that **ke + iro** does not have [e:] even in sloppy pronunciation unless the speaker does not recognize the morpheme division. My impression, however, is that /e + i/ and /o + u/ frequently become [e:] and [o:] in rapid speech.

3.2.2 Phonemicization

Bloch (1950:139) phonemicizes long vowels as two identical vowel phonemes in succession and says that a long vowel is equal in duration to two short vowels. Han (1962a:69–70), however, reports measurements showing that a long vowel is approximately twice as long as a short vowel only when no consonant precedes. In words of the form CV and CV̄, the duration of the long vowel is considerably greater than twice the duration of the short vowel. When the durations of the entire words are compared, however, Han's measurements show a one-to-two ratio. I will argue in Chapter 7 that Japanese has short and long syllables and that a short syllable like CV consists of one mora while a long syllable like CV̄ consists of two moras. Han's results indicate that a long syllable is approximately twice as long as a short syllable, and she interprets a long syllable like CV̄ as consisting of the mora /CV/ followed by the mora /V/, with the two moras roughly equal in length.

Other writers have argued that a long vowel should be phonemicized as a short vowel followed by a length phoneme. Kindaichi (1950), for example, adopts this position on the basis of pairs like **sato + oya** 'foster parent' (from **sato** 'village' and **oya** 'parent') and **satō + ya** 'sugar shop' (from **satō** 'sugar' and **ya** 'shop'). Martin (1952:13) says that in slow speech, VOWEL REARTICULATION (Catford 1977:89) sometimes occurs between vowels belonging to different morphemes. Bloch (1950:139) describes vowel rearticulation as "a diminution in loudness between the two vowels (sometimes accompanied by a slight glottal constriction) and a renewed pulse of expiration on the second," and Martin treats it as an allophone of his glottal stop phoneme (section 3.1.2). Kindaichi claims that ordinarily **sato + oya** is [satoʔoja] (where [ʔ] is presumably vowel rearticulation) and **satō + ya** is [sato:ja]. This difference leads Kindaichi to the conclusion that **sato + oya** should be phonemicized as /satooya/ and **satō + ya** as /sato:ya/, where /:/ is a length phoneme. Martin says that the rearticulation in slow speech disappears in more rapid speech, and it generally does, but Bloch (1950:139–140) points out some phonological environments that favor the retention of rearticulation even at faster tempos. The two words under consideration here, however, are doubtless both [sato:ja] at a fast tempo.

Kawakami (1977:74–76) considers the distinction between **mā** 'well' and the **ma a** in **Iku ma aru?** 'Is there time to go?'. He transcribes **mā** as [ma:] and describes it as "indivisible," by which he means that it constitutes a single long syllable. He transcribes **ma a** as [maa] and describes it as "divisible." This statement apparently means that it consists of two short syllables, and vowel rearticulation is undoubtedly one signal of the difference. In addition, there is an accent (Chapter 8) on the second **a**, also indicating that there are two syllables (sections 7.3.2 and 8.3.1). The words **ma** and **aru** in Kawakami's example sentence are separated by a major syntactic division, and the vowel rearticulation is probably less likely to disappear than in **sato + oya**. Nonetheless, [mɑːɾɯ] is certainly possible in rapid speech.

Pike (1947) argues that grammatical information such as word and morpheme boundaries has always been a prerequisite for phonemicization, and such boundaries are used freely in generative phonology. If we attribute vowel rearticulation to the presence of a boundary, it is unnecessary to distinguish between divisible and indivisible in terms of a difference in segmental makeup. The fact that vowel rearticulation seems to be more resistant to elimination in **ma aru** than in **sato + oya** is a natural consequence of a "stronger" boundary. As Hamada (1955b:37–38) points out, once we allow reference to a boundary, we can represent **sato + oya** as /sato + oya/ and **satō + ya** as /satoo + ya/, and there is no need for a length phoneme.

Maeda (1971:150–163) notes that when recent borrowings are written in katakana in modern Japanese orthography, the same symbol (a straight line) is used to represent the second mora of any long-vowel syllable. This is an obvious orthographic parallel to a length phoneme. According to Nihon Onsei Gakkai (1976:755), this spelling convention was introduced for all long vowels in elementary school textbooks in 1900. It was later restricted to borrowings written in katakana, and Maeda says that there has been no resistance to adopting it. Nonetheless, Maeda himself argues against a length phoneme. His suggestion is that long-vowel syllables are indivisible units that extend over two moras. The mora for Maeda is simply a timing unit, and a syllable that occupies two moras need not be divisible into two mora-length parts. In any event, the treatment of long vowels is controversial, but I will phonemicize them as /VV/. (I will transcribe morphemes that can have [ei] with /ei/; see section 3.2.1.)

I have already noted that **sato + oya** and **satō + ya** merge as [satoːjɑ] at faster tempos, but Kawakami (1977:76) points out that the distinction between the two also disappears in a kind of overly precise pronunciation. He says that it is possible to pronounce long-vowel syllables as two short syllables when reading a word list very slowly and with great care, and in this style the two words merge as [satoʔojɑ], where [ʔ] represents vowel rearticulation.

Linell (1979:54–56) distinguishes CAREFUL PRONUNCIATION from ELABORATED PRONUNCIATION, and says that phonological representations should be based on the former. Elaborated pronunciation is used when a speaker wants to articulate the sounds of a word very distinctly. Linell says that SHARPENING PROCESSES apply in elaborated pronunciation, and that some of them neutralize phonemic distinctions. An example from English is the overly precise pronunciation of *train* as [tʰɹ̩ein], with a syllabic [ɹ]. This pronunciation obliterates the distinction between *train* and *terrain*.

It seems reasonable to attribute pronunciations of Japanese long-vowel syllables as two short syllables to a sharpening process of this kind, and this treatment makes such pronunciations irrelevant to determining phonological representations. It is clear from Kawakami's (1977:76) discussion that he would be comfortable with this conclusion.

Sakuma (1973:35) compares the nonpast verb form **suu** 'suck' (which can be analyzed as a stem **su** plus an inflectional suffix **u**; see section 12.3) with the noun **sū** 'number' and says that the vowel quality shifts in the former but remains steady in the latter. As we saw in section 3.1.1, Japanese /u/ is commonly described as having a front allophone after alveolars, and I will follow Sakuma in transcribing the back allophone as [ɯ] and the front allophone as [ü]. Sakuma says that **su + u** is pronounced [süɯ], while **sū** is pronounced [sü:].

Kindaichi (1950:146–147) cites this example in support of his argument for a length phoneme. He would phonemicize the two words as /suu/ and /su:/, but the boundary treatment will obviously work just as well. Neither Sakuma nor Kindaichi mentions anything about vowel rearticulation in **su + u**, but I suspect that the vowel quality shift disappears when the rearticulation does. According to Kindaichi, not all Tokyo speakers make the vowel quality distinction in words of this type.

3.3 NONIDENTICAL VOWEL SEQUENCES

In Old Japanese, syllables consisting entirely of a vowel almost never occurred except word-initially (Hashimoto 1948:240–241). Since all syllables at that time had the form /(C)V/ (or perhaps /(C)(G)V/, where G is a glide; see sections 7.1 and 11.1.1), there were almost no word-internal vowel sequences. Hashimoto notes that when vowel sequences arose in compounds, or even in phrases, they were sometimes eliminated by vowel deletion, and he cites examples like those in [3].

[3] **a.** hanare 'isolation' + iso 'beach'
      hanareso 'isolated beach'
   b. wa 'I' + ga (genitive particle) + ihe 'house' wagihe 'my house'

In other cases, the two consecutive vowels were replaced by a single vowel of intermediate quality (Miller 1967:193), as in **sakeri** 'are blooming', from **saki** 'blooming' + **ari** 'are'.

Borrowings and historical consonant losses in native words have left modern Japanese with many word-internal vowel sequences. All possible /V_1V_2/ combinations occur, although many are rare morpheme-internally (Martin 1952:13). Given a sequence of nonidentical vowels in modern standard Japanese, it is not obvious whether the second vowel should be analyzed as a separate syllable or as the second half of a diphthong. The answer will not necessarily be the same in every case, and I will return to this problem in section 7.5.

Chapter *4*

CONSONANTS

4.1 CONSERVATIVE AND INNOVATING VARIETIES

Massive borrowing from English and other European languages over the last century or so has had a substantial impact on the Japanese phonological system. Modern Tokyo speakers fall along a continuum in terms of how thoroughly recent borrowings are assimilated to the native phonemic pattern. At one extreme, which I will call the CONSERVATIVE VARIETY, such borrowings are completely assimilated. At the other extreme, which I will call the INNOVATING VARIETY, several phones occur in new environments, and in some cases the result has been a PHONEMIC SPLIT (Bynon 1977:29–30). These labels correspond to Bloch's (1950: 116) "innovating dialect" and "conservative dialect." There are also intermediate varieties that have some but not all of the innovations. My description of the consonant system will cover the two extremes of this continuum. Any intermediate variety can be described by eliminating a subset of the extra sequences allowed in the extreme innovating variety.

4.2 STOPS

4.2.1 Place of Articulation

There are six distinctive stops in Japanese, as illustrated by **pan** 'bread', **ban** '(one's) turn', **tan** 'cinnabar', **dan** 'level', **kan** 'can', and **gan** 'cancer'. The bilabials [p b] and the velars [k g] are essentially identical in place of articulation to their English counterparts, but [t d] are somewhat different. Edwards (1903: 52–53) and Sakuma (1929:151–152) both describe Japanese [t d] as "intermediate" between the similar sounds in French and English. Someda (1966:335) says that the Japanese sounds are "lamino-alveolar," which means that the blade of the tongue (the part just behind the tip) is the lower articulator and the alveolar ridge is the upper articulator (Catford 1977:143). He describes French [t d] as "lamino-dental" and English [t d] as "apico-alveolar." Nihon Onsei Gakkai (1976:492) labels Japanese [t d] "blade-point" sounds and describes them as having the tip of the tongue touching the back of the upper front teeth and the blade of the tongue pressing against the gums to make the closure.

As we saw in the discussion of articulatory setting (section 2.2), in English [t d] the tip of the tongue is tapered and curled up to the alveolar ridge. This position makes the body of the tongue slightly concave to the roof of the mouth. Someda (1966:335) says that the body of the tongue is convex to the roof of the mouth in Japanese and French [t d]. He also says that the tapering in English makes the tongue tenser and increases the pressure of the closure. Edwards (1903:52–53) remarks that the tongue is very flat in Japanese [t d], and Sakuma (1929:151–152) attributes this flatness to a relative lack of tongue tension in the Japanese sounds. Presumably, the lack of lateral constriction for tapering leaves the tongue relatively flat from side to side.

I will transcribe the Japanese stops phonemically as /p b t d k g/.

4.2.2 Aspiration

Impressionistic descriptions of Japanese /p t k/ show a curious lack of agreement about aspiration. Sakuma (1929:208) says that they are almost always unaspirated. Bloch (1950:129) says that they are "slightly aspirated" except in the second half of a geminate (i.e., after the mora obstruent; see section 5.2). Hattori (1951:138) says that word-initial /p t k/ are aspirated, although not as strongly as their English counterparts. Kawakami (1977:72, 103) simply says that word-initial /p t k/ are usually aspirated.

Lisker and Abramson (1964) describe voicing and aspiration in stops in terms of VOICE ONSET TIME (VOT), which is the time between the release of a stop closure and the onset of vocal cord vibration in a CV sequence. VOT is relatively easy to measure on spectrograms, and Lisker and Abramson indicate that typical VOT is 0–25 milliseconds for voiceless unaspirated stops and 60–100 milliseconds for voiceless aspirated stops. In voiced stops, the onset of vibration precedes the release of the closure, and the VOT is negative.

Homma (1980:9) reports a mean VOT of 25 milliseconds for word-initial /t/ in Japanese and argues that this mean falls between the typical means for voiceless unaspirated /t/ and voiceless aspirated /tʰ/ in several other languages. If Japanese /p t k/ really are intermediate in this sense, they would be counterevidence to Lisker and Abramson's (1971:770) claim that "by and large, there is rough agreement across languages in the placement of category boundaries along the dimension of voice onset timing, yielding three phonetic types: voiced, voiceless unaspirated, and voiceless aspirated stops."

It is important to remember, however, that phonological context can have an effect on VOT. Lisker and Abramson (1967:16) note that VOT for both voiceless unaspirated and voiceless aspirated stops is greater in stressed syllables, and Homma (1981:276) reports greater VOT for Japanese /p t k/ in accented syllables, although Japanese has pitch accent rather than stress accent (Chapter 8). This factor would account for Hattori's (1951:138) claim that the aspiration of the /k/ in /kata/ 'shoulder' is stronger than that of the /k/ in /naka/ 'middle', since both words have first-syllable accent. Homma also compares VOT after single and geminate stops, but finds no difference.

All the tokens of /t/ measured in Homma (1980) were in the word /tada/ 'free', which has first-syllable accent. The mean VOT of 25 milliseconds therefore does not seem out of line with the Lisker and Abramson suggestion of three universal phonetic types. Keating, Mikoś, and Ganong (1981:1261–1262) report the VOT of initial stops in isolated disyllabic words in Polish. All these words have first-syllable stress, and the measured mean for Polish /t/ is 27.9 milliseconds. These authors describe Polish voiceless stops as "unaspirated or slightly aspirated," and they do not hesitate to assign them to Lisker and Abramson's voiceless unaspirated category.

In summary, there is no solid evidence that Japanese /p t k/ fall between the putatively universal voiceless unaspirated and voiceless aspirated types in terms of VOT. We must simply keep in mind that unaspirated stops do not ordinarily have a VOT of zero but rather a relatively short VOT. I therefore tentatively conclude that Japanese /p t k/ are voiceless unaspirated, but VOT in Japanese certainly deserves further study.

4.2.3 Intervocalic Weakening

Japanese /b g/ are sometimes pronounced as fricatives [β γ] intervocalically, but /d/ does not weaken in parallel fashion (Kawakami 1977:33). Many standard speakers have [ŋ] noninitially, but whether [g] and [ŋ] are allophones of a single phoneme or separate phonemes for such speakers is a difficult question. I will consider this problem in depth in Chapter 9. Kana orthography does not distinguish between [g] and [ŋ], and I will phonemicize all orthographic **g**'s as /g/.

4.3 FRICATIVES

4.3.1 Articulation

The word **fune** 'boat' begins with a sound that is commonly described as a voiceless bilabial fricative [ɸ] (Nihon Onsei Gakkai 1976:817, Catford 1977:146). Sakuma (1929:139–142) says that the friction is generally very weak, and this statement seems accurate. Bloch (1950:131) describes this sound as bilabial or labiodental, and he also says that in most environments [h] can occur instead, although it rarely does. I suspect that Bloch's observations are another reflection of the lack of lip activity in the articulatory setting for Japanese (sections 2.2 and 3.1.1). My impression is that a weak bilabial fricative is the norm in careful speech. In less careful pronunciation, the lips are less likely to come together, but the lower lip and upper teeth happen to be approximated, and a weak labiodental fricative sometimes results. Although this labiodental is quite different from the voiceless labiodental fricative in English, I will transcribe it as [f]. Sometimes the opening between the lower lip and upper teeth is so large or the airstream so weak that there is no audible supraglottal turbulence. This possibility accounts for Bloch's [h] in place of [ɸ] or [f], and in fact, this [h] is probably rather common.

The words **asa** 'morning' and **aza** '(village) section' contain alveolar fricatives [s z] that are essentially identical to their English counterparts. Bloch (1950:131, 133) describes them as grooved alveolar fricatives. Catford (1977: 127, 153–155) explains that in a GROOVED FRICATIVE, air escapes through a relatively narrow central depression or groove running from front to back between the tongue and the roof of the mouth. In a SLIT FRICATIVE such as English [θ], on the other hand, the tongue is flatter and air escapes through a relatively wide and flat channel. Catford argues, however, that the shape of the channel is far less important than its location and its cross-sectional area in determining the acoustic quality of a fricative.

The word **shima** 'island' begins with a voiceless fricative somewhat farther back than [s]. The IPA symbol for this sound is [ɕ], and Catford (1977:159) describes it as dorso-prepalatal, which means that the lower articulator is the dorsum and the upper articulator is the area just behind the alveolar ridge. Catford (1977:143) defines the blade of the tongue as the first 10 to 15 millimeters behind the tip, and the dorsum as the remainder of the tongue's upper surface. [ɕ] involves the more anterior portion of the dorsum. Bloch (1950:131) says that Japanese [ɕ] is a grooved prepalatal fricative, and this description seems accurate, although the groove is not as narrow as it is in [s].

Bloch (1950:133) also mentions [ʑ], the voiced counterpart of [ɕ], but he says that some speakers do not have it. My impression is that it does not occur in careful speech. I will mention [ʑ] again in section 4.4.2.5.

The word **himo** 'string' begins with a voiceless dorso-palatal fricative [ç], which is somewhat farther back than [ɕ]. This sound occurs in many English dialects as the first sound in words like *huge*, but it is probably best known as German "**ich-laut**." Sakuma (1929:138–139) says that in most environments a "palatalized *h*" [h,] can appear instead of [ç]. This [h,] is presumably like the initial sound of words like *heat* in many English dialects. In my own speech, the supraglottal constriction generally produces audible friction for the first sound in *huge* but not for the first sound in *heat*. Kawakami (1977:49) says that it is only when a voiceless vowel (Chapter 6) follows that [ɸ ç] can never be replaced by [h h,].

The word **hema** 'blunder' begins with a glottal fricative [h] essentially identical to its English counterpart. According to Yoshioka (1981:38), so-called voiced *h* [ɦ] frequently occurs instead intervocalically, as it does in English in words like *behind*. Kawakami (1977:49) says that this does not happen in very careful pronunciation. According to Abercrombie (1967:59), the vocal cords are vibrating along part of their length and are just close together along the rest of their length in [ɦ].

4.3.2 Distribution

4.3.2.1 [ɸ f ç h, h ɦ]

It is clear from the discussion in section 4.3.1 that [ɸ] and [f] are variants of a single phoneme. The same is true for [ç] and [h,] and also for [h] and [ɦ], since [ɦ] is an intervocalic variant of [h]. In this section I will consider the distribution of [ɸ f], [ç h,], and [h ɦ], and for convenience I will refer to them simply as [ɸ], [ç], and [h].

There is general agreement that [ɸ], [ç], and [h] are in complementary distribution in the conservative variety, although Bloch (1950) is forced to conclude otherwise because of his treatment of voiceless vowels (section 6.5). The conditioning factor is the following segment, and we find [ɸ] before /u/, [ç] before /i y/, and [h] elsewhere, i.e., before /e a o/. In the innovating variety, [ç] and [h] have this same distribution, but [ɸ] occurs before all vowels. For example, we find [ɸi] in **firumu** 'film', [ɸe] in **feruto** 'felt' [ɸɑ] in **fan** '(sports) fan', and [ɸo] in **fōku** 'fork'. Conservative speakers pronounce these words with [ɸuV], [hV], or [çV] instead of [ɸV]. I will transcribe [ç h] as /h/ and [ɸ] as /f/.

4.3.2.2 [s ç]

In the conservative variety, [s] and [ç] contrast before /a o u/, as in **sakai** 'boundary', **sōkai** 'general meeting', and **sūkai** 'several times', with initial [s], versus **shakai** 'society', **shōkai** 'introduction', and **shūkai** 'assembly', with initial [ç]. Only [s] occurs before /e/, and only [ç] occurs before /i/. In the innovating variety, [ç] also occurs before /e/, as in **sherī** 'sherry', and there are probably very few modern Tokyo speakers who do not pronounce any words with [çe].

Hattori (1955:287) says that both [çe] and [si] occur in recent loans but that they are hard for most people to pronounce. This account is not satisfactory, however, because, as Kawakami (1977:46) points out, Japanese speakers find [çe] very easy to pronounce. [si], on the other hand, is very difficult, and loans from English like **shīsō** 'seesaw' and **shīzun** 'season' begin with [çi]. Neither Umegaki (1966) nor Masuda (1974) lists any word as having initial [si].

I will transcribe [s] as /s/ and [ç] as /š/. Although the relevant historical developments are not completely clear (Miller 1967:192–193, 202, Okumura 1972:119–121), /s/ and /š/ are both descendants of a single Old Japanese phoneme. One reflection of this fact is the /s/~/š/ alternation in modern standard verb morphology (section 12.2.5.1); we find /š/ before /i/ and /s/ before other vowels, as in /kaš + ita/ 'lent' versus /kas + u/ 'lend'. In fact, an alternative analysis of modern standard Japanese treats [s] and [ç] as allophonic variants, with [ç] appearing before /i/ and /y/, but I will argue against this analysis in section 4.8.

4.3.2.3 Merger of [ç] with [ɕ]

One of the features invariably cited to distinguish Yamanote speakers from Shitamachi speakers (section 1.1) is the merger of [çi] with [ɕi] in the Shitamachi dialect. Nakamura and Kindaichi (1955), for example, say that Shitamachi speakers pronounce **hibachi** 'brazier' as **shibachi** and **hidoi** 'terrible' as **shidoi.** Martin (1952:12) points out that the pronunciation with the merger is considered substandard, and he also notes that Shitamachi speakers have [ç] instead of [çj] (e.g., [ço:] for **hyō** 'chart'). Hattori (1958:360) defines the Tokyo dialect he analyzes as the one that differentiates /hi hya hyo hyu/ from /ši ša šo šu/.

Many standard speakers sometimes pronounce [ɕi] instead of [çi], but my impression is that the replacement is generally confined to certain common words in which the /i/ is devoiced (Chapter 6), such as **hito** 'person' and **hitotsu** 'one'.

There is also an interesting lexical shift that is apparently related to the [ç ɕ] merger. Many Yamanote speakers say **futon o hiku** to mean 'spread out a futon'. The "correct" verb is **shiku** 'spread out', but **hiku** 'pull' is also semantically reasonable, since a **futon** is folded up for storage and must be pulled on to spread it out for use. This use of **hiku** almost certainly originated as a HYPERCORRECTION (Bynon 1977:185–186) by speakers with only [ɕi] in their native dialect. In attempting to imitate the prestige standard, such speakers are likely to go too far and replace some standard [ɕi] sequences with [çi]. Because of the semantic plausibility of **hiku** in this particular case, it has caught on to some extent among standard speakers, and the desire to avoid sounding like a Shitamachi speaker probably works in favor of **hiku**. Even if a Yamanote speaker knows that **shiku** is "correct," there is always the danger that it will be taken as a stigmatized pronunciation of **hiku** by listeners.

4.3.2.4 [z]

[z] is an allophone of a phoneme that I will transcribe as /z/. The other principal allophone is an affricate, and I will discuss their distribution in detail in section 4.4.2.3.

4.4 AFFRICATES

4.4.1 Articulation

The word **tsu** 'harbor' begins with the voiceless alveolar affricate [ts], and the word **zu** 'illustration' begins with the corresponding voiced affricate [dz]. The initial sound in **chi** 'blood' is a voiceless affricate with the same dorso-prepalatal place of articulation as the fricative [ç] (section 4.3.1). Catford (1977:159) transcribes this affricate as [cç], where [c] alone stands for a voiceless palatal or prepalatal stop. The initial sound in the word **ji** 'letter' is the voiced counterpart of [cç], which Catford transcribes as [ɟʑ].

4.4.2 Distribution

4.4.2.1 [t ts]

According to Bloch (1950:130), the only vowel that can follow [ts] in the conservative variety is /u/. Since [t] cannot occur before /u/, it would seem reasonable to treat [ts] as an allophone of the phoneme /t/, but Bloch's treatment of voiceless vowels makes this analysis impossible for him (section 6.5). Hattori (1958:361) cites examples like **otottsan** 'father' and **gottsō** 'feast' as instances of [tsɑ] and [tso] in native words, but Kawakami (1977:52) describes these as nonstandard Tokyo dialect forms. One Yamanote speaker that I asked told me that only "country people" use such forms.

In the innovating variety, [ts] appears before /e a o/, as in **tsetsebae** 'tsetse fly', **tsaitogaisuto** 'Zeitgeist', and **kantsōne** 'canzone', and standard speakers find [tse tsɑ tso] very easy to pronounce. I do not know of any well-established loanwords with [tsi], and we might expect this sequence, like [si] (section 4.3.2.3), to be difficult for standard speakers. Momoi (personal communication, 1984) informs me, however, that when the movie **South Pacific** appeared in Japan, Mitzi Gaynor's first name was spelled **mittsi**, and many speakers pronounced it with [tsi]. In any case, [t] and [ts] clearly contrast in the innovating variety, and I will transcribe them phonemically as /t/ and /c/.

The sequence /tu/, if it occurs at all, is rare in the innovating variety. The only word listed in Masuda (1974) with initial /tu/ is the musical term **tutti** 'tutti'. Bloch (1950:162) does not list /tu/ as a possible sequence in the innovating variety, and English /tu/ is usually borrowed as /cu/, as in **tsūran** 'two-run homerun'.

4.4.2.2 [t ts cç]

In the conservative variety, [t] and [cç] clearly contrast before /a o/, as in **ta** 'field' versus **cha** 'tea' and **tō** 'ten' versus **chō** 'trillion', and [ts] and [cç] contrast before /u/, as in **tsūka** 'currency' versus **chūka** 'minting'. [cç] also occurs before /e/ in the interjection **chĕ** (section 3.1.2), and [te] sequences, as in **te** 'hand', are common. Only [cç], and not [t] or [ts], occurs before /i/, as in **chi** 'blood'. I will transcribe [cç] phonemically as /č/.

In the innovating variety, /t/ occurs before /i/, as in **aisutī** 'ice tea', as well as before /e a o/. Bloch (1950:159) says that /t/ is palatalized in this environment and that conservative variety speakers have /č/ instead. In addition, /č/ is common before /e/ in recent borrowings like **chekku** 'check' and **chero** 'cello'.

/t/, /c/, and /č/ are all descendants of a single earlier phoneme. It appears that this phoneme was a stop in all environments in Old Japanese and that affricate allophones developed before high vowels in the fifteenth or sixteenth century in Kyoto (Okumura 1972: 124–125). There is a /t~c~č/ alternation in modern standard verb morphology (section 12.2.5.1); we find /c/ before /u/, /č/ before /i/, and /t/ before other vowels, as in /kac + u/ 'win' versus /kač + i/ 'winning' versus /kat + oo/ 'let's win'. An alternative analysis of modern standard Japanese treats [t] and [cç] as allophonic variants, with [cç] appearing before /i/ and /y/, but I will argue against this analysis in section 4.8.

4.4.2.3 [dz z]

There is no contrast between [dz] and [z] in either the conservative or the innovating variety. Apparently there used to be a distinction between [zɯ] and [dzɯ], but missionary accounts indicate that it was disappearing in Kyoto by about 1600, and it probably had already disappeared in the Tokyo area by then (Toyama 1972:198–202). Bloch (1950:141) does not recognize a [dz] phone at all, and Sakuma (1973:46) recognizes only [dz]. Arisaka (1940:57–58) claims that [dz] always occurs in careful speech, but my impression is that consistent [dz] is characteristic only of elaborated pronunciation (section 3.2.2). According to Kawakami (1977:52–53), [dz] always appears word-initially and after the mora nasal (section 5.1), but [z] usually appears intervocalically, although not always. Kawakami's account is certainly the most accurate for the standard speakers I have observed, although I think [z] may sometimes appear word-initially when a pause does not precede.

4.4.2.4 [d dz z]

In both the conservative variety and the innovating variety, [d] and [dz z] contrast before /e o a/, as in **den** 'palace' versus **zen** 'goodness', **danki** 'warmth' versus **zanki** 'remaining time', and **dō** 'how' versus **zō** 'elephant'. I will transcribe [d] and [dz z] phonemically as /d/ and /z/.

4.4.2.5 [ɟʑ ʑ]

There is no contrast between [ɟʑ] and [ʑ] in either the conservative or the innovating variety. It appears that a distinction between [ʑi] and [ɟʑi] was disappearing by 1600 in Kyoto, and like the [zɯ] versus [dzɯ] distinction (section 4.4.2.3), it probably had already disappeared in the Tokyo area (Toyama

1972:198–202). As noted in section 4.3.1, [z̧] does not seem to occur in careful pronunciation, and Bloch (1950:133) says that some speakers have [z̧] as a rare variant of [ɟ̧z̧]. Kawakami (1977:54) claims that [z̧] is frequent intervocalically, and perhaps it is in rapid speech, but standard speakers find this sound difficult or impossible to produce when asked. I will ignore [z̧] hereafter.

4.4.2.6 [d dz z ɟ̧z̧]

In the conservative variety, [ɟ̧z̧] contrasts with /d/ before /a o/, as in **jakyō** 'heresy' versus **dakyō** 'compromise' and **jōken** 'condition' versus **dōken** 'same prefecture'. [ɟ̧z̧] also contrasts with /z/ before /a o u/, as in **jama** 'obstruction' versus **zama** 'state', **jōsen** 'embarkation' versus **zōsen** 'shipbuilding', and **jukei** 'serving time' versus **zukei** 'diagram'. Only [ɟ̧z̧] occurs before /i/, and /d/ does not occur before /u/. I will transcribe [ɟ̧z̧] phonemically as /ǰ/.

In the innovating variety, /d/ appears before /i/, as in **dīzeru** 'diesel'. Bloch (1950:160) notes that /d/ is palatalized in this environment and that conservative speakers use /ǰ/ instead. In addition, /ǰ/ appears before /e/, as in **jesuchā** 'gesture'. Conservative speakers use /z/ instead.

4.5 NASALS

Japanese has two contrasting nasals before all vowels and /y/, as in **mi** 'body' versus **ni** 'two', **me** 'eye' versus **ne** 'root', **ma** 'interval' versus **na** 'name', **mo** 'also' versus **no** 'field', **mushi** 'neglect' versus **nushi** 'owner', and **myō** 'strange' versus **nyō** 'urine'. I will transcribe these sounds phonemically as /m/ and /n/. Many Tokyo speakers also have [ŋ] noninitially in the same environments, but as noted in section 4.2.3, it is not obvious whether this is a separate phoneme or an allophone of /g/. I will consider this problem in detail in Chapter 9.

The bilabial /m/ is essentially identical to its English counterpart. Bloch (1950:134) notes that Japanese /m/ is palatalized before /i y/, and the English sound shows similar COARTICULATION (Catford 1977:188) in words like *meat* and *music*. Japanese /n/ has the same lamino-alveolar place of articulation as /t d/ before /e a o u/ (section 4.2.1). Before /i y/, however, it is dorso-prepalatal (section 4.3.1) and quite different from the English /n/ in a word like *need*. There is no special symbol for a prepalatal as opposed to a palatal nasal [ɲ] (Catford 1977:159). Sakuma (1929:159–162) uses his own symbol [ṅ] for the Japanese allophone and does not identify it with the [ɲ] in Spanish **año** 'year' or French **ligne** 'line'. I will return to the question of palatalization in section 4.8.

4.6 GLIDES

4.6.1 [ɰ]

Sakuma (1929:110) says that the Japanese back glide is articulated exactly like the high back vowel, and he transcribes it phonetically as [ɰ], that is, as a nonsyllabic [ɯ]. This glide thus has the same kind of lip activity as /u/ (section 3.1.1), and I will transcribe it phonemically as /w/.

When the hiragana came into use around 900 (Miller 1967:125), there were letters for /wa/, /wi/, /we/, and /wo/. /wi we wo/ appear to have merged with /i e o/ by about 1200 in Kyoto (Tsukishima 1964:29, Okumura 1972:99–102), and most accounts of modern standard Japanese say that /w/ occurs only before /a/ (Bloch 1950:135). Kawakami (1977:55), however, gives examples that he says contain /wo/ and /we/.

Kawakami's first example involves what Kuno (1973:19) calls the "superpolite" form of adjectives. In general, in an adjective with a citation form ending in /ai/, /oo/ replaces /ai/ and the word /gozaimasu/ follows. For example, /takai/ 'high' becomes /takoo gozaimasu/. If the adjective /kowai/ 'afraid' follows the same pattern, the superpolite form should begin with /kowoo/.

Kawakami's other example involves the substitution of /ee/ for /ai/ in what he labels "vulgarisms." As Nakamura and Kindaichi (1955) note, the use of /ee/ instead of /ai/ in certain forms is the norm in the Shitamachi dialect (section 1.1). But standard speakers, especially men, replace their normal /ai/ in these forms with /ee/ as a kind of "tough guy" speech. For example, /takai/ 'high' can be pronounced /takee/, and if /kowai/ follows the same pattern, it should become /kowee/.

Kawakami claims that speakers do in fact say /kowoo/ and /kowee/. Of course, one problem with these forms is that speakers probably do not distinguish between /owV/ and /oV/ in ordinary speech. Another problem is that younger standard speakers never use the superpolite form of most adjectives, and when I tried to elicit forms like /kowoo/ from several such speakers in 1978, none of them could produce the morphologically "correct" forms. More recently, one of these speakers (KH) pronounced what sounded to me like [koɰe:], and when I asked her to write it in hiragana, she began the second syllable with the letter for /u/ followed by a reduced-size letter for /e/. This spelling convention is ordinarily confined to katakana renderings of [we] in foreign words in language textbooks, although some dictionaries spell certain recent borrowings this way.

Bloch (1950:160) says that /w/ occurs before all vowels except /u/ in the innovating variety, but neither Umegaki (1966) nor Masuda (1974) lists any words with initial /w/ before a vowel other than /a/. Even younger speakers fluent in English seem to feel that recent borrowings such as **uīkuendo** 'weekend', **uētā** 'waiter', and **uotchi** 'watch' begin with /u/ when used as Japanese words. I therefore conclude that aside from forms like /kowoo/ and /kowee/, /w/ occurs only before /a/ even in the innovating variety.

4.6.2 [j]

Sakuma (1929:109–110) says that when the Japanese front glide precedes /u/, it begins with the tongue in the position for [i]. Before /a/, however, he says it usually begins at about [ɛ], and before /o/, somewhere in between. We might tran-

scribe these sequences phonetically as [iɯ], [ẹo], and [ɣɑ], but phoneticians ordinarily use the symbol [j] for any front unrounded glide to or from a point higher
than the contiguous vowel (Catford 1977:131). I suspect that in very careful pronunciation something approximating [i̯] will occur in all environments. I will
transcribe this sound phonemically as /y/.

According to Bloch (1950:135, 162), /y/ occurs only before the back vowels
/a o u/ in both the conservative variety and the innovating variety. We might expect that the "tough guy" form (section 4.6.1) of an adjective like /hayai/ 'fast'
would be /hayee/, and when I asked the same speaker who pronounced [koɰe:]
(KH), she very clearly pronounced [haje:]. According to Umegaki (1966) and
Masuda (1974), recent borrowings like **iesuman** 'yes man' begin with /i/.

On the basis of Portuguese missionary records, it appears that word-initially
or after a vowel, sixteenth-century Kyoto Japanese had [je] where modern standard Japanese has /e/ (Toyama 1972:238–239). Toyama surmises that the shift
from [je] to [e] took place about 1750, but then it is hard to understand why the
word for the Japanese monetary unit, **en**, was borrowed into English as *yen*. The
earliest citation for *yen* in the *Oxford English Dictionary* is from 1875, which
suggests that [je] has disappeared only in the last century. This conclusion is re-
inforced by the common use of **ye** in pre–World War II romanization. Shand
(1907:9) says, "In the syllable **ye** the **y** is mute in most words, and is sometimes
omitted in the Roman character." His glossary lists /ezoraičoo/ 'grouse' as
yezoraichō (page 15), /ie/ 'house' as **iye** (page 23), and /e/ 'to' as **ye** (page 71),
but most syllables corresponding to modern standard /e/ are written as **e**. This
fact suggests that perhaps the last vestiges of [je] had not quite disappeared in
early twentieth-century Tokyo.

4.7 THE LIQUID

Kawakami (1977:50) says that the Japanese liquid is ordinarily the apico-alveolar TAP [ɾ]. Ladefoged (1971:50–51) defines a tap as a sound formed by throw-
ing one articulator against another, and in [ɾ] the tip of the tongue is thrown
against the alveolar ridge. This is essentially the same sound as the /r/ in Spanish,
Russian, and many other languages. In American English, this sound often occurs instead of [t] or [d] in pronunciations of words like *butter* and *ladder*. This
American English [ɾ] is traditionally called a FLAP, but Ladefoged defines a flap
as a sound in which one articulator strikes against another in passing. Catford
(1977:51), on the other hand, calls both these articulation types flaps and uses
the term FLICK for taps like [ɾ]. I will transcribe the Japanese liquid phonemically
as /r/.

Kawakami (1977:51) claims that in word-initial /r/ the tip of the tongue is already resting very lightly on the alveolar ridge and that the sound is produced by
rapidly releasing this contact. The environment for this allophone is undoubtedly
utterance-initial rather than word-initial, but, in any case, Kawakami describes
the resulting sound as a kind of [d]. According to Nihon Onsei Gakkai (1976:

493), this is why children sometimes mispronounce words like /raǰio/ 'radio'/ as /daǰio/.

Bloch (1950:133) mentions specifically that /r/ is palatalized before /i y/, and it certainly is. In fact, in any sequence /rV/, the /r/ shows coarticulation (Catford 1977:188) in anticipation of the following vowel, to the extent that this coarticulation does not interfere with producing the tap. I will return to the question of palatalization in section 4.8.

Kawakami (1977:51) notes that [l] is sometimes heard for /r/, and Bloch (1950:133) also mentions this pronunciation. Jones (1967:205–206) claims that individual speakers indiscriminately pronounce /r/ as [ɾ], [ɹ] (the English r-sound), a kind of [l], a kind of retroflex stop [ḍ], and other intermediate sounds. He uses the pronunciations of /r/ as an example of what he calls a VARIPHONE, which he says arises when a language has relatively few phonemes and does not require absolute precision in the pronunciation of some of them. There is certainly a great deal of individual variation in the pronunciation of Japanese /r/, but I doubt that most standard speakers are quite as erratic as this account suggests.

Kawakami (1977:51) says that when /r/ is lengthened for emphasis, it is pronounced as [l:], and he argues that if a tap [ɾ] were lengthened, it would become [d:]. As Sakuma (1929:171) points out, however, [ɾ] involves closing off the airstream only in the center, not completely. This means that a lateral results automatically when the contact between the tip of the tongue and the alveolar ridge is held for emphasis. On the other hand, it does seem that the utterance-initial allophone described above begins from a complete, although weakly held, oral closure.

Kawakami (1977:50) points out that an apico-alveolar TRILL [r] (Ladefoged 1971:50) for /r/ is felt to be "rough pronunciation" in Japanese. This trill is another feature of the "tough guy" speech mentioned in section 4.6.1.

4.8 PALATALIZATION AND CONSONANT-GLIDE SEQUENCES

4.8.1 /Cy/ Sequences

According to Bloch (1950:152), /y/ can follow any of several consonants in the conservative variety. I will ignore the mora nasal (section 5.2) here and confine the discussion to tautosyllabic /Cy/ sequences. I will also ignore the velar nasal (Chapter 9). Bloch (1950:129) recognizes /ty/, but only in /tyuu/, a contraction of /toyuu/ (**to iu**) 'saying'. I will tentatively dismiss this example as rapid speech, but I will return to the problem it raises in section 4.8.4. The remaining /Cy/ sequences in Bloch's account are /py by ky gy hy my ny ry/, as in **pyonto** 'hop', **byōki** 'illness', **kyō** 'today', **gyō** 'line', **hyō** 'chart', **myō** 'strange', **nyō** 'urine', and **ryō** 'quantity'.

The consonants /p b k g m r/ are all palatalized before /y/, just as they are before /i/, and /n/ is prepalatal (section 4.5). Bloch (1950:135) says that the voiceless allophone [j] appears after /p k/, but not after /h/. As we saw in sections 4.3.1 and 4.3.2.1, /h/ is usually [ç], but sometimes [h,], before /i/. Bloch (1950:131) says that a word like **hyō** 'chart' can be either [ço:] or [h, jo:], and his treatment of voiceless vowels (section 6.5) forces him to assign [ç] to a phoneme other than /h/. In fact, however, the [j] that appears after /p k/ usually has audible friction at the supraglottal constriction and is therefore phonetically identical to [ç]. In addition, the [ç] at the beginning of the [ço:] pronunciation of **hyō** is distinctly longer than the [ç] at the beginning of, for example, **himo** [çimo] 'string'. A more accurate transcription of **hyō** would be [ç:o:], and we could interpret the extra length of [ç:] as [j]. This would make **hy** parallel to **py** and **ky**, that is, phonetically [Cj] and phonemically /Cy/.

4.8.2   A Four-Vowel Analysis

Bloch (1946a:3, n. 4) suggests a phonemicization for Japanese that greatly increases the symmetry of the system by reducing the number of vowel phonemes to four. As McCawley (1968:64) points out, this analysis is possible only if we exclude certain sequences found in recent borrowings in the innovating variety, and in fact, the /če/ in the native interjection **chě** (sections 3.1.2 and 4.4.2.2) must also be excluded. Bloch (1950:161–165) eventually repudiates the four-vowel analysis even for the conservative variety because his treatment of voiceless vowels (section 6.5) leaves him little choice. But since my treatment of this problem is consistent with the four-vowel analysis of the conservative variety (excluding **chě**), I will consider it here.

Since /y/ occurs only before /a o u/ (aside from forms like /hayee/; see section 4.6.2), the /Cy/ sequences considered in section 4.8.1 all occur only before /a o u/. If we treat [ç] as palatalized /h/ and the prepalatal nasal (section 4.5) as palatalized /n/, we can say that /p b k g h m n r/ are palatalized preceding /i ya yo yu/ and nonpalatalized preceding /e a o u/. If we translate Bloch's (1946a:3, n. 4) suggestion into a more recent framework, we might say that we can set up an underlying /ye/ for what appears on the surface as [i]. We then need a rule to palatalize a consonant before /y/ and another rule to change /ye/ into [i]. This gives us only four underlying vowels and makes all /CV/ and /CyV/ sequences (where /C/ is one of /p b k g h m n r/) admissible in underlying forms.

The phonemes /s š t č z ǰ/ can also be neatly integrated into this analysis. /š č ǰ/ occur only before /i a o u/, and /s t z/ occur only before /e a o u/. (Recall that [ts] can be treated as an allophone of /t/ in the conservative variety; see section 4.4.2.1.) If we analyze /šV čV ǰV/ as underlying /syV tyV zyV/, we simply need to complicate our rules a little so that /sy ty zy/ become [ç cç j̵z] instead of [s, jt, j z,j]. I give sample derivations in [1] for **i** 'stomach', **e** 'picture', **ki** 'tree', **ke** 'hair', **kyō** 'today', **chi** 'blood', **te** 'hand', and **chō** 'trillion'.

[1] Underlying form	/ye/	/e/	/kye/	/ke/	/kyoo/
e → i/y —	yi	—	kyi	—	—
Palatalization	—	—	k,yi	—	k,yoo
y → ∅/ — i	i	—	k,i	—	—
Surface form	[i]	[e]	[k,i]	[ke]	[k,jo:]

Underlying form	/tye/	/te/	/tyoo/
e → i/y —	tyi	—	—
Palatalization	cçi	—	cçoo
y → ∅/ — i	—	—	—
Surface form	[cçi]	[te]	[cço:]

4.8.3 Against the Four-Vowel Analysis

The four-vowel analysis obviously will not work for the innovating variety. The sequences /še če ǰe/ (sections 4.3.2.2, 4.4.2.2, and 4.4.2.6) make it impossible to treat /ši či ǰi/ as underlying /sye tye zye/, and the sequence /ti/ (section 4.4.2.2) also rules out the analysis of /či/ as underlying /tye/. Umegaki (1966) lists four recent borrowings with initial /ty/ and gives initial /č/ as an alternative for two of them (**tyūba/chūba** 'tuba' and **tyūbu/chūbu** 'tube'). Masuda (1974) lists only these two, both with initial /č/. If some speakers do in fact use /ty/ in these words, this pronunciation also rules out underlying /ty/ for /č/. As Kawakami (1977:65) notes, /dy/ seems to be well established in recent borrowings like **dyuetto** 'duet', but if we take /ǰ/ in words like **jū** 'ten' as underlying /zy/, these /dy/ sequences do not disrupt the four-vowel analysis.

Even in the conservative variety, however, the four-vowel analysis is implausible. Notice that it is the sequences /še če ǰe/ that disrupt this analysis in the innovating variety. Neither variety has the sequences /pye bye kye gye hye mye nye rye/. In short, the novel environments for /e/ in the innovating variety are just those environments that I analyzed previously as single consonants (i.e., /š č ǰ/) and not those that I analyzed as /Cy/. Since the syllable /ye/ does not occur in either variety (aside from forms like /hayee/; see section 4.6.2), it is not surprising that /Cye/ sequences do not occur either. Given the phonemicization proposed earlier in this chapter, the difference between the conservative and innovating varieties is relatively minor. But if we adopt the four-vowel analysis for the conservative variety, the appearance of /še če ǰe/ forces a drastic reorganization of the entire system. It seems unlikely that /še če ǰe/ would have been adopted so easily if this latter scenario were accurate.

4.8.4 Contractions

Although the four-vowel analysis does not seem viable, it is still possible to argue that the phonemic inventory can be reduced by analyzing /š č ǰ/ as /sy ty zy/.

If we analyze both the conservative variety and the innovating variety this way, the difference between the two phonological systems is minor. This analysis would require that words like **chekku** 'check' in the innovating variety be phonemicized with initial /tye/, but we have already seen that /ye/ occurs in forms like /hayee/ (section 4.6.2), and even the conservative variety has the interjection **chĕ** section 4.4.2.2), which we could treat as /tye/. This analysis will not work for innovating speakers who have [t, j] in words like **tyūba** 'tuba', but as I noted in section 4.8.3, this [t, j] is not well established.

As we saw in section 4.8.1, however, [t, j] occurs even in the conservative variety in a contraction of **to iu** 'saying', and both [t, j] and [s, j] occur in another common contraction. As Martin (1975:558, n. 117) points out, a conditional verb form that ends /Ceba/ contracts to /Cya(a)/, as in /mireba/ → /mirya(a)/ 'if one looks' and /ikeba/ → /ikya(a)/ 'if one goes'. There are many conditionals ending in /teba/ and /seba/, and these contract to [t, jɑ(:)] and [s, jɑ(:)], as in /mateba/ → [mɑt, jɑ(:)] 'if one waits' and /hanaseba/ → [hɑnɑs, jɑ(:)] 'if one speaks'.

If we dismiss contractions as rapid-speech phenomena, they present no problem for the /sy ty zy/ analysis of /š č ǰ/. It is well known that fast-speech reductions often produce segments and sequences that speakers will judge unpronounceable or phonologically deviant in careful speech (Linell 1979:120). Hasegawa (1979), however, draws an important distinction between FAST SPEECH and CASUAL SPEECH: fast-speech reductions are sensitive to tempo; casual-speech reductions are sensitive to the degree of formality of the situation. The forms traditionally labelled "contractions" in most languages probably originated as fast-speech reductions, but synchronically they are not sensitive to tempo. English *can't*, for example, is not a fast-speech reduction of *cannot* but a less formal equivalent.

Standard Japanese speakers seem to be able to pronounce contracted conditionals at very slow tempos, but, on the other hand, they seem to have more trouble slowing down those ending in [t, jɑ(:) s, jɑ(:)] than those ending in other sequences. In any event, it is not obvious that we can ignore these contractions as fast-speech forms, and if we cannot, they are a problem for the analysis of /š č/ as /sy ty/, even in the conservative variety.

It may be, however, that we can rescue the /sy ty zy/ analysis by referring to morpheme boundaries. The verb stems in the conditional examples cited above are ordinarily taken to be /hanas/ for 'speak' and /mat/ for 'wait' (sections 12.3.2 and 12.4.2), and this makes /eba/ the uncontracted conditional suffix. If we say that the contracted form of the suffix is /ya(a)/, we have /hanas + ya(a)/ and /mat + ya(a)/, and it looks as if we could say that /sy/ and /ty/ are pronounced [ɕ] and [cɕ], whereas /s + y/ and /t + y/ are pronounced [s, j] and [t, j]. This will also work for the contraction of /to yuu/ 'saying' to [t, juː], since this can be treated as /t + yuu/. The alternative contraction [cɕuː] would be a problem, but Martin (1975:1001) says this form is "little used by Tokyo speakers."

4.8.5 /Cw/ Sequences

The sequences /kw gw/ entered Japanese in borrowings from Chinese, but according to Toyama (1972:204–207) and Shibata (1955), they survived only before /a/ after the thirteenth century. Toyama says that there is clear evidence for confusion between /kwa gwa/ and /ka ga/ in the fifteenth century, and he cites a few even earlier examples. In modern standard Japanese, /kw gw/ have merged completely with /k g/. The distinction was maintained in kana orthography until after World War II, but Shand (1907:9) says, "After **k** or **g**, **w** is not sounded except as a provincialism." This statement suggests that /kwa gwa/ disappeared in Tokyo before /ye/ did (section 4.6.2).

4.9 VOICED LABIODENTAL FRICATIVES

Bloch (1950:161) says that the voiced labiodental fricative [v] occurs in recent borrowings in the innovating variety and constitutes a separate phoneme /v/; the conservative variety has /b/ instead. It is not clear, however, that any modern standard speaker ever pronounces [v] when using a borrowing as a Japanese word. Most Japanese speakers have great difficulty pronouncing [v], and even those who can find it virtually impossible to discriminate [v] from [b] auditorily.

There is a method for spelling /v/ in the kana syllabary, and according to Umegaki (1963:98), it was invented by Yukichi Fukuzawa in 1860 for transliterating English words. This orthographic device is still widely used, but the 1954 report of the National Language Council (Kokugo Shingikai) recommended restricting it to words for which the "consciousness of the original pronunciation" still remains (Umegaki 1963:127–131). It is not clear to what extent the orthographic **v** has ever represented a pronunciation distinct from /b/ in words used as Japanese, but I will assume hereafter that there is no separate /v/ phoneme, even in the innovating variety.

4.10 GLOTTAL STOPS

As we saw in section 3.1.2, a glottal stop [ʔ] generally appears after a short vowel before a pause. In section 3.2.2, I discussed vowel rearticulation, which sometimes involves glottal constriction. I argued in both cases that there was no need for a glottal stop phoneme. Martin (1952:13) notes that a glottal stop can also occur before a vowel in interjections and emphatic speech. Kawakami (1977:39–40) says that [ʔ] can appear before a word-initial or phrase-initial vowel even when the speaker is not being emphatic, and his description suggests that consistent [ʔ] in such cases is characteristic of certain groups or individuals. Kawakami also points out that a glottal stop can be pronounced before any word-initial vowel to enhance clarity, which seems to me just the extreme case of vowel rearticulation. My impression is that, in both Japanese and English, an utterance-initial vowel is generally preceded by a glottal stop, and emphasis simply makes this rapid opening of the glottis more salient. I suspect that this is why Hockett (1958:65), sounding very much like Martin, says that in English "an emphatic exclamation such as *ouch!*" often begins with [ʔ].

McCawley (1968:67) claims that a glottal constriction precedes any syllable-initial vowel and consistently transcribes /ʔV/ rather than /V/ in his underlying forms. McCawley identifies this glottal constriction with the phoneme that Hattori (1950, 1958) writes /'/, but Hattori does not define this phoneme as a glottal stop or glottal constriction. It is clear from Hattori's (1955:290–291) discussion that he proposes the phoneme /'/ for two reasons. First, it simplifies the phonotactics by eliminating vowel-initial syllables, and second, it provides a way of discriminating phonemically between long vowels and sequences of two short vowels in cases like /satoo + ya/ 'sugar shop' versus /sato + oya/ 'foster parent' (section 3.2.2).

The phonetic correlates of /'/, however, is just extra length in a syllable-initial vowel. Hattori (1955:290) says that the first vowel in /aka/ 'red' is longer than the first vowel in /baka/ 'fool', and he treats this extra length as a consonant parallel to the initial /b/ of /baka/. He also compares the onset of /aka/ with the onset of /haka/ 'grave'. I described [h] as a glottal fricative in section 4.3.1, but as Catford (1977:250, n. 1) points out, we can also describe [h] as a voiceless vowel, depending on whether we are thinking in terms of phonation or articulation. Under the voiceless vowel interpretation, we could transcribe /haka/ as [ɑ̥ɑkɑ]. Since Hattori identifies the extra length of the first vowel in /aka/ as an initial phoneme, we could transcribe /aka/ as [ɑɑkɑ]. He argues that the initial [ɑ] in the transcription of /aka/ is the voiced counterpart of the initial [ɑ̥] in the transcription of /haka/, and for this reason he classifies /'/ as a glottal phoneme along with /h/. Hattori (1950:753) refers to /'/ as a "zero-phoneme."

Although it is true that /'/ simplifies the phonotactics of Japanese, I do not find this analysis very attractive. For one thing, the idea that words like /aka/ 'red' begin with some kind of consonant does not conform to native speakers' intuitions. No standard Japanese speaker learning to write in romanization wonders what consonant /aka/ begins with. Secondly, we have already seen in section 3.2.2 that the distinction between items like /satoo + ya/ and /sato + oya/ can be handled naturally if boundaries are a part of phonological representations. I therefore conclude that, on the basis of the evidence considered in this section and in sections 3.1.2 and 3.2.2, it is unnecessary to propose a phoneme /'/ or /ʔ/. I will return to this question one more time, however, in section 5.2.4.

Chapter 5

MORA CONSONANTS

5.1 THE MORA NASAL

5.1.1 Phonetic Description

5.1.1.1 Before a Pause

The word **hon** 'book', spoken in isolation, ends with a long nasal sound that Sakuma (1929:164, 168–169) describes as an unreleased [ŋ]. There is general agreement that this sound does not involve the release of an oral closure (Hattori 1930:41, Kindaichi 1954:162–164, Naitō 1961:118), but Hattori says that the place of articulation is generally farther back, and he transcribes it with [N], the IPA symbol for a uvular nasal. Nakano (1969:220) gives a tracing of an x-ray photograph of a speaker articulating this sound, and Naitō says that the back of the tongue touches the roof of the mouth "as far back as possible." I will adopt the phonetic transcription [N:ˆ], using the symbol [ˆ] to indicate that the closure is not released. Bloch (1950:143) says that this sound is in free variation with a long alveolar nasal, but his definition of free variation is idiosyncratic (1950: 118, n. 11). I know of no evidence for such free variation in the ordinary sense of the term.

Hattori (1930:42) also says that the uvular closure in [N:ˆ] is weak, and Arisaka (1940:83–84) describes the sound as a lax uvular nasal. Sakuma

34

(1929:166) reports a simple experiment and says that no air flows out of the mouth during [N:ˆ]. This statement indicates that while the closure may be weak, it is nonetheless complete, but other writers disagree. Kawakami (1977:43) claims that the closure is not complete, and Aoki (1976:204–205) gives kymograph recordings that show air flowing out of the mouth during the articulation of this sound.

Jones (1967:88, n. 3) says that the sound in question varies between an ordinary nasal consonant and a nasalized fricative. Bloch (1950:134–135) says that the variant is a "voiced frictionless nasalized . . . spirant." A spirant is the same thing as a fricative, however, and a "frictionless fricative" is a contradiction in terms. Bloch presumably meant to describe an APPROXIMANT (Catford 1977: 118–122), and if he is correct, the final sound in a word like **hon** can be pronounced with or without complete closure. Perhaps this is a case of variation among speakers rather than free variation, since Bloch (1950:118, n. 11) uses the term "free variation" to cover both. In either case, it would account for the disparity in descriptions. The symbol [N] is, of course, inappropriate for an approximant, but I will hereafter ignore variation and continue to transcribe the final sound in words like **hon** as [N:ˆ].

Hattori (1930:42) remarks that the tongue is close to its "neutral state" in [N:ˆ]. Arisaka (1940:84) characterizes the articulation of [N:ˆ] as a step in the return to the rest configuration of the articulators. In this configuration, says Arisaka, the mouth is closed, the velum is open for breathing through the nose, and the tongue is lightly touching the palate. Aside from some marginal exceptions, [N:ˆ] always follows a vowel (section 5.1.3), and in the transition from the open mouth for the vowel, the first contact between the tongue and palate as they come together is naturally in the back.

The notion of a return to a position of rest strikes me as a little farfetched, but I think we can relate the feeling that the articulation of [N:ˆ] is somehow neutral to the articulatory setting for Japanese. We saw in section 2.2 that the anchorage of the tongue in Japanese involves a slightly raised dorsum and that back consonants are apparently much more frequent in Japanese than in English. It may be, therefore, that the configuration for [N:ˆ] reflects not some absolute position of rest but the articulatory setting.

5.1.1.2 Before Stops, Affricates, and Nasals

When a word like **hon** 'book' is not followed by a pause, the nasal appears as a wide variety of sounds. The examples in [1] illustrate a few of the possibilities. (I continue to use the symbol [ˆ] to make it clear that the oral closure is not released at the point where the symbol appears.)

[1]	**a.** hon mo 'book too'	[hõm:ˆmo]
	b. hon da 'is book'	[hõn:ˆda]
	c. hon ni 'in book'	[hõɲ:ˆɲi]
	d. hon ka 'book?'	[hõŋ:ˆka]

In each case, we find a long, unreleased nasal, but the place of articulation varies widely. In general, when a nasal precedes a consonant that begins with a complete oral closure (i.e., a stop, affricate, or nasal), the nasal is long and unreleased and has an identical closure. When the following consonant is a nasal, as in [1a] and [1c], the result is phonetically a long, uninterrupted, intervocalic nasal. When the following consonant is an obstruent, as in [1b] and [1d], the velum is raised before the closure is released, but the closure itself is uniform throughout.

5.1.1.3 Before /r/

A long, unreleased nasal occurs before /r/ in words like **honrai** 'originally'. We saw in section 4.7 that /r/ is phonetically a tap, and this means that ordinarily no closure is maintained. As we noted, however, utterance-initial /r/ does seem to involve a preparatory closure. My impression is that a nasal before /r/ has a complete oral closure. If a speaker were to prepare to articulate utterance-initial /r/, hold that configuration, and pronounce a long, unreleased nasal, I think the resulting sound would be the nasal that appears before /r/. Maeda (1971:135) is absolutely right, of course, that this sound is not identical to the [n:ˆ] that appears before /t d c n/.

5.1.1.4 Before Vowels and Glides

When the word **hon** 'book' appears before a vowel or glide, its final sound is long and nasalized, but there is no complete oral closure. The examples in [2] illustrate **hon** followed by each of the five short vowels (section 3.1) and two glides (section 4.6).

[2] **a.** hon iru 'need book'
   b. hon e 'to book'
   c. hon aru 'book exists'
   d. hon o 'book (direct object)'
   e. hon uru 'sell book'
   f. honya 'bookstore'
   g. hon wa 'book (topic)'

Nakano (1969:225) would transcribe **hon o** [2d] as [hoõo], with the nasal as a nasalized copy of the surrounding vowels. One problem with this transcription is that the vowel preceding the nasal is nasalized in anticipation (section 5.1.3). A more serious problem is that [õ] is too low a vowel for the final sound of **hon** in **hon o**. Something like [hoũo] would be more accurate.

Nasals without complete oral closure always follow a vowel (section 5.1.3), and Hattori (1930:46) says that if we ignore small differences, those that also precede a vowel are something like [ĩ] before /i e/ and something like [ũ] before /a o u/. (The rounded [ũ] in [hoũo] is due, of course, to the rounding of [o]; see section 3.1.1.) Hattori is careful to point out, however, that the preceding vowel also has an influence, and Arisaka (1940:83–84) gives several examples in a very NARROW TRANSCRIPTION (Sloat, Taylor, and Hoard 1978:48). Arisaka also suggests that the pronunciation of **hon o** may approach [hõõo] as the tempo increases. There is general agreement that **honya** [2f] and **hon wa** [2g] are [hõĩja] and [hõũɰa] (Hattori 1930:42, Arisaka 1940:83, Nakano 1969:225), or perhaps [hõĩja] and [hõũ̃ɰ̃a].

As Arisaka (1940:83) emphasizes, the nasals in examples like [2] never involve complete oral closure. If a closure were made, it would, of course, have to be released to pronounce the following vowel or glide. If, for example, **hon o** were pronounced with a closure, Arisaka says that the auditory impression would be that the speaker had pronounced [hõŋ:ˆŋo].

5.1.1.5 Before Fricatives

When the word **hon** 'book' appears before the emphatic particle **sa**, the final sound in **hon** is long and nasalized, but there is no complete oral closure. Hattori (1930:42) transcribes this sound as a nasalized high central unrounded vowel. Maeda (1971:143–144) argues for transcribing it as a nasalized voiced fricative [z̃], but since there is no audible friction, Hattori's nasalized vowel is certainly preferable.

The examples in [3] show that a nasal can occur before any of the voiceless fricatives discussed in section 4.3.1. (As I noted in section 4.4.2.3, /z/ appears after a nasal as [dz] rather than [z].) Hattori (1930:46) says that a nasal before [ɕ], as in [3b], is something like [ĩ], and a similar sound occurs before [ç], as in [3c]. For the nasal before [ɸ], as in [3d], a reasonable transcription would be [ũ].

[**3**] **a.** hon sa 'book, of course' (before [s])
   b. hon shika 'book only' (before [ɕ])
   c. hinhin 'neigh-neigh' (before [ç])
   d. funfun 'sniffle-sniffle' (before [ɸ])
   e. senhekutāru 'a thousand hectares' (before [h])
   f. yonhon 'four (long objects)' (before [h])
   g. hanhan 'half-and-half' (before [h])

The character of a nasal before [h] varies considerably. As we saw in section 4.10, it is possible to think of [h] as a voiceless vowel, and the configuration of the supraglottal vocal tract anticipates the vowel to follow. As a result, the [h] sounds in the syllables /ha he ho/ differ, although they have glottal friction in common. A nasal before /he/ is auditorily quite different from a nasal before /ha/ or /ho/, and the character of the vowel preceding the nasal also has an effect. As Arisaka (1940:83) points out, this means that the nasals that appear before [h] are like those that appear before vowels (section 5.1.1.4). We might transcribe the nasals in [3e], [3f], and [3g] as [ĩ], [ũ], and [ũ].

My impression is that, in general, the position of the oral constriction in a nasal before a fricative anticipates the position for the fricative. Since a fricative involves a narrow constriction but not a complete closure, the nasal does not have a complete closure either. If a complete closure were made during such a nasal, it would have to be released to pronounce the fricative, and this release would blur the distinction between, for example, **konshū** 'this week' and **konchū** 'insect'. (Compare the distinction between words like *prince* and *prints* in English, which is blurred; see Bloch 1941.) This does not happen, however, and we can describe nasals before fricatives as unreleased, just like the nasals discussed in sections 5.1.1.1–5.1.1.4. It may be that the constriction for a nasal before a fricative is just as narrow as the constriction for the fricative. Since the velum is lowered, however, most of the air from the lungs escapes through the nose, and airflow through the mouth is not sufficient to produce audible friction.

5.1.1.6   Length

I have described all the nasal sounds treated in sections 5.1.1.1–5.1.1.5 as long. This description reflects a consensus that these nasals have approximately the same duration as ordinary CV syllables (Bloch 1950:149, Kindaichi 1954:155, Jones 1967:88, n. 1). Han (1962a:70) reports duration measurements of pairs like **shinin** 'dead person' versus **shinnin** 'new appointment' that show an approximate three-to-four ratio. I will argue in Chapter 7 that Japanese has short and long syllables and that a short CV syllable consists of one mora, while a long CVN syllable (like a CVV syllable; see section 3.2.2) consists of two moras.

5.1.2   Phonemicization

why isn't it /n/?

There is general agreement that all the nasal sounds described in section 5.1.1 should be treated as allophones of a single phoneme (Bloch 1950:149, Naitō 1961:117, Jones 1967:88–89), and I will transcribe this phoneme as /N/. Arisaka (1940:82) describes /N/ as a special nasal phoneme that transcends any oral place of articulation. Kindaichi (1954:155) says that while /N/ is realized phonetically as various sounds, phonologically it is a nasal that, unlike /m n/, constitutes a mora. In addition to nasality and mora length, all allophones of /N/ are unreleased (Kindaichi 1954:162–164). I will refer to /N/ as the MORA NASAL.

Jones (1967:89, n. 4) notes that alternations in the pronunciation of individual morphemes support the identification of all the sounds described in section 5.1.1 as allophones of a single phoneme. As we have seen, a word like **hon** 'book' appears with a wide variety of final nasals, depending on the following segment. There are countless alternations of this kind in Japanese, all perfectly regular.

Kana orthography also supports the grouping of the various allophones of /N/, since the allophones are all written with the same letter. This letter was a later addition to the original syllabary; it apparently came into use in the twelfth century (Hamada 1955a). I will briefly consider the historical development of /N/ in section 7.1.

5.1.3 Distribution

Bloch (1950:133–134) says that /N/ can occur after a pause in words like **uma** 'horse' and **umi** 'ocean', which he transcribes as [m:ˆmɑ] and [m,:ˆm,i]. Martin (1952:13) claims that /N/ occurs utterance-initially before /ma me mo/ (which would exclude **umi**) in most words spelled **umV-**, although he says there are some exceptions. There is no doubt that words of this kind are sometimes pronounced with an initial nasal rather than a vowel, but I do not think this tendency is characteristic of careful pronunciation for speakers I have observed closely. I will therefore treat such pronunciations as fast-speech reductions and phonemicize **uma** as /uma/ and not as /Nma/. The glottal stop that characteristically appears before an utterance-initial vowel (section 4.10) remains, even when /u/ is realized as a long nasal. Thus, a more accurate transcription of this pronunciation of **uma** would be [ʔm:ˆmɑ].

Sakuma (1929:164) notes that orthographic **un** 'yeah' is actually pronounced [ʔN:ˆ] or [ʔm:ˆ]. We might consider this a case of initial /N/, but my feeling is that it belongs in the same category as English *uh-huh*, which is often pronounced something like [ʔm̩m̩m̩]. What I am suggesting is that both languages have a phonotactically anomalous expression of affirmation, and this need not concern us in stating the distribution of phonemes.

There are, however, some examples that are not so easily dismissed. Another source of initial long nasals is the reduction of the morpheme /naN/ (meaning something like 'several') when it occurs before a word denoting a quantity. Authors sometimes render this kind of pronunciation when writing dialogue; Komatsu (1978:171), for example, writes **njūoku**, with the katakana symbol for /N/ as the first letter, for /naNjuuoku/ 'several billion' (cf. /juu/ 'ten' and /oku/ 'hundred million'). This pronunciation of /naN/ may be a casual-speech reduction rather than a fast-speech reduction (section 4.8.4), and if so, we cannot ignore it in discussing the distribution of /N/.

Aside from marginal examples like those in the preceding paragraph, /N/ occurs only after a vowel. We expect a vowel before a nasal to be nasalized (Sloat, Taylor, and Hoard 1978:112–113), and a vowel before /N/ certainly is (Bloch 1950:133–135, Jones 1967:88, n. 3, Nakano 1969:224).

5.2 THE MORA OBSTRUENT

5.2.1 Phonetic Description

Phonetic long voiceless obstruents are frequent in Japanese, and the examples in [4] illustrate some of the possibilities.

[4]	a.	happa 'leaf'	[hɑp:ˆpɑ]
	b.	hatta 'stuck'	[hɑt:ˆtɑ]
	c.	hakka 'ignition'	[hɑk:ˆkɑ]
	d.	hassha 'departure'	[hɑɕ:ɕɑ]
	e.	hatchū 'ordering'	[hɑc:ˆcɕɯ:]

Han (1962a:70) reports duration measurements of pairs like **ita** 'was' versus **itta** 'went' that show approximately a two-to-three ratio, and this means that a word with a long voiceless obstruent has an extra mora (section 5.1.1.6). I use [C:] to indicate this extra mora's worth of consonant and [ˆ] to indicate (as in section 5.1.1.2) that an oral closure is not released at the point where the symbol appears. Thus, [hɑp:ˆpɑ] [4a], for example, contains a voiceless bilabial stop that is uninterrupted and slightly longer than one mora.

Sakuma (1929:149, 272) claims that long voiceless stops have stronger closure than their short counterparts, with the articulators exerting more pressure on each other. He says that long voiceless obstruents give an impression of tension; and we might be tempted to describe them as TENSE. As Catford (1977:199–208) points out, however, linguists have used the label *tense* for a variety of phonetic characteristics, and experiments have often failed to detect the putative physiological correlates of tenseness. Since I am unaware of any experimental corroboration, I will not ascribe stronger closure to long voiceless stops.

5.2.2 Phonemicization

5.2.2.1 The Traditional Japanese Analysis

Japanese linguists traditionally analyze all long voiceless obstruents as consisting of a phoneme that I will transcribe as /Q/ followed by a voiceless stop, affricate, or fricative (Hashimoto 1950b:286, Arisaka 1940:94, n. 7, Hattori 1958:360–361). Thus, for example, [hɑt:ˆtɑ] [4b] is phonemically /haQta/. Arisaka suggests that the target for /Q/ is an abrupt suspension of articulatory movements. This target is not quite achieved when a fricative follows because air continues to flow from the lungs. Kindaichi (1954:161) says that what is essential for /Q/ is sustaining an oral closure or constriction; the particular place of articulation, like that of /N/ (section 5.1.2), depends on the following segment. Kawakami (1977:85, 87) describes /Q/ as a sustained portion, one mora in length, of a long obstruent. He also notes that /Q/ does not include the "off-glide," by which he presumably means the release in the case of a stop. All the allophones of /Q/, like those of /N/ (section 5.1.2), lack the release of an oral closure. I will adopt this phonemicization of long voiceless obstruents and refer to /Q/ as the MORA OBSTRUENT, but I will consider an alternative phonemicization in section 5.2.2.2.

As in the case of /N/ (section 5.1.2), widespread alternations support the identification of all the sounds described in section 5.2.1 as allophones of a single phoneme. The words in [4c]–[4e] for example, are transparently analyzable as beginning with a morpheme /haQ/ 'origination', and the fact that the same kanji is used to write /haQ/ in each case reinforces this morphemic analysis. Kana orthography also supports the phonemicization as /Q/, since the allophones are all written with the same letter, namely, the letter for the syllable **tsu** (/cu/) reduced in size. I will briefly consider the historical development of /Q/ in section 7.1.

5.2.2.2 An Alternative Analysis

Bloch (1950:146–147) notes that long voiceless stops are in complementary distribution with each other and with the corresponding short voiceless stops. A long voiceless stop must precede a homorganic voiceless stop or affricate, whereas a short voiceless stop must precede a vowel. Bloch says that [t:] precedes /s/ in **otottsan** 'father', but as we saw in section 4.4.2.1, this should probably be considered a nonstandard dialect form. In any case, I would treat it as an example of [t:] before /c/. It is possible, therefore, to group all long voiceless stops together as allophones of a single phoneme. Bloch considers this possibility and suggests /q/ as a transcription.

Long voiceless fricatives, on the other hand, are not in complementary distribution with each other for Bloch. This is a consequence of his analysis of vowel devoicing (Chapter 6). For example, Bloch (1950:131–132) transcribes **hito** 'person' as [çto], and he would transcribe **suto** 'strike' as [s:to] and **futo** 'suddenly' as [ɸ:to]. As we will see in section 6.5, these transcriptions are probably accurate for some rapid pronunciations, but in more careful speech, we find [çito̥], [su̥to], and [ɸu̥to]. Bloch (1950:157–159) would phonemicize **suto** as /sto/, and since a word like **hassō** [has:so:] 'sending' also has [s:], the PHONETIC SIMILARITY criterion (Sommerstein 1977:21–22) requires that **hassō** be phonemicized /hassoo/. This treatment makes long fricatives the preconsonantal allophones of fricative phonemes.

Bloch (1950:146–147) gives two reasons for rejecting the grouping of long voiceless stops into a single phoneme /q/. First, he argues that the distribution of /q/, limited to the environment V—C, would be unique. Hattori (1958:361) notes that phonetic long voiceless stops sometimes occur after /N/, as in **Rondonkko** 'Londoner', but even taking this fact into account, the distribution of Bloch's /q/ remains unique. Bloch would be willing to adopt /q/ in spite of this if it made the overall phonemic description of Japanese more economical, but he says, "The effect of adopting /q/ would be to make the descriptive statements more numerous and less general." By "more numerous," Bloch means that if we group all long voiceless stops together as /q/, rather than group each with its corresponding short stop, we have an extra phoneme. By "less general," he means that the phoneme /q/ could not include all long voiceless obstruent phones, since his treatment of vowel devoicing leads him to analyze long fricatives as allophones of the ordinary fricative phonemes.

I will adopt a treatment of vowel devoicing in section 6.5 that allows us to phonemicize words like **hito** 'person' and **suto** 'strike' as /hito/ and /suto/. This makes it possible to group long fricatives with long stops in the phoneme /Q/, as in section 5.2.2.1. The analysis with /Q/ does, of course, have an extra phoneme with a unique distribution, but there can be little doubt that it is a much better reflection of native speakers' intuitions.

5.2.3   /Q/ Before Voiced Obstruents

All the phonetic long obstruents considered so far have been voiceless, and except for recent borrowings, we do not find /Q/ before voiced obstruents. Dictionaries spell words like **beddo** 'bed', **baggu** 'bag', and **mobbu** 'mob' with small **tsu** before a voiced obstruent (Nihon Hōsō Kyōkai 1966, Shinmura 1969), and Arisaka (1940:94, n. 7) says that pronunciations like [bed:ˆdo] are possible. Kawakami (1977:90) agrees, and Bloch (1950:160) says that long voiced obstruents are a feature of the innovating variety (section 4.1).

Arisaka (1940:94, n. 7) claims that if a speaker wants to manifest /Q/ more strongly, there is a temporary suspension of voicing in words like **beddo** 'bed'. Kawakami (1977:90) agrees and says that [bak:ˆgɯ] is probably more common than [bag:ˆgɯ] for **baggu** 'bag'. Kawakami also claims that as a word comes into popular use in Japanese, a voiced consonant after /Q/ becomes voiceless, and it is interesting that Masuda (1974) lists **betto** as an alternative for **beddo**. Tagashira (1979) says that orthographic sequences representing /Q/ plus voiced obstruent are quire generally pronounced as long voiceless obstruents, and I think this observation is correct. It means that the orthographic distinction between, for example, **baggu** and **bakku** 'back' is generally not reflected in pronunciation. (I recall using the word /peepaabaQku/ 'paperback' in a conversation and having a Japanese friend ask if I meant /kamibukuro/ 'paper bag'.)

Homma (1981:274–276) had speakers read nonsense words like **pabba**, **tadda**, and **kagga** and measured voice onset time (section 4.2.2) for the stops. These words contain orthographic sequences that should represent /Q/ followed by a voiced stop in medial position, but Homma's measurements show no cases of voice onset preceding the release of medial stop closure. This might mean that only the last portion of the phonetic long stop is voiceless (as Homma suggests), but I suspect they are simply voiceless throughout.

The tendency for orthographic sequences of /Q/ plus voiced obstruent to be pronounced voiceless is especially interesting in view of the fact that standard speakers seem to have no trouble lengthening voiced obstruents for emphasis. For example, it is not uncommon to hear words like /sugoi/ 'amazing' and /kudaranai/ 'absurd' pronounced emphatically as [sɯg:oi] and [kɯd:aranai]. It is important to keep in mind, of course, that lengthening of this kind is not fixed at one mora but varies according to the degree of emphasis. It is true, nonetheless, that writers use a small **tsu** to indicate emphatic lengthening in print. Hamada (1955c) notes that /taQta/ 'only' developed as an emphatic form of

/tada/, and in this case devoicing apparently occurred. Perhaps conventional emphatic forms like /taQta/ undergo devoicing as they become established.

Emphatic forms have sometimes displaced their unemphatic counterparts over time. Hamada (1955c) notes that /maQtaku/ 'completely' originated as an emphatic version of /mataku/, but /maQtaku/ is the only form now in use in standard Japanese. The long stop can be lengthened even further for emphasis, of course, but the unemphatic form is clearly /maQtaku/. In other cases, a semantic distinction has developed between emphatic and unemphatic forms. Hamada mentions that /saQki/ 'a little while ago' originated as an emphatic form of /saki/ 'before', but the two are clearly separate words in modern standard Japanese and should be phonemicized differently.

Since standard speakers seem to be able to pronounce phonetic long voiced obstruents for emphasis, we cannot very well attribute the tendency toward devoicing in recent loanwords to a simple phonetic difficulty. It does, of course, take considerable energy to keep air flowing from the lungs and maintain vocal cord vibration while air pressure is building up behind a supraglottal closure. Perhaps speakers avoid expending this kind of energy in unemphatic utterances. Something a little more subtle may also be at work. Long voiced obstruents are ordinarily confined to emphatic pronunciations, and speakers may feel that they are somehow out of place in unemphatic pronunciations of recent loanwords.

5.2.4 /Q/ and Glottal Stops

In the discussion of utterance-final glottal stops in section 3.1.2, I noted that exclamatory interjections like ă 'oh' generally end with [ʔ]. I argued that any utterance-final short vowel is followed by a glottal stop and that emphasis simply makes this glottal stop more salient. I concluded that there was no need for a separate glottal stop phoneme, but in this section I will consider the possibility of treating utterance-final [ʔ] as an allophone of /Q/.

Naitō (1961:119) notes that ă [aʔ] 'oh' appears in /aQto sakebu/ 'shout ă'. The word /to/ is a quotative particle (Martin 1975:996), and another example with ă is /aQto yuu ma ni/ 'as quick as you can say ă'. Other relevant examples are hă [haʔ] 'oh', which appears in /haQto omou/ 'think hă', and kyakkyă [k,jak,:^k,jaʔ] 'eek-eek', which appears in /kyaQkyaQto yuu/ 'say kya kkyă'. (Note that kyakkyă itself is reduplicated, with /kyaQ/ as the first half.) On the basis of alternations like this, Naitō argues that utterance-final [ʔ] is an allophone of /Q/. I mentioned in section 3.1.2 that the spelling convention for representing utterance-final [ʔ] is a small **tsu**, that is, the same as the spelling of /Q/ (section 5.2.2.1), and this fact certainly supports the assignment of [ʔ] to /Q/.

Emphatic phrases are not always spelled with a small **tsu** before the quotative particle /to/. For example, the entry for /donaru/ 'shout' in Masuda (1974) gives /kešite kure to taroo ga donaQta/ '"Turn it off!" barked Tarō' as an illustration, and even though /kešite kure/ 'Turn it off!' is exclamatory, no small **tsu** appears before /to/. In actual pronunciation, however, we get something like /kešite kure [t:ˆt]o donaQta/. It thus appears that this phonetically long stop is not consistently spelled as /Qt/ would be, and the spelling in cases like /aQto/ and /haQto/ is perhaps a matter of tradition.

Speakers presumably do not notice an utterance-final glottal stop unless emphasis makes it salient. When they do notice, they apparently always assign it to the phoneme /Q/. When an emphatic expression is quoted, we get [t:ˆ] before the quotative particle /to/, and when speakers notice this, they assign it to /Q/ as well. We can avoid saying that individual words, such as interjections like ă 'oh', end in /Q/ by attributing such occurrences of /Q/ to the emphasis itself rather than to the word emphasized. The apparently inconsistent orthographic practice remains to be accounted for, however, and the entire question of utterance-final glottal stops deserves further study.

5.3 MORA CONSONANTS IN GENERATIVE PHONOLOGY

As we will see in greater detail in section 12.4, generative phonology handles allomorphy by setting up invariant underlying forms and deriving surface forms by rules. Kuroda (1965:201–230) points out that this approach leads to an analysis of Japanese with no level on which the mora consonants /N Q/ are represented uniquely. In this section I will look at Kuroda's analysis carefully enough to see how this problem arises.

We will see in Chapter 12 that Japanese verb forms involve considerable allomorphy, and examples like those in [5] are relevant here.

[5] *Nonpast*   *Past*

/yomu/	/yoNda/	'read'
/yobu/	/yoNda/	'call'
/karu/	/kaQta/	'cut'
/kacu/	/kaQta/	'win'

Kuroda (1965:204) argues that the stems of the verbs in [5] should have the underlying forms //yom//, //yob//, //kar//, //kat//, and that the past-tense suffix should have the underlying form //ta//. (I enclose underlying forms in double slashes to distinguish them from phonemic transcriptions.) McCawley's (1968:93–110) treatment of verb morphology involves the same underlying forms (section 12.4), and the discussion here will focus on three of the rules necessary to derive the phonetic representations of the forms in [5].

First, the underlying //t// in the past-tense suffix becomes voiced when a voiced obstruent or a nasal precedes. Second, a voiced consonant becomes a nasal when another voiced consonant follows. Third, the first consonant in a cluster assimilates to the second in all features except nasality. The derivations in [6] show how these three rules apply to produce the past-tense forms in [5]. The phonetic representations in [6] also show the effects of additional rules that are not of immediate concern.

[6] Underlying form $\qquad$ //yom + ta// $\qquad$ //yob + ta//

t → d / $\begin{bmatrix} + \text{vce} \\ \{ + \text{obs} \} \\ \{ + \text{nas} \} \end{bmatrix}$ — $\qquad$ yomda $\qquad$ yobda

C → [+ nas] / — C $\qquad$ — $\qquad$ yomda
$\qquad\qquad$ [+ vce]

Assimilation $\qquad$ yonda $\qquad$ yonda

Phonetic representation $\qquad$ [jõn:ˆdɑ] $\qquad$ [jõn:ˆdɑ]

Underlying form $\qquad$ //kar + ta// $\qquad$ //kat + ta//

t → d / $\begin{bmatrix} + \text{vce} \\ \{ + \text{obs} \} \\ \{ + \text{nas} \} \end{bmatrix}$ — $\qquad$ — $\qquad$ —

C → [+ nas] / — C $\qquad$ — $\qquad$ —
$\qquad\qquad$ [+ vce]

Assimilation $\qquad$ katta $\qquad$ —

Phonetic representation $\qquad$ [kɑt:ˆta] $\qquad$ [kɑt:ˆta]

We will see in section 11.2 that alternations like those in [7] are characteristic of Sino-Japanese morphemes.

[7] /gaku/ ~ /gaQ/ $\qquad$ /gaku + neN/ $\qquad$ 'school year'
$\qquad\qquad\qquad\qquad$ /gaQ + ki/ $\qquad$ 'school term'
$\qquad$ /kecu/ ~ /keQ/ $\qquad$ /kecu + acu/ $\qquad$ 'blood pressure'
$\qquad\qquad\qquad\qquad$ /keQ + sei/ $\qquad$ 'blood serum'

Kuroda (1965:206–207) argues that the underlying forms of the alternating morphemes in [7] should be //gaku// and //ketu// and that the final vowel is deleted by a rule. McCawley (1968:115–120) adopts the same solution, and I will consider this problem in more detail in section 11.2.2.1. In addition to this vowel deletion rule, the rule that assimilates the first consonant in a cluster to the second in all features except nasality will apply in the derivation of /keQ + sei/. The derivations in [8] illustrate this point, and here again, the phonetic representations show the effects of some additional rules.

[8] Underlying form $\qquad$ //gaku + ki// $\qquad$ //ketu + sei//

Vowel deletion $\qquad$ gakki $\qquad$ ketsei

Assimilation $\qquad$ — $\qquad$ kessei

Phonetic representation $\qquad$ [gak,:ˆk,i] $\qquad$ [kes:se:]

Kuroda (1965:205–206) also incorporates certain mimetic adverbs that he calls "intensified adverbs" into his analysis. The examples in [9] illustrate the type of word in question.

[9] **a.** /baQtari/ 'suddenly' $\qquad$ cf. /batabata/
$\qquad$ **b.** /yuQkuri/ 'slowly' $\qquad$ */yukuyuku/
$\qquad$ **c.** /zaNburi/ 'with a splash' $\qquad$ cf. /zabuzabu/
$\qquad$ **d.** /boNyari/ 'vacantly' $\qquad$ cf. /boyaboya/

As Kuroda points out, these intensified adverbs have the form /CVMCVri/, where /M/ stands for either /N/ or /Q/. Many of them are arguably related to reduplicated mimetic adverbs of the form /CVCV + CVCV/, although many others, such as [9b], are not. In general, an intensified adverb contains /Q/ if the following consonant is voiceless and /N/ if it is voiced. Kuroda treats this /Q/ or /N/ as an infix with an underlying form that specifies it only as a consonant. I will represent this underlying segment as //X//, and since it always occurs before a consonant, it is subject to the nasalization and assimilation rules mentioned above. The derivations in [10] illustrate this point, with additional rules reflected in the phonetic representations.

[10]	Underlying form	//ha + X + ki + ri//	//bo + X + ya + ri//
	C → [+ nas] / — C	—	boX̃yari
	[+ vce]		
	Assimilation	hakkiri	boȳyari
	Phonetic representation	[hɑk,:ˆk,iɾ,i]	[bōjjɑɾ,i]

It is clear at this point that there is no unique representation for either /N/ or /Q/ in Kuroda's underlying forms. /N/ can originate as //m//, //b//, or //X//, and /Q/ can originate as //r//, //t//, //k//, or //X//. It is also clear that neither /N/ nor /Q/ has a unique representation in phonetic forms, and of course we already knew this from the discussion in sections 5.1.1 and 5.2.1.

It also turns out, as Kuroda (1965:220–221) demonstrates, that there is no level between the underlying and the phonetic at which /N/ or /Q/ has a unique representation, as the derivations in [11] illustrate.

[11]	Underlying form	//yob + ta//	//bo + X + ya + ri//
	Vowel deletion	yobta	boX̃yari
	t → d / [+ obs] —	yobda	boX̃yari
	[+ vce]		
	C → [+ nas] / — C	yomda	boX̃yari
	[+ vce]		
	Assimilation	yonda	boȳyari
	Underlying form	//kar + ta//	//gaku + ki//
	Vowel deletion	karta	gakki
	t → d / [+ obs] —	karta	gakki
	[+ vce]		
	C → [+ nas] / — C	karta	gakki
	[+ vce]		
	Assimilation	katta	gakki

A glance at [11] shows that there is no rule after which the /N/ in /yoNda/ is identical to the /N/ in /boNyari/ or the /Q/ in /kaQta/ is identical to the /Q/ in /gaQki/.

Early generative phonologists, following Halle (1959:19–24), came to the conclusion that phonemes are irrelevant in phonological analysis. Since there is, in general, no one level in a generative analysis at which each phoneme has a unique representation, the traditional phonemic level had no theoretical status in generative phonology. Most linguists were probably never really convinced that the phoneme was dead, and dissenters eventually appeared even among phonologists trained in the generative model (Johns 1969, Darden 1971, Schane 1971). Many recent works treat the phoneme as fully rehabilitated (Linell 1979:88–116, 257–267).

It is interesting in this connection that Kuroda (1965:220–228) is unwilling to accept the conclusion that /N/ and /Q/ are irrelevant units in Japanese phonology. He says, "It seems beyond doubt that . . . native intuition identifies the [mora nasal] and the [mora obstruent] as definite entities." Sommerstein (1977:121) notes that generative arguments against the phonemic level "[tell] us nothing about the role that such a level might play in speech production or, more importantly, in speech perception," and Kuroda suggests that "phonemic representation [may be] significantly involved in perceptual behavior." Kuroda tries to reconcile the perceptual importance of /N/ and /Q/ with his generative treatment of Japanese phonology, but the exact nature of his proposal need not concern us here. What is significant is that even in the heyday of generative phonology, the widely accepted arguments against the phoneme could not shake Kuroda's phonemic intuition.

Chapter 6

VOWEL DEVOICING

6.1 HIGH AND NONHIGH VOWELS

Japanese is frequently cited as an example of a language with voiceless vowels. Martin (1952:14) suggests treating these voiceless vowels as independent phonemes, but most linguists working in a phonemic framework have regarded them as allophones of the ordinary voiced vowels. Fromkin and Rodman (1983:87) say, "In Japanese, high vowels are devoiced when preceded and followed by voiceless obstruents." This rule is a good illustration of assimilation for an introductory textbook, and it is easy to formalize, but the actual situation in Japanese is much more complicated. For one thing, a high vowel between a voiceless obstruent and a pause is also generally devoiced (Nihon Onsei Gakkai 1976:748). A minor change in the rule will accommodate this fact, but there are several more serious difficulties.

One problem is that nonhigh vowels sometimes devoice, although not as frequently or as consistently as high vowels. Sakuma (1929:231–232) says that the italicized vowels in /haha/ 'mother', /kakaru/ 'hang', and /koko/ 'here' are devoiced on occasion, and that the one in /kokoro/ 'heart' always is. In other cases, Sakuma says that devoicing applies only in careless pronunciation: /tataku/ 'hit', /sotobori/ 'outer moat', /seQkaku/ 'with effort'. Bloch (1950:136) gives examples of devoicing for each vowel except /e/, and his statements about /i u/ are quite different from those about /a o/. He says that [i̥ ɯ̥] can be replaced by [i ɯ] "especially in slow or careful speech," but that [ɑ̥ o̥] can occur "in rapid speech only." Martin (1952:14) says that devoicing of nonhigh vowels varies from individual to individual and that it usually occurs in an initial syllable preceding an identical syllable (e.g., /kokoro/). Kawakami (1977:69) says that while devoicing in /katana/ 'sword' varies from speaker to speaker and from occasion to occasion, devoicing in /kusuri/ 'medicine' is obligatory, except in unnaturally precise speech. According to Nihon Onsei Gakkai (1976:748), the final /a/ in an utterance ending with a polite past-tense verb form (i.e., with /-mašita/) is usually devoiced. The example given is the sentence /arimašita/ '(It) was (there)', and supposedly it is usually [ɑrimɑ̥çitɑ].

To the best of my knowledge, Sakuma is the only writer to claim that the first vowel in /kokoro/ is obligatorily devoiced. Han (1962b:84–85) simply says that /a e o/ are not devoiced at normal tempo, whereas /i u/ are, and this is certainly a concise statement of the consensus. Han defines normal tempo as what she uses "in normal polite conversation with native speakers of Japanese."

Sakuma (1929:232–233) argues that /i u/ are more likely to devoice than /a e o/ because they are generally shorter. The idea is that the voicelessness of the environment is more likely to spread across a shorter vowel, since a shorter time span provides less leeway for executing voicing. This accounts for the increased likelihood of devoicing at faster tempos, since the length of each segment decreases as the tempo increases.

Lehiste (1970:18–19) says that "other factors being equal, a high vowel is shorter than a low vowel." The figures Lehiste quotes from Elert (1964) show that for short allophones in Swedish, if the average duration of high vowels is taken as 1.00, that of mid vowels is 1.08 and that of low vowels is 1.17. The figures from Han (1962a:67) show much greater differences for Japanese vowels. Taking the average duration of /u/ as 1.00, the averages for the other vowels are as follows: /i/ 1.17, /o/ 1.26, /e/ 1.37, and /a/ 1.44. Lehiste says, "It is quite probable that the differences in vowel length according to degree of opening are physiologically conditioned and thus constitute a phonetic universal." Han's figures suggest that the physiologically conditioned differences have been exaggerated in Japanese. This kind of exaggeration is sometimes known as PHONOLOGIZATION (Hyman 1975:171–173).

Sakuma (1929:233) tries to relate length to the tendency Martin suggests for initial syllables with nonhigh vowels to devoice if an identical syllable immediately follows. Sakuma says that in words like /kokoro/ and /kakaru/, there is a tendency for the consecutive identical syllables to be pronounced very rapidly. Such pronunciation would shorten each vowel, of course, and therefore make devoicing more likely, but I know of no concrete evidence for Sakuma's claim.

6.2 ACCENT AND INTONATION

Another problem is that devoicing interacts with accent. As we will see in detail in Chapter 8, a Japanese word can be accented or unaccented. The essential part of the accent pattern on an accented word is the location of a change from high pitch to low pitch. I will call the last high-pitched syllable in an accented word the accented syllable and indicate it with an acute accent mark over the vowel. (We will see in section 7.3.2 that the description of Japanese accent involves moras as well as syllables, but this problem need not concern us here.)

An unaccented word has no such fall in pitch, and in isolation, a word with final accent and a word with no accent have the same pattern. When an ENCLITIC (Bloomfield 1933:187) is added, however, the difference shows up. For example, when the enclitic topic particle /wa/ is added to final-accented /haší/ 'bridge', /wa/ is on a low pitch, but when it is added to unaccented /haši/ 'edge', it is on a high pitch. Han (1962b:81) notes that devoicing generally applies only to vowels in unaccented syllables, although there are some exceptions.

One way to avoid an accent on a devoiced syllable is to shift the accent to another syllable. McCawley (1977:266) and Haraguchi (1977:40–41) both discuss accent shift phenomena. One of McCawley's examples involves a regular pattern in accented adjectives like /takái/ 'high'. In general, such adjectives have the accent on the last syllable of the stem in the nonpast form (/taká + i/) and on the penultimate syllable of the stem in the past form (/táka + kaQta/). The corresponding forms of /fukái/ 'deep', however, are /fuká + i/ and /fuká + kaQta/. The accent in the past-tense form has apparently shifted because the vowel in the first syllable of the stem is devoiced.

According to Nihon Onsei Gakkai (1976:748), the power of devoicing to cause accent shifts has apparently weakened considerably in recent times. The example given is /akíkaze/ 'autumn wind', in which the devoiced second syllable carries the accent. Han (1962b:81–82) says that the first syllables of /šíku/ '4 times 9' and unaccented /šíku/ 'spread' are both devoiced at normal tempo. The former has the accent pattern high-low and the latter has the pattern low-high, and Han says, "In actual speech the pitch fall or rise on the syllable /ku/ distinguishes the two."

Another way to avoid an accent on a devoiced syllable is to pronounce an accented syllable with a voiced vowel even if it is in the devoicing environment. Martin (1952:14) says that prepausal /i u/ after a voiceless consonant are devoiced only if there is a fall in pitch somewhere in the word. For a fall in pitch to occur in the word, some syllable other than the last must be accented, and this means that words with final accent or no accent do not meet Martin's conditions for devoicing. The entries in Hirayama (1960), a pronunciation dictionary, seem to be consistent with this description. For example, /tánuki/ 'raccoon dog' is listed with final [i], but /katakí/ 'enemy' and unaccented /misaki/ 'promontory' are listed with final [i̥]. It thus appears that devoicing generally does not apply to a high-pitched final syllable, whether or not that syllable is accented. According to Kawakami's (1977:70–71) discussion, devoicing in /katakí/ and /misaki/ should be usual, although not obligatory, while devoicing in /tánuki/ should be obligatory, but I know of no evidence for this claim.

Intonation also interacts with devoicing. According to Nihon Onsei Gakkai

(1976:748), when a final syllable in the devoicing environment must carry a rising intonation, the vowel does not devoice. One of the examples given is the sentence **Nani ka arimasu?** 'Is there something?', which is distinguished from a statement by question intonation. The essential part of this intonation contour is a rise on the last syllable /su/, and the requirements of this intonation pattern override devoicing.

6.3 CONSONANT ENVIRONMENT

Another problem is that different voiceless consonants seem to have slightly different effects on the probability of devoicing. Han (1962b:88–90) reports experiments in which sentences beginning with words of the form /Cuku/ (where /C/ is a voiceless consonant) were spoken at various tempos. The spectrograms of these utterances suggest that the strength of the devoicing effect of the consonant preceding the relevant vowel can be described as follows: fricatives > affricates > stops. Han says that the fricatives /s/ and /š/ are the strongest. These experiments do not take into account the following consonant, and Martin (1952:14) says that devoicing between two fricatives, while common, is not obligatory at normal tempo.

Han (1962b:86–87) claims that /i u/ sometimes devoice even at normal tempo when the following consonant is the voiced glide /y/. Otherwise, she says, both consonants in a sequence [CVC] must be voiceless. The example Han gives is /soo desu yo/ 'That's right!', which she says can be pronounced [so:desɯjo]. I would argue, however, that this example involves a contraction restricted to the polite copula /desu/ and the polite verb suffix /-masu/ before the emphatic particle /yo/. A more accurate transcription of Han's example would probably be [so:des,jo], with a voiceless [j]. My guess is that this contraction of /suy/ to [s,j] originated as a fast-speech reduction and has become a casual-speech option (section 4.8.4) for /desu/ and /-masu/ before /yo/. A parallel reduction of the /suy/ sequence in, for example, /dasu yoo ni/ 'so as to put out' would certainly not occur at normal tempo. I think it is misleading, therefore, to suggest that a following /y/ somehow favors devoicing.

6.4 CONSECUTIVE SYLLABLES

A final problem is the behavior of words and phrases containing two or more consecutive syllables with vowels in the devoicing environment. Han (1962b:91) says, "In normal speech, the unvoicing of vowels in two consecutive syllables is rare, and the unvoicing of three successive vowels does not occur." Han and Martin (1952:14) agree that if one of the syllables in such a sequence is accented, it will generally not devoice. Martin compares /číšiki/ 'knowledge' and /cukúsu/ 'exhaust' and says that they are pronounced /číšiki/ and /cukúsu/. (To avoid cumbersome phonetic transcriptions in this section, I will simply indicate devoiced vowels with italics in phonemic transcriptions.) The entry in Hirayama (1960) for /číšiki/ agrees, but /cukúsu/ is listed as /c*u*kús*u*/. This last pronunciation conforms to a principle suggested by Han that alternate syllables devoice rather than contiguous ones. In /číš*i*ki/ the accented first syllable remains voiced, and the third syllable must also remain voiced to avoid consecutive devoiced syllables. In /c*u*kúsu/, on the other hand, the accented second syllable remains voiced, and the first and third syllables can both devoice without producing consecutive devoiced syllables.

Martin (1952:14) says that when none of the syllables in the sequence is accented, "there is usually some variation, and the first of the sequence is more often unvoiced." His example is /šikicuméru/ 'spread over', which he says can be /š*i*kicuméru/ or /šik*i*cuméru/. Han (1962b:91–92) says that vowels preceded by nonstops are more often devoiced than those preceded by stops. If there really are differences in the strength of the devoicing effects of preceding consonants (section 6.3), this principle is presumably related. Assuming that preceding nonstops do in fact favor devoicing more than preceding stops, this too predicts that the first syllable in /šikicuméru/ is more likely to devoice than the second syllable. Han's argument, however, is not very convincing. She compares pronunciations of the sentences /sukusuku to nobita/ 'Grew fast' and /kusukusu to waraQta/ 'Giggled', and the spectrograms she gives do in fact show /s*u*kus*u*ku/ versus /kus*u*kus*u*/. The problem is that accent is also involved here. Hirayama (1960) gives /sukúsuku/, with second-syllable accent, as /sukús*u*ku/ but lists both /kusúkusu/ and /kúsukusu/ and, not surprisingly, gives the former as /kus*ú*k*u*su/ and the latter as /kús*u*kus*u*/. It is therefore not clear whether Han is justified in proposing an independent principle depending on the preceding consonant.

Han (1962b:91) also claims that /u/ is more likely to devoice than /i/ if both are involved in a sequence of the type under discussion. Her example is /pikúpiku to/ 'twitch-twitch', which she says is more often pronounced /pik*ú*pik*u* to/ than /p*i*kúp*i*ku to/. The greater susceptibility of /u/ to devoicing presumably follows from its shorter inherent duration (section 6.1), and if Han's claim about this example is correct, this preference for devoicing /u/ is strong enough to override accent considerations. The entry in Hirayama (1960), however, is /p*i*kúp*i*ku/.

One factor that deserves more attention is the apparent preference for devoicing a vowel that is morpheme-medial rather than morpheme-final. For example, in a word like /oši + cukéru/ 'push against', both the /i/ and the first /u/ are in the devoicing environment and neither is in the accented syllable. In spite of the tendency mentioned above for the first vowel in such a sequence to devoice, both Hirayama (1960) and Nihon Hōsō Kyōkai (1966) give /oši + c*u*kéru/.

6.5 DEVOICING VERSUS DELETION

The last question I will consider in this chapter is whether vowels in the devoicing environment are just devoiced or deleted entirely. Bloch's phonemicized text (1950:157–159) and list (1950:164–165) make it clear that he treats many orthographic CVC sequences as phonemically /CC/. For example, leaving aside the pitch markings, he gives **kimashita** 'came', **hitorigoto** 'talking to oneself', **chikai** 'near', **futsū** 'ordinary', and **desukara** 'therefore' as /kimašta/, /xtorigoto/, /čkai/, /hcuu/, and /deskara/, that is, all without vowels. In general, when the orthography indicates a sequence of a fricative or affricate followed by /u/ or /i/ followed by a stop, affricate, or pause, Bloch phonemicizes with no vowel. The only exception seems to be that when the consonant at the end of the sequence is the mora obstruent (section 5.2), Bloch recognizes a voiceless vowel. For example, he transcribes **suppai** 'sour' and **shitta** 'knew' phonetically as [sɯp:pɑi] and [çit:tɑ] (Bloch 1950:136). Since he does not accept /Q/ (section 5.2.2.2), he would phonemicize these as /suppai/ and /šitta/.

Using Ladefoged's (1971:55) feature system, in which consonants that end as fricatives (i.e., fricatives and affricates) are [+ fricative] and consonants that begin as stops (i.e., stops and affricates) are [+ stop], we can say that sequences of the form [1a] do not occur in Bloch's treatment and that sequences of the form [1b] occur instead.

[1] a. $\begin{bmatrix} + \text{fricative} \\ - \text{voice} \end{bmatrix}$ $\begin{matrix} V \\ [+ \text{high}] \end{matrix}$ $\left\{ \begin{matrix} \begin{bmatrix} + \text{stop} \\ - \text{voice} \end{bmatrix} & V \\ \\ \# \end{matrix} \right\}$

   b. $\begin{bmatrix} + \text{fricative} \\ - \text{voice} \end{bmatrix}$ $\left\{ \begin{matrix} \begin{bmatrix} + \text{stop} \\ - \text{voice} \end{bmatrix} & V \\ \\ \# \end{matrix} \right\}$

Han (1962b:82) argues that not recognizing voiceless vowels in sequences of this kind greatly complicates the phonotactics of Japanese. She says that Bloch phonemicizes **kutsu** 'shoe' as /kcu/, and although she is in error about this particular example, her point is well taken. Bloch's analysis gives Japanese a large number of obstruent clusters and word-final obstruents of the form [1b]. Han's position seems to be that an analysis with voiceless vowels is preferable because it simplifies the phonotactics. Phonotactic simplification of this kind is one of the things traditionally labelled PATTERN CONGRUITY (Sommerstein 1977:22), and it is a common criterion in phonemic analysis. (I considered and rejected a phonotactic simplification argument for the phoneme /'/ in section 4.10.)

I mentioned in section 4.8.2 that Bloch's treatment of vowel devoicing leads him to reject the four-vowel analysis, and we are now in a position to see exactly why. To give just one example, we saw that Bloch phonemicizes **kimashita** as /kimašta/. The four-vowel analysis replaces /i/ with /ye/ and derives [ç] from

/sy/. If [ç] appears before /t/, however, we would have to phonemicize **kimashita** as /kimasyta/, with the outlandish cluster /syt/. It is not hard to see that the four-vowel analysis entails several other /CyC/ clusters for Bloch, and he is not willing to go this far.

Bloch's treatment also requires extra phonemes that would not be necessary if he recognized voiceless vowels. In the conservative variety (section 4.1), [ɸ] and [h] do not contrast and can be treated as allophones of a single phoneme /h/ (section 4.3.2.1). The fricative [ç], however, contrasts with [ɸ], as in **hito** 'person' versus **futo** 'suddenly', which Bloch would transcribe phonetically as [ç:to] versus [ɸ:to]. Bloch must therefore assign [ç:] to a separate phoneme /x/. In parallel fashion, [ts] and [t] (section 4.4.2.1) contrast for Bloch in **katsute** 'once' versus **katte** 'raise (gerund)', which he would transcribe phonetically as [kɑts:te] versus [kɑt:te].

Han (1962b:83) also argues that devoiced vowels are identifiable on spectrograms as energy at the characteristic frequencies of formant 1 and formant 2. She says that since vowels are audible even in whispered speech, devoiced vowels are auditorily distinguishable from other sounds. Bloch recognizes the phonetic existence of voiceless vowels in words like /kucu/ 'shoe' and /susumu/ 'advance', but not in words like /arimasu/ 'is' and /šikata/ 'way of doing'. Bloch's (1950:131) phonetic transcriptions of these last two items are [ɑr,imɑs:] and [ç:kɑtɑ], both with a long fricative, and he analyzes these long fricatives as just positional allophones of fricative phonemes. Han's spectrograms seem to show, however, that voiceless vowels are sometimes phonetically present even in words of this latter type at normal tempo.

A final, rather weak argument in favor of recognizing voiceless vowels is an appeal to native speakers' intuitions. There can be little doubt that Japanese speakers "feel" that they pronounce vowels in all the syllables to which devoicing applies, and the writing system is almost certainly involved in some way. For example, /cuki/ 'moon' begins with the same letter as /cugi/ 'next' in kana spelling, but the exact role of orthography is not clear. It may be that kana spelling simply reinforces intuitions that speakers would have anyway, but perhaps it actually determines intuitions to some extent. I will raise this problem again in section 7.3.5.

I do not mean to claim that a voiceless vowel is necessarily articulated in every case, and Han (1962b:92) says that at a fast tempo, a voiceless vowel after a fricative may be "reduced to a mere durational feature." Kawakami's (1977: 71−74) discussion of devoicing implies that a devoiced vowel is sometimes deleted when preceded by a fricative or affricate. He says that such a vowel is usually retained when followed by a consonant identical to the preceding consonant or by /Q/. Otherwise, he says, the voiceless vowel is usually reduced to zero. He claims, however, that even when the vowel is deleted, an [i] or [ɯ] coarticulation (section 4.7) remains on the preceding consonant, and that one might regard such a pronunciation as consisting of a consonant and a voiceless vowel articulated simultaneously.

In any event, it would be foolish to deny that in rapid speech (and probably even in moderately slow speech), at least some voiceless vowels disappear. As Linell (1979:120) points out, however, intuitions about phonotactic correctness seem to be based on careful pronunciations. I noted in section 4.8.4 that fast-speech reductions often produce phonetic segments or segment combinations that native speakers would consider phonologically impossible in isolation. Thus, although voiceless vowel deletion undoubtedly produces phonetic obstruent clusters at rapid tempos in Japanese, this apparently does not happen in the kind of pronunciation to which speakers' intuitions apply. A phonemic treatment of Japanese should therefore include vowels in all the relevant cases, and I will continue to use a phonemic transcription consistent with this conclusion.

Lexical control, + ref. to strength and rate!

Chapter 7

SYLLABLES AND MORAS

7.1 HISTORICAL BACKGROUND

Japanese is frequently cited as an example of a language with relatively simple syllable structure (Sloat, Taylor, and Hoard 1978:62–63), and the structure of Old Japanese was even simpler. All Old Japanese syllables had the form /(C)V/ (or perhaps /(C)(G)V/, where G is a glide; see section 11.1.1), and as I noted in section 3.3, /V/ syllables were generally restricted to word-initial position. At this stage there presumably were no doubts about the locations of syllable boundaries or about the number of syllables in any given word.

Massive borrowing from Chinese and a heterogeneous group of phonological changes known collectively as ONBIN altered the Old Japanese pattern substantially. Most of the mora consonants in modern Japanese derive from these two sources. The onbin changes apparently began about the ninth century, and some of them were probably triggered, or at least accelerated, by the influence of Chinese loans (Endō 1955).

Many of these loans had syllable-final /m/, /n/, or /ŋ/ in the original Chinese. /m/ and /n/ have developed into modern Japanese /N/, but /ŋ/ was generally replaced by a high vowel (Okumura 1972:73–78). It appears that vowels derived from /ŋ/ were originally nasalized but later merged with /i/ or /u/ (Miller 1967: 204–205). The examples in [1] illustrate the correspondences between modern standard Japanese and modern Cantonese. (In these and all subsequent examples, the Cantonese tones are omitted.)

[1] *Cantonese*   *Japanese*

/taŋ/	/too/ (</tau/)	'lamp'
/meŋ/	/mei/	'name'
/san/	/saN/	'mountain'
/kan/	/kaN/	'dry'
/sam/	/saN/	'three'
/nam/	/naN/	'south'

According to Okumura, orthographic practice suggests that a distinction between /m/ and /n/ in this position may have existed in Japanese until the twelfth century. One way (among others) of maintaining the distinction in writing was to use the kana letter for /mu/ for syllable-final /m/ and a new kana symbol, now used for modern standard /N/, for syllable-final /n/ (Toyama 1972:222). In modern standard Japanese, we find only /N/.

Japanese verb morphology shows the effects of the onbin changes very clearly. The examples in [2] illustrate the development of /N/ in verb forms that I will refer to as GERUNDS (Bloch 1946a:6). (In these and all subsequent examples, the Old Japanese forms will not reflect the eight-vowel system discussed in section 11.1.1.)

[2] *Old Japanese*   *Modern Japanese*

/yomite/	/yoNde/	'read'
/yobite/	/yoNde/	'call'
/sinite/	/šiNde/	'die'

There were also loans that had syllable-final /p/, /t/, or /k/ in the original Chinese. In many cases these /p t k/ have developed into modern Japanese /Q/ (Okumura 1972:78–82). The examples in [3] illustrate some correspondences between modern standard Japanese and modern Cantonese.

[3] *Cantonese*   *Japanese*

/čip + kʌn/	/seQ + kiN/	'approach'
/yʌt + pou/	/iQ + po/	'one step'
/tʰit + sin/	/teQ + seN/	'iron wire'
/čit + tʌi/	/teQ + tei/	'thoroughness'
/kwok + ka/	/koQ + ka/	'nation'

In general, in two-morpheme combinations like those in [3], Chinese syllable-final /t/ has become modern Japanese /Q/ before all voiceless obstruents. Chinese syllable-final /p/ in some (but not all) morphemes has also become /Q/ before all voiceless obstruents. Chinese syllable-final /k/ has become /Q/ only before /k/ (with a few exceptions). I will consider these developments in more detail in section 11.2.1.

The onbin changes produced /Q/ in native Japanese words, and again, verb morphology provides good examples. The forms in [4], like those in [2], are gerunds.

[4] *Old Japanese*   *Modern Japanese*
    /matite/   /maQte/   *[mɑt:e]*   'wait'
    /yoɸite/   /yoQte/   'get drunk'
    /yorite/   /yoQte/   'approach'

The Old Japanese phoneme that I transcribe as a bilabial fricative /ɸ/ was undoubtedly /p/ at some earlier stage, and there is some disagreement about whether in fact it had already become /ɸ/ in Old Japanese (Okumura 1972: 126–130). I will follow Hashimoto (1928) and assume that it was already a fricative, but nothing I will say depends on this assumption being correct.

Chinese loans also introduced long vowels into Japanese (Okumura 1972: 82–87, Inoue 1977). Orthographic evidence suggests that even in Old Japanese some words occasionally had lengthened vowels, but it does not appear that there was a long/short contrast. In most cases, Chinese loans with long vowels in modern Japanese were first borrowed with /V₁V₂/ sequences. The long vowels in their modern reflexes are due to subsequent assimilations. See the examples in [5].

[5] *As Borrowed*   *Modern Japanese*
    /guu/   /guu/   'palace'
    /riu/   /ryuu/   'flow'   (/iu/>/yuu/)
    /kou/   /koo/   'public'   (/ou/>/oo/)
    /kau/   /koo/   'high'   (/au/>/oo/)
    /keu/   /kyoo/   'teaching'   (/eu/>/yoo/)

Long vowels have also developed in native Japanese words because of consonant losses. For example, the loss of /k/ in verb and adjective forms (one of the onbin changes) produced results like those in [6].

[6] *Old Japanese*   *Modern Japanese*
    /kikite/   /kiite/   'hear (gerund)'
    /kanasiki/   /kanašii/   'sad (nonpast)'

Another important change was the shift of Old Japanese intervocalic /ɸ/ to /w/ (to Ø before /u/) and the subsequent loss of /w/ everywhere except before /a/ (Matsumoto 1977a, 1977c). This development produced many /VV/ sequences, some with identical vowels from the start and others with nonidentical vowels that have since undergone the same assimilations as the Chinese loans in [5]. The examples in [7] are illustrations.

[7] *Old Japanese*   *Modern Japanese*
    /oɸokami/   >   /owokami/   >   /ookami/   'wolf'
    /yuɸu/   >   /yuu/   'evening'
    /keɸu/   >   /keu/   >   /kyoo/   'today'

In addition, some loans with syllable-final /p/ in the original Chinese developed final /ɸu/ in Japanese. As the examples in [8] show, the same loss of intervocalic /ɸ/ and contiguous vowel assimilations produced long vowels in the modern reflexes.

[8] *As Borrowed*   *Modern Japanese*
/kaɸu/ > /kau/ > /koo/   'tortoise shell'
(Modern Cantonese /kap/)

/kiɸu/ > /kiu/ > /kyuu/   'sudden'
(Modern Cantonese /kʌp/)

Some of the /V_1V_2/ sequences in Chinese loans have not coalesced into long vowels. The examples in [9] illustrate the correspondences between modern standard Japanese and modern Cantonese.

[9] *Cantonese*   *Japanese*
/tai̯/   /tai/   'large'
/söi̯/   /sui/   'water'
/lʌi̯/   /rei/   'example'
/meŋ/   /mei/   'name'

We saw in section 3.2.1 that although /ei/ is ordinarily pronounced [e:] in modern standard Japanese, it can be pronounced [ei] under certain circumstances and is therefore distinct from /ee/.

The /ɸ/ > /w/ > ∅ change and the loss of /k/ in verb and adjective forms produced many /V_1V_2/ sequences in native Japanese words.

[10] *Old Japanese*   *Modern Japanese*
/kakite/ >   /kaite/   'write (ger.)'
/samuki/ >   /samui/   'cold'
/koɸi/   >   /kowi/ >   /koi/   'love'

In the remainder of this chapter I will consider the effect these various changes have had on Japanese syllable structure. In particular, I will try to determine the status of /VV/, /VN/, and /VQ/ sequences. As I mentioned in sections 3.2.2, 5.1.1.6, and 5.2.1, I will argue that modern standard Japanese should be analyzed in terms of both syllables and moras, but we will see that this conclusion is not beyond dispute.

7.2 DEFINITIONS

7.2.1 Syllables

Ladefoged (1982:219–224) divides attempts to define syllables into two categories: definitions in terms of acoustic properties and definitions in terms of speaker activity. One well-known acoustic definition is based on the notion of SONORITY. Ladefoged characterizes the sonority of a speech sound as its intrinsic loudness, that is, "its loudness relative to that of other sounds with the same length, stress, and pitch." There is general agreement that the ranking of sounds on a scale of sonority is roughly as follows: low vowels > high vowels > nasals > voiced fricatives > voiceless fricatives > voiced stops > voiceless stops. According to this definition, the number of syllables in a word is equal to the number of peaks of sonority.

This criterion works perfectly well much of the time, but it does not square with speakers' intuitions in many cases. The examples in [11] illustrate with the English words *rotation* and *spin*.

[11]   *Sonority Scale*

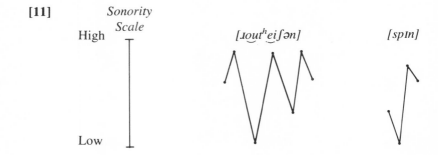

There are three peaks of sonority in *rotation*, and English speakers would certainly agree that there are three syllables. There are two peaks in *spin*, however, and I doubt that any English speaker would say there are two syllables. Ladefoged also points out that the sonority criterion fails to distinguish pairs like *lightening* [lʌitn̩ɪŋ] (three syllables) versus *lightning* [lʌitnɪŋ] (two syllables). The problem here is that an [n] in the same surroundings can be either syllabic or nonsyllabic.

To avoid the problems of the sonority criterion, some linguists have defined syllables in terms of PROMINENCE. Ladefoged (1982:223–224) describes prominence as "some combination of sonority, length, stress, and pitch," and by this criterion, the number of syllables in a word is equal to the number of peaks of prominence. As Ladefoged points out, however, this definition is completely subjective, because prominence is not measurable.

One definition in terms of speaker activity is Stetson's (1951) suggestion that each syllable corresponds to a CHEST PULSE, which Ladefoged (1982:223) describes as "a contraction of the muscles of the rib cage that pushes more air out of the lungs." Experiments by Ladefoged (1967:11–25) have shown, however, that there is no simple one-to-one relationship between this kind of muscular activity and syllables.

Catford (1977:63–92) also defines syllables in terms of speaker activity, but to understand his definition of the syllable, we will first have to consider some preliminary definitions. Catford defines an INITIATOR as "an organ or organ-group . . . which generates positive or negative pressure in the part of the vocal

tract adjacent to it, that is, between the initiator and the place of articulation."
The initiator is the lungs for most of the speech sounds in all languages. The air
expelled from the lungs produces a positive pressure in the vocal tract, and the
outward airflow is known as the PULMONIC-EGRESSIVE airstream. All the speech
sounds in Japanese and in English are produced this way.

The various articulatory structures formed in the vocal tract during speech
impede the outward flow of air to varying degrees. Catford defines INITIATOR
POWER in straightforward mechanical terms as the product of the pressure created
by the initiator and the rate of airflow. Intuitively, it is clear that initiator power
must increase, that is, the initiator must "work harder" to maintain a given rate of
outward airflow when the pressure due to the impedance of articulatory strictures
increases.

Catford (1977:85–92) claims that "in all languages initiator power is deliv-
ered in quantum-like bursts, containing a single peak of power." He also says
that these initiator power pulses are ISOCHRONOUS, that is, roughly equal in
duration at any given tempo. In some languages he says, these power pulses
coincide with syllables, and such languages have SYLLABLE-TIMED rhythm
(Abercrombie 1967:96–98). French is commonly cited as an example of a syllable-timed language. In English, however, Catford says that initiator power
peaks coincide with stressed syllables, and each pulse may span more than one
syllable. Abercrombie (1967:96–98, 131) says that English has STRESS-TIMED
rhythm and labels each isochronous pulse a FOOT. This means that stressed syllables occur at roughly equal intervals, but Ladefoged (1982:109–110, 224) cau-
tions that this is only a tendency. The example in [12] is Abercrombie's; the ver-
tical lines mark foot boundaries, and the feet obviously do not all contain the
same number of syllables.

[12] Whích is the | tráin for | Créwe, | pléase?

Catford (1977:88–92) says that in a two-syllable foot like *tráin for* in [12],
the narrow strictures for [nf] impose a momentary retardation on initiator power.
He then defines syllables as "minimal intra-foot smooth stretches of initiator
power bounded either by major foot boundaries or by minor intra-foot retarda-
tions of initiator activity." In a foot like *sáw all the* (as in *Hárriet | sáw all the |
péople*), of course, the two syllables [sɔ:] and [ɔ:l] are not separated by an articulatory stricture. Catford says, "If any syllable division at all is produced in [such]
sequences . . . it is marked either by very slight self-imposed initiator retardation, or, by the insertion of a glottal stop." This self-imposed retardation is presumably what Martin (1952:13) describes as vowel rearticulation (section 3.2.2).
It is not quite so clear that a momentary retardation is involved in a foot like *téa
out* (as in *Hárriet | thréw the | téa out*). Catford says that the sudden change in
vowel quality in the transition from [tʰi:] to [ɑut] may cause listeners to perceive
a "pseudo-syllable-division."

Ladefoged (1982:219–221) says that leaving aside some minor difficulties,
native speakers of a language seem to agree on how many syllables any given

word contains. This claim is widely accepted, although it has not gone unchal-
lenged (Bell 1975). Even when native speakers do agree, however, the phonetic
definitions I have considered are all inadequate. The number of syllables they
specify is not always the same as the number that native speakers recognize.
Catford's definition is certainly the best, but he is still forced to invoke the notion
of a pseudo-syllable-division in a few cases. This problem has led some linguists
to draw a distinction between PHONETIC SYLLABLES and PHONOLOGICAL SYLLA-
BLES. O'Connor and Trim (1953:104), for example, say that there are "many
cases in which a phonetic syllable can be correlated with no phonological syllable and vice versa."

Hattori (1954:246, n. 4) distinguishes between phonetic and phonological
syllables in Japanese, and he uses the word /háši/ 'chopsticks' to illustrate. When
this word appears in a phrase like /háši to/ 'and chopsticks', vowel devoicing
(Chapter 6) applies, and as I noted in section 6.5, voiceless vowels sometimes
disappear completely. As a result, /háši/ can be pronounced [haç:], and Hattori
treats this as one phonetic syllable but two phonological syllables. He argues that
since /háši/ also appears as [haçi] (as in /háši de/ 'with chopsticks'), it is phonologically two syllables.

When a devoiced vowel is morpheme-internal, of course, there will be no alternations of this kind. For example, the /i/ in /ašitá/ 'tomorrow' is always in the
devoicing environment. It seems clear that in cases like this Hattori would have
to invoke the notion of careful pronunciation (section 3.2.2). He would then be
able to say that a pronunciation like [aç:ta] has two phonetic syllables but three
phonological syllables, since the more careful pronunciation [açita] is also possible. I will return to the problem of careful pronunciation and the distinction between phonetic and phonological syllables in Japanese in section 7.3.1.

7.2.2   Moras

According to McCawley (1978:114), "there is only one workable definition of
'mora': something of which a long syllable consists of two and a short syllable
consists of one." Ladefoged (1982:226), however, says the following: "A mora
is a unit of timing. Each mora takes about the same length of time to say." In
McCawley's analysis of Japanese, the units he identifies as moras are supposed
to fit both these definitions. He says that "the mora functions as the unit of length
in the language; . . . the length of a phrase [is] roughly proportional to the number of moras it contains."

I have already noted that some languages seem to have syllable-timed
rhythm (section 7.2.1). In Catford's (1977:85–88) terms, the syllables in these
languages coincide with the feet, that is, the isochronous initiator power pulses.
If Japanese has two-mora long syllables and one-mora short syllables, and if the
moras are isochronous, then it cannot be a syllable-timed language. It cannot be
stress-timed either. Japanese accent involves pitch rather than stress (section
8.2), and in any case, we certainly do not find roughly equal intervals between

accents. As a result, Japanese rhythm is sometimes called MORA-TIMED. We will see in section 7.3.5, however, that there is serious doubt about whether moras in Japanese are isochronous units.

7.3 SYLLABLES, MORAS, OR BOTH?

7.3.1 Background

According to Kindaichi (1967c:70–71), when Western scholars first introduced the concept of the syllable into Meiji Japan, words like /keQkoN/ 'marriage' and /šookai/ 'introduction' were described as having two syllables each: /keQ-koN/ and /šoo-kai/. Kindaichi says it was his father, Kindaichi Kyōsuke, who first argued that such words contain four syllables each: /ke-Q-ko-N/ and /šo-o-ka-i/. He also claims that before the influence of Western linguistics, no Japanese would have thought of dividing a word like /keQkoN/ into the units /keQ/ and /koN/. One reason he suggests for the initial acceptance of the two-syllable analysis is uncritical application of a European language perspective to Japanese.

In terms of the phonetic definitions discussed in section 7.2.1, there is little doubt that words like /keQkoN/ and /šookai/ have two syllables. At normal tempos there are certainly two peaks of sonority in each word, and probably two initiator power pulses as well. Arisaka (1940:106–107), for example, acknowledges that words of this kind are commonly pronounced with two syllables. He argues, however, that they can be pronounced with four syllables in careful speech. To pronounce /koN/ and /šoo/ as two syllables, there presumably must be a self-imposed initiator retardation (section 7.2.1) between /ko/ and /N/ and between /šo/ and /o/. An abrupt transition from the vowel quality [ɑ] to the vowel quality [i] is probably sufficient to make /kai/ two syllables. The sequence /keQ/ is more problematical, but Arisaka argues that in very slow and careful speech, /Q/ can be a separate syllable, even though its acoustic realization is silence. His position is that the syllables in this kind of pronunciation are the phonological syllables of Japanese, whereas the two syllables in a pronunciation of /keQkoN/ or /šookai/ at a faster tempo are phonetic syllables. The phonological and phonetic syllables coincide only in very slow and careful pronunciation.

In the discussion of long vowels in section 3.2.2, I introduced Linell's (1979:54–56) distinction between careful pronunciation and elaborated pronunciation. I argued that a sharpening process is responsible for pronunciations of sequences like the /šoo/ in /šookai/ as two short syllables, and that such pronunciations need not be considered in determining phonological representations. I suggest, therefore, that the pronunciations on which Arisaka bases his argument are elaborated rather than careful.

Kindaichi (1963:113–114) defines Japanese syllables as the units of rhythm, and he says there is no doubt that words like /keQkoN/ and /šookai/ contain four units. In general, /N/, /Q/, and the second /V/ in a /VV/ sequence are all separate units, just like /CV/ syllables. These are the metrical units in Japanese poetry, and the examples in [13] illustrate the 5-7-5 pattern in a haiku by Bashō Matsuo and in a verse contributed to a linked poem by Bonchō Nozawa. The translations are by Ueda (1982:48, 98).

[13] **a.** Ran no ka ya   'The fragrant orchid
        Chō no tsubasa ni   Into a butterfly's wings
        Takimono su   It breathes the incense.'
        /ra-N-no-ka-ya/
        /čo-o-no-cu-ba-sa-ni/
        /ta-ki-mo-no-su/

    b. Goroppon   'Five or six pieces
        Namaki tsuketaru   Of freshly cut timber
        Mizutamari   Over a muddy pool.'
        /go-ro-Q-po-N/
        /na-ma-ki-cu-ke-ta-ru/
        /mi-zu-ta-ma-ri/

In [13a], /raN/ 'orchid' and /čoo/ 'butterfly' both count as two units, and in [13b], /goroQpoN/ 'five or six pieces' counts as five units. Ordinary native speakers refer to these units as **onsetsu** (usually translated as 'syllables'), but Kindaichi adopts the musical term BEAT (**haku**) to avoid confusion.

Hattori (1954:246, n. 4, 1958:360–362) recognizes these same units of rhythm but refers to them as "moras" rather than "beats." He differs from Kindaichi in recognizing phonological syllables in addition to moras. For Hattori, the words /keQkoN/ and /šookai/ each contain four moras and two phonological syllables, and in general, all Japanese syllables (except the rare overlong syllables; see section 7.4) conform to the schema in [14].

$$[14] \quad (C)(y)V \left(\begin{cases} V \\ N \\ Q \end{cases} \right)$$

Thus, for Hattori, phonological syllables can be short (one mora) or long (two moras). As we saw in section 4.10, Hattori argues that vowel-initial syllables actually begin with the consonant phoneme /'/. I rejected this analysis, however, and I treat the initial consonant in [14] as optional.

Kindaichi (1967c:61) criticizes Hattori's approach as a violation of parsimony. He claims that the concept of beat/mora alone is sufficient. Bloch (1950:120–121) refers to these same beat/mora units as the "syllables of Japanese," and recognizes no longer units that would correspond to Hattori's syllables. Hockett (1955:59) takes the same position and says that "the Japanese syllable is defined fundamentally in terms of duration and nothing else." Hattori's discussion does not make it clear why syllables are necessary in addition to moras, but as we will see in section 7.3.2, there are arguments involving accent that support his analysis.

7.3.2 Syllables, Moras, and Accent

McCawley (1968:133–134) says that the mora is "the unit of phonological distance" in Japanese, by which he means that there are rules that depend on the number of moras. In particular, the third mora from the end of a sequence seems to be a kind of "neutral" location for accent. As we will see in section 8.3.1, the essential part of the accent pattern on an accented Japanese word is the location of the change from high pitch to low pitch, and I will call the last high-pitched mora the "accented mora." McCawley says that strings of meaningless syllables and recent borrowings tend to be accented on the third mora from the end, and the examples in [15] illustrate this point. (An acute accent marks the accented mora in each case.)

[15] /kakikúkeko/   (a line of the kana syllabary)
/pájama/   'pajamas'
/pairóQto/   'pilot'
/hoomúraN/   'home run'

At the same time, other facts about accent provide evidence for Hattori's phonological syllables. As we will see in section 8.3.1, a noun of n short syllables (and therefore n moras) can have any of $n + 1$ possible accent patterns: the pitch may fall after any syllable, or it may not fall at all. The examples in [16] illustrate the three possibilities for two-syllable nouns of this type.

[16] **a.** /háši/   'chopsticks'
     b. /haší/   'bridge'
     c. /haši/   'edge'

As we saw in section 6.2, the difference between [16b] and [16c] is realized when an enclitic like the topic marker /wa/ follows. In /hašíwa/, /wa/ is on a low pitch, and in /hašiwa/, /wa/ is on a high pitch.

In a noun of n long syllables (and therefore $2n$ moras), there are still only n + 1 possible accent patterns and not $2n + 1$. The examples in [17] illustrate the three possibilities for nouns with two long syllables.

[17] /sáNsei/   'third-generation immigrant'
/seNséi/   'teacher'
/saNsei/   'agreement'

Only the first mora of a long syllable can be the accented mora. This means that Hattori's phonological syllable is, in McCawley's (1968:59) words, the "prosodic unit" of Japanese, that is, the accent-bearing unit. The neutral location for accent mentioned above can be stated more accurately as the syllable that contains the third mora from the end. In other words, when the third mora from the end is the second mora of a long syllable, the fourth mora from the end is accented, as the examples in [18] show.

[18] /karéNdaa/   'calendar'
     /esukaréetaa/   'escalator'

There is also an accent loss phenomenon that is most conveniently formulated as a rule referring to syllables rather than moras. As Okuda (1971:24–25) points out, when the genitive particle /no/ follows a noun accented on the final syllable, the accent usually disappears. The rule does not apply, however, unless the noun has more than one syllable. Thus, both the rule and the exception involve counting syllables. The examples in [19] illustrate this point.

[19] /kawá/   'river'   /kawano/
     /kinóo/   'yesterday'   /kinoono/
     /há/   'tooth'   /háno/
     /hóN/   'book'   /hóNno/
     /kása/   'umbrella'   /kásano/

7.3.3 Internal and External Justification

I have considered three kinds of justification for asserting the existence of moras in Japanese. First, there is a kind of INTERNAL JUSTIFICATION, that is, evidence that depends on a particular theoretical perspective (Sommerstein 1977:9–12). Second, there is a kind of PHONETIC JUSTIFICATION, that is, evidence that the linguistic unit corresponds to some phonetic reality. Third, there is a kind of PSYCHOLOGICAL JUSTIFICATION, that is, evidence that the linguistic unit plays some role in behavior. Both phonetic justification and psychological justification are types of EXTERNAL JUSTIFICATION (Sommerstein 1977:13–15).

The internal justification I cited for the existence of the mora is the claim that it is the unit of phonological distance (section 7.3.2). By referring to moras, we can specify the neutral location of accent as a neat generalization: the third mora from the end. The theoretical perspective involved is a preference for more general statements over less general statements in a linguistic description. This view is hardly controversial, but we must keep in mind that the generalization made possible by reference to moras, in and of itself, does not provide any direct evidence that native speakers of Japanese actually organize their utterances in terms of moras.

The phonetic justification I cited for the existence of the mora is the claim that the rhythmic organization of Japanese utterances involves isochronous moras (sections 7.2.2 and 7.3.1). It is widely believed that the duration of an utterance is proportional to the number of moras it contains, but we will see in section 7.3.5 that this belief may well be erroneous.

The psychological justification I cited for the existence of the mora is the claim that it is the metrical unit in Japanese poetry (section 7.3.1). There can hardly be any doubt that this claim is correct, although there is an interesting phenomenon known in Japanese as JIAMARI (literally, 'excess of letters'). The metrical pattern for a haiku, for example, is 5-7-5, and jiamari is the use of more than the required five or seven moras in a line. It would be interesting if there were a tendency for jiamari lines to contain long syllables more frequently than standard-length lines. This does not appear to be the case in the haiku of Bashō, but it might be worthwhile to check the work of more recent poets. In any event, the mora's role in Japanese poetry is beyond dispute, and it seems reasonable to interpret this role as evidence for the psychological reality of this unit. We will see in section 7.3.5, however, that another interpretation is possible.

The internal justification I cited for the existence of the syllable is the claim that the phonological syllable is the accent-bearing unit (section 7.3.2). This claim does not mean that unless we can refer to syllables it is impossible to specify which combinations of phonemes comprise two moras but allow only one possibility for accent placement. The claim is, rather, that a description in terms of moras alone is needlessly messy; it misses a generalization that can be captured by recognizing the syllable as a unit in addition to the mora.

The phonetic justification I cited for the existence of the syllable is straightforward. Even the definition in terms of peaks of sonority (section 7.2.1) works perfectly well in Japanese, and initiator power pulses (section 7.2.1) probably correspond to the same units.

I have not yet suggested any psychological justification for the existence of the syllable, and I will now attempt to remedy this situation in section 7.3.4.

7.3.4 Words and Music

Poetic practice is often cited as psychological evidence, but as we saw in section 7.3.1, the metrical conventions of traditional Japanese poetry involve only moras. The conventions for setting words to music, however, seem to provide psychological evidence for the existence of syllables. I will examine these conventions by citing some well-known children's songs, but the same principles apply in contemporary pop music.

The mora obstruent /Q/ poses an obvious problem in songs because its phonetic realization is generally a voiceless obstruent (section 5.2.1). When a voiceless stop follows, the acoustic correlate of /Q/ is silence. Nonetheless, /Q/ can be assigned to a note of its own by singing it as a short vowel, identical to the preceding vowel, followed by the appropriate voiceless obstruent. On the other hand, /Q/ can also be assigned to the same note as the preceding mora. The examples in [20] illustrate these two possibilities, and apparently both are equally felicitous. (All the musical examples in this section are from Iizuka Shoten Henshūbu (1977), and I cite them by page number.) In [20a] /Q/ is assigned to its own note, whereas in [20b] /Q/ and the preceding /či/ are assigned together to a single note.

[20] a. "Teruteru Bōzu" (page 220, verse 3, line 2)

b. "Sat-chan" (page 318, verse 1, line 2)

da - ke - do   či_Q-ča - i   ka - ra

The mora nasal /N/ (section 5.1) also allows two equally felicitous assignments to notes; see the example in [21]. The first /N/ in this line is assigned to the same note as the preceding mora, but the second /N/ is assigned to a note of its own.

[21] "Genkotsuyama no Tanuki-san" (page 328, line 1)

geN - ko - cu - ya - ma no ta - nu - ki - sa - N

Long vowel syllables (section 3.2) also allow two felicitous assignments, as the examples in [22] illustrate. In [22a] /roo/ is assigned to a single note, but in [22b] /šo/ and /o/ are assigned to separate notes.

[22] "Momotarō" (page 85)

a. mo - mo - ta - r̦oo - saN   (verse 1, line 1)
b. ya - ri - ma - šo - o   (verse 2, line 1)

As we will see in section 7.5, not all /(C)(y)V₁V₂/ sequences that occur in modern Japanese are analyzed as long syllables even by linguists who accept the existence of syllables distinct from moras. I will suggest in section 7.5, however, that words like /nagái/ 'long' and /nasái/ 'do (imperative)', with the accent on the mora before the final /i/, have two syllables: /na-gái/, /na-sái/. The long syllables /gai/ and /sai/ in these words, like long vowel syllables, seem to allow two felicitous assignments to notes. See the examples in [23]. In [23a] /gai/ is assigned to two notes, but in [23b] /sai/ is assigned to one note.

[23] **a.** "Zō-san" (page 141, verse 1, line 1)

o - ha - na ga na - ga - i no ne

b. "Tonton Tomodachi" (page 289, verse 1, line 4)

go - me - N   na - sai

Thus, long syllables apparently coincide with those sequences of two moras that can be assigned with equal felicity to one or two notes. It is possible to argue, of course, that assignments of two moras to a single note simply reflect sloppiness on the part of songwriters. For example, since a quarter note can always be replaced with two eighth notes on the same pitch, we could argue that assigning two moras to a single quarter note is equivalent to assigning them to two eighth notes. However, this line of argument is not very plausible.

In the vast majority of cases, assignments of two moras to one note involve sequences that I have identified as long syllables. This is not to say, of course, that two short syllables are never assigned to a single note, as the examples in [24] illustrate. In [24a] the four-mora word /okašii/ 'funny' is assigned to four notes, but in [24b] the five-mora word /kawaisoo/ 'unfortunate' is squeezed onto the same four notes, and the first two syllables are assigned to the first note. Examples like [24b], however, are relatively rare. Assignments of long syllables to single notes are overwhelmingly more frequent, and it is not clear why this should be so if syllables distinct from moras do not exist in Japanese.

[24] "Sat-chan" (page 318)

a. o - ka - ši - i   na   (verse 1, line 4)
b. kawa - i - so - o   ne   (verse 2, line 4)

When a song has two short syllables in one verse at the same point where it has one long syllable in another verse, some songwriters are careful to put in an extra note for the more crowded verse, as the example in [25] illustrates. If long syllables do not exist in Japanese, it is hard to imagine why the songwriter would add an extra note for /te/ in [25b] and deliberately refrain from adding the same extra note for /N/ in [25a].

[25] "Kurisumasu Dakara" (page 312)

a. ta - ku - saN   ta - ku - saN   (verse 1, line 1)
b. do - o - ši - te   do - o - ši - te   (verse 2, line 1)

One question remains to be considered with respect to words and music. Devoiced vowels (Chapter 6) present a problem in singing, since a syllable containing such a vowel cannot be assigned to a note if the vowel remains voiceless. In most cases, such vowels are voiced in songs, but Sakuma (1973:60) says that they often remain devoiced. Although I have not found any examples in children's songs, it is certainly true in pop music that sequences like /šite/ are sometimes pronounced [çite] or [ç:te] and sung on a single note.

Devoiced vowels occur only in short syllables, and a short syllable with a normally devoiced vowel is probably significantly more likely to be assigned to the same note as a neighboring mora than is a short syllable with a normally voiced vowel. Assuming this surmise is correct, I think the way to resolve the difficulty is to say that although sequences like /šite/ contain two syllables, the natural assignment to two notes in a song can only be bought at the price of the unnatural pronunciation that results from voicing the normally devoiced vowel. This approach maintains the analysis of sequences like /šite/ as two phonological syllables and treats assignments to one note as exceptions. I attribute these exceptions to an additional factor, namely, the pressure to avoid voicing vowels that are ordinarily pronounced voiceless.

This approach makes the interaction between vowel devoicing and music analogous to the interaction between vowel devoicing and accent (section 6.2). Since an accented syllable in a phrase is the syllable containing the last high pitch, syllables with devoiced vowels do not make good accent sites. To avoid this problem, as we saw, the accent can be shifted or the vowel can be voiced.

7.3.5 The Phonetic Status of Moras

The results of some experiments by Beckman (1982) cast serious doubt on the widely held belief that Japanese moras are isochronous units (sections 7.2.2, 7.3.1, and 7.3.3). Beckman pays particular attention to /CV/ moras in which vowel devoicing (Chapter 6) applies. As I mentioned in section 6.1, Sakuma (1929:232–233) says that /i u/ are more susceptible to devoicing than /a e o/ because they are intrinsically shorter. I also noted in section 6.5 that devoiced vowels are sometimes deleted entirely.

Homma (1981:280) argues that mora lengths remain roughly equal because of TEMPORAL COMPENSATION. As Beckman (1982:114) explains, this means that "the lengths of adjacent segments vary inversely with each other so that mora lengths are maintained in spite of widely varying intrinsic lengths of the component segments." When a devoiced vowel is deleted, the mora involved is realized phonetically as just a consonant. If temporal compensation maintains isochronous moras, the duration of this consonant should be about the same as the duration of /CV/ moras with voiced vowels. Beckman's (1982:118–119) measurements indicate, however, that when a devoiced vowel is deleted, the duration of the remaining consonant is not significantly longer than the duration of the consonant in a /CV/ mora with a voiced vowel.

Beckman also reports measurements of the mora obstruent /Q/ (section 5.2). As I mentioned in section 5.2.1, Han (1962a:70) reports results indicating that the duration of a phonetically long stop (phonemically, /Q/ followed by a stop) is roughly one mora longer than the duration of a short stop. Homma (1981:275) reports similar ratios, but Beckman's (1982:121–124) replications of the Han and Homma experiments indicate that the average duration of /Q/ is approximately two-thirds the average duration of a /CV/ mora.

In her conclusion, Beckman (1982:133–134) says that her investigation provides "no convincing evidence for the phonetic reality of the mora." As we saw in section 7.3.1, however, moras are the metrical units in Japanese poetry and the units into which native speakers intuitively divide words. Beckman attributes such phenomena to the influence of writing. As she points out, the kana spelling system and traditional poetic meter both date back to the time of Old Japanese. We saw in section 7.1 that Old Japanese syllables all had the form /(C)V/ (or perhaps /(C)(G)V/), and the units identified by all the criteria I have discussed in this chapter would have coincided. The various phonological changes we saw in section 7.1 have produced syllables written with two kana letters that count as two units in traditional poetic meter. Beckman argues that since virtually all Japanese are literate, kana orthography mediates their intuitions about poetic length and dividing words into smaller units.

It would be interesting to know whether careful replications of Han's experiments on the second moras of long-vowel syllables (section 3.2.2) and the mora nasal /N/ (section 5.1.1.6) would show that the average duration of these moras, like that of /Q/, is significantly less than the average duration of /CV/ moras. In any case, the shorter duration of /Q/ is certainly consistent with what Beckman (1982:118–120) calls a "weaker version" of the claim that moras are isochronous. According to this weaker version, a segment's intrinsic duration constrains temporal compensation. In the case of /Q/, as long as the average duration of a phonetic long stop is significantly longer than twice that of a short stop, we can maintain the weaker claim.

It seems likely that /CV/ moras with devoiced vowels are also consistent with the weaker claim. Beckman (1982:115) instructed her subjects to use a "comfortable speaking rate," but I argued in section 6.5 that phonological intuitions are based on careful pronunciation (section 3.2.2). We saw in section 6.5 that devoiced vowels apparently do not delete in careful pronunciation, and although I would not expect the average duration of [CV̥] moras to be as long as that of [CV] moras, the difference is probably consistent with the weaker version of the claim that moras are isochronous.

Further investigation is clearly required, but I am not yet willing to abandon the claim that moras are phonetically real units in Japanese. In any event, the psychological reality of moras is hard to deny. It may well be that kana orthography mediates native speakers' intuitions, but such mediation does not necessarily make these intuitions nonlinguistic. Bloomfield (1933:21) says, "A language is the same no matter what system of writing may be used to record it," and I think it is fair to say that most phonologists work under this assumption. Jones (1967:63) mentions that the labiodental nasal [ɱ] occurs in Italian before /f v/, and he says that the inclination to treat it as an allophone of /n/ rather than /m/ is due to the fact that it is spelled **n**. He cites this as an example of what he interprets as a "prejudice," caused by literacy, that obscures a native speaker's "natural linguistic sense." It is certainly possible, however, that orthography shapes natural linguistic sense to some extent in literate cultures.

If we accept the idea that orthography can influence phonological representations, we must reconsider the arguments I have given that depend on the distinction between careful and elaborated pronunciation. I suggested in sections 3.2.2 and 7.3.1 that each mora of a long syllable is pronounced as a separate short syllable only in elaborated pronunciation, and there is little doubt that this kind of letter-by-letter pronunciation is mediated by kana orthography. Linell (1979:54–56) says that speakers use elaborated pronunciation when they want to articulate the sounds of a word very distinctly, and it is not surprising that orthography influences the elaborated pronunciation of literate speakers. I suggested in section 6.5 that native speakers' intuitions apply to careful pronunciations, but if orthography can in fact mediate intuitions, the situation is more complicated. In any case, this problem deserves more careful consideration than I can give it here.

7.4 OVERLONG SYLLABLES

Hattori (1958:361) says that certain morphological processes sometimes produce three-mora syllables. Using hyphens to delimit these overlong syllables, his examples are /-tóoQ-ta/, the past tense of the verb /tóoru/ 'pass'; /roN-doNQ-ko/ 'Londoner', which contains the suffix /Qko/ (cf. /edo/ 'Edo', /edoQko/ 'Edoite'); and /arima-séNQ-te/ 'that (there) isn't', which contains the colloquial quotative particle /Qte/ (cf. /iku/ 'go', /ikuQte/ 'that (it) will go'). Adding the common adjective-forming suffix /Qpoi/ can also produce overlong syllables. Typical examples are /ni-hoNQ-pói/ 'Japanesey' (from /nihóN/ 'Japan') and /fu-ryooQ-pói/ 'delinquentlike' (from /furyoo/ 'delinquent').

In addition, many recent loanwords are spelled with /V_1V_1N/ sequences that may represent three-mora syllables. A few examples are /rabu-šíiN-/ 'love scene', /gureeto-déeN-/ 'Great Dane', and /-zóoN-/ 'zone'. /$V_1 + V_1N$/ sequences, with a morpheme boundary between the vowels, are common in Sino-Japanese words, but these sequences have a syllable boundary at the morpheme boundary. For example, words like /í + iN/ 'committee member' and /soo + oN/ 'noise' clearly end with /VN/ syllables. There are no morpheme boundaries in the /V_1V_1N/ sequences in the recent borrowings cited just above, however, and they apparently do not contain syllable boundaries.

At normal conversational tempos, there seems to be a strong tendency to reduce overlong syllables to ordinary long syllables. /V_1V_1Q/ sequences are reduced to /V_1Q/, and /VNQ/ sequences are reduced to /VN/. Thus, /tóoQta/

'passed' is often indistinguishable from /tóQta/ 'took', and /nihoNQpói/ 'Japanesey' sounds like /nihoNpói/. At least some of the /V_1V_1N/ sequences in recent borrowings seem to reduce to /VN/, which suggests that they are in fact overlong syllables. For example, /gureetodéeN/ 'Great Dane' usually sounds like /gureetodéN/ to me. Some experimental work would certainly help clarify the status of overlong syllables.

7.5 NONIDENTICAL VOWEL SEQUENCES

We saw in section 3.3 that all possible /V_1V_2/ sequences occur in modern standard Japanese. As I noted, it is not obvious when /V_2/ initiates a separate phonological syllable (section 7.3.1) and when it is the endpoint of a diphthong. As a first approximation, it seems safe to say that unless /V_2/ is a high vowel (/i/ or /u/), there is generally a syllable boundary between two nonidentical vowels. I will consider a few apparent exceptions to this generalization below.

Most /Vu/ sequences contain a morpheme boundary between the two vowels and are clearly not diphthongs. This is because some of the phonological changes discussed in section 7.1 eliminated such sequences within morphemes. Some examples of /V + u/ are: /ki + uke/ 'popularity', /ame + uri/ 'candy seller', /ma + ura/ 'right behind', /go + uči/ 'go player'. In recent borrowings, however, we find many /au/ sequences within morphemes, and at least some of these may be diphthongs. The /au/ in /áuto/ 'out (in baseball)', for example, may be a single phonological syllable. In a word like /káuNtaa/~/kauNtaa/ 'counter', the /kauN/ sequence may be an overlong syllable (section 7.4).

/Vi/ sequences within morphemes are not confined to recent borrowings. As we saw in section 7.1, /ai/ and /ui/ have remained in Sino-Japanese morphemes, and consonant losses have produced /ai/, /ui/, and /oi/ sequences in many native morphemes. The /i/ moras in native Japanese /cúi/ 'just', Sino-Japanese /ái/ 'love', and the recent borrowing /boikóQto/ 'boycott' may not be separate phonological syllables, and the recent borrowing /kóiN/ 'coin' may be a single overlong syllable.

Hattori (1950:751, n. 1, 1958:360–361) says that the second vowel in /V_1V_2/ sequences in Tokyo Japanese usually initiates a separate phonological syllable. He mentions, however, that some speakers pronounce /(C)(y)Vi/ sequences as single long phonological syllables. He does not explain how such a sequence pronounced as a long syllable differs from the same sequence pronounced as two short syllables, but he transcribes his /'/ phoneme (section 4.10) between the two vowels if they are in separate syllables. This presumably means that /V_2/ is longer when it initiates a separate syllable. It may also be that the change in vowel quality is more abrupt when the two vowels are in separate syllables.

If Japanese syllables coincide with initiator power pulses, as I suggested in section 7.3.3, then it should be possible to determine objectively whether careful pronunciations of a given /(C)(y)Vi/ sequence contain one syllable or two. Recall, however, that an abrupt vowel quality transition can apparently give rise to a perceived syllable division even when there is no retardation of initiator activity (section 7.2.1).

In some cases, it is clear even without any phonetic experimentation that the second mora in a /V_1V_2/ sequence initiates a separate phonological syllable. As we saw in section 7.3.2, an accented long syllable has a high pitch on the first mora and a low pitch on the second mora. If the last high pitch in a word is on the second vowel in a /V_1V_2/ sequence, that vowel must be a separate syllable, since the second mora of a long syllable cannot bear accent. Thus, for example, the accented /i/ in /hiroízumu/ 'heroism' is clearly a syllable.

When the accent does not fall on the second vowel of a /V_1V_2/ sequence, it tells us nothing about whether /V_2/ is a separate syllable. As we saw in section 7.3.2, however, a polysyllabic word with final accent loses its accent before the genitive particle /no/. Thus, if a polysyllabic word ends /(C)(y)V́$_1$V$_2$/ and loses its accent before /no/, this sequence must be a long syllable.

Another type of accentual evidence I will consider is the location of accent in accented verbs. As we will see in section 8.3.2, if a verb is accented, the accent generally falls on the second mora from the end in the citation form, as the examples in [26] illustrate.

[26] /tabéru/   'eat'
     /yómu/   'read'
     /oboéru/   'remember'
     /kuíru/   'regret'

There are a few exceptions, however, as the examples in [27] show.

[27] **a.** /háiru/   'enter'
     b. /máiru/   'go (humble)'
     c. /káeru/   'return home'
     d. /kotáeru/ (~/kotaéru/)   'answer'

The verbs in [27] suggest that the /ai/ and /ae/ sequences are diphthongs, allowing us to maintain a completely general rule for accent placement in verbs by referring to the second syllable from the end. If this conclusion is correct, examples [27c] and [27d] contain long syllables ending in the nonhigh vowel /e/. I should point out in this connection that there is a tendency for Tokyo speakers to pronounce /ae/ and /oe/ within morphemes as /ai/ and /oi/, although this pronunciation is considered substandard (Martin 1952:13).

Accentual evidence also indicates that the /(C)Vi/ sequence at the end of the citation form of an unaccented adjective is a long syllable. According to Hirayama (1960:918, 928) and Akinaga (1966:66–69, 75), when the enclitic /ga/ 'but' is added to an unaccented verb, an accent appears on the last syllable of the verb, as in /iku/ 'go' versus /ikúga/ 'go, but'. When this same /ga/ is added to an unaccented adjective, the accent appears on the penultimate mora, as in /asai/ 'shallow' versus /asáiga/ 'shallow, but'. It is interesting that these long syllables appear to span a morpheme boundary. The final /i/ in the citation form of an adjective is usually considered an inflectional ending, but when an enclitic like /ga/ contributes an accent, it falls on the preceding vowel.

To conclude this chapter, I will mention a potential source of nonaccentual evidence for the syllable structure of word-final /(C)(y)V₁V₂/ sequences. In the discussion of utterance-final glottal stops in section 3.1.2, I said that a nondistinctive glottal stop appears after an utterance-final short vowel. This fact suggests that a word-final /i/ that constitutes a separate syllable will be followed by [ʔ] utterance-finally.

As we saw in section 5.2.4, when emphasis makes an utterance-final glottal stop salient, speakers seem to identify it as /Q/. I will now consider instances of utterance-final glottal stops after long syllables. According to Nihon Onsei Gakkai (1976:480), /ikoo/ 'let's go' can be pronounced emphatically as [ʔikoʔ], with a final glottal stop following a shortened vowel. It appears that a glottal stop can also follow a /(C)(y)VN/ syllable at the end of an emphatic utterance, and when this happens, the entire syllable seems to be squeezed into the duration of a single mora. An example from a comic book (Takahashi 1982:19) is the word /kaNriniNsaN/ 'manager' in the utterance **Kanrininsaň!!** 'Manager!!'. As in section 3.1.2, the breve indicates that there is a reduced-size kana letter **tsu** at the end of the word in the Japanese orthography. This small **tsu** is the conventional spelling of a salient utterance-final glottal stop.

Words ending in /Vi/ are also sometimes spelled with a final glottal stop in comic books, as the examples in [28] illustrate.

[28] **a.** /urusái/   'noisy'   Urusaĭ!
                                   (Fujikawa and Hio 1974:76)

b. /hái/   'yes'   Haĭ!
                        (Fujikawa and Hio 1974:121)

c. /abunái/   'dangerous'   Abunaĭ!
                                  (Fujimoto and Abiko 1974:27)

These spellings apparently represent final [ɑiʔ], with the diphthong squeezed into a single mora. This kind of shortening seems to apply only to /(C)(y)Vi/ sequences that are long syllables and not to those that are two short syllables. For example, unaccented /hai/ 'ash' is apparently two syllables, since even if it is shouted emphatically, it remains two moras [hɑ-iʔ] and is not shortened.

All the words in [28] have final-syllable accent, which means that the last high-pitched mora is the one before /i/. When there is a fall in pitch between the two moras, a morpheme-internal /(C)(y)Vi/ sequence is probably always a single long syllable. The words /urusái/ [28a] and /abunái/ [28c], however, are both adjectives, and as I mentioned above, the final /i/ is usually considered an inflectional ending. Nonetheless, utterance-final shortening applies to emphatic pronunciations of these words, and this shortening indicates that /sa + i/ and /na + i/ are long syllables. Since even unaccented adjectives seem to end in long syllables, as we saw above, it should come as no surprise that the same is true of accented adjectives.

The various criteria mentioned in this section for determining syllable structure are nothing more than preliminary suggestions. There are, of course, many /(C)(y)V_1V_2/ sequences to which they do not apply, and the entire problem certainly deserves more thorough study.

Chapter 8

ACCENT

8.1 PREVIOUS WORK

Accent is undoubtedly the most widely studied aspect of Japanese phonology. In the preface to the collection of articles on Japanese phonology in Shibata, Kitamura, and Kindaichi (1980:iii), Shibata says that the large proportion of accent studies reflects the volume of Japanese scholarship in this area. These papers provide a fine introduction to the development of accent studies in Japan, and the commentary by Shibata (1980) is excellent.

Japanese accent has also been a popular topic for generative studies in the United States in recent years. Growing interest in suprasegmental phenomena has led to a proliferation of theoretical models, and the Japanese accent system provides a convenient body of well-known data against which such proposals can be tested.

Even a cursory survey of the literature on Japanese accent would have to be very long, and I will not attempt one here. I will simply try to provide enough background to allow an intelligible comparison of the approaches in McCawley (1977) and Haraguchi (1977). I will confine my attention to the system in standard Japanese and ignore the wealth of material on other Japanese dialects.

8.2 HIGH AND LOW PITCH

The pitch of a sound is the perceptual correlate of FUNDAMENTAL FREQUENCY. The fundamental frequency of speech sounds is determined by the rate at which the vocal cords open and close in voicing, and this rapid opening and closing, or vibration, is known as PHONATION. Voiceless sounds, therefore, do not have fundamental frequency. Kaplan (1971:203–204) gives a good account of the anatomical and physiological factors involved in phonation. The most important factors in determining fundamental frequency are the rate at which air is expelled from the lungs, the tension of the vocal cords, and the length and mass of the vibrating portions. All of these factors are under voluntary control to a certain extent, but anatomical and physiological factors set the absolute limits on each individual's voice range.

A speaker does not use this entire range when speaking, and the portion in use does not remain constant. Emotional state, for example, can have a considerable effect on what part of the range a person uses; the average fundamental frequency generally rises when the speaker is angry or afraid. Abramson (1962:14) refers to the range determined by anatomical, physiological, and emotional factors as the UNDERLYING VARYING VOICE REGISTER. It is convenient to think of other variations in fundamental frequency as being superimposed on this underlying register.

There is general agreement that the accent patterns of isolated Japanese words can be represented by specifying which moras carry high pitch and which moras carry low pitch. The examples in [1] illustrate, using H to represent a high mora and L to represent a low mora.

[1] /haǰimeru/   'begin'   LHHH
    /zárazara/   'rough'   HLLL
    /tatémono/   'building'   LHLL
    /širabéru/   'investigate'   LHHL

The use of H and L does not mean, however, that when a given speaker pronounces a given word in isolation, H and L correspond to two particular fundamental frequencies, or even two narrow ranges of fundamental frequency. Weitzman's (1969) measurements, for example, show that in a sequence HH or LL, the second mora is on a significantly lower pitch than the first mora.

Kawakami (1977:103–104) and Higurashi (1983:87–90) both suggest that Japanese utterances involve a kind of natural DOWNDRIFT, that is, the mean pitch falls gradually from the beginning to the end of a syntactic unit such as a phrase or clause. Fromkin (1972:84–86) says that downdrift may be due to a gradual decrease in airflow within what Lieberman (1967:26) calls a BREATH GROUP, that is, one expiration of air from the lungs. Other things being equal, the smaller the airflow, the lower the rate of vibration of the vocal cords. Higurashi suggests the same explanation and refers to the gradual fall in pitch within a breath group as "phonetic tonal fade."

We might represent the effect of downdrift schematically as in [2]. If a certain decrease in pitch from one mora to the next is due to downdrift, the change from H to L in the first two moras of a word like /zárazara/ (HLLL) must be a significantly steeper drop, as [2] shows.

[2]

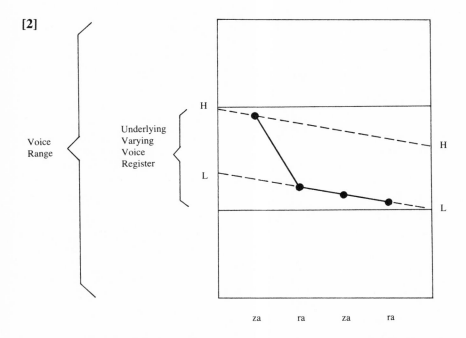

Representation in terms of H and L seems to make intuitive sense to native speakers of standard Japanese. It is quite easy for them to learn to "sing" words so that all the H moras are on the same pitch, and accent dictionaries compiled for the general public, such as Hirayama (1960) and Nihon Hōsō Kyōkai (1966), use notational variants of this system. I will assume hereafter that this kind of two-level description is adequate for isolated words and words followed by enclitics.

8.3 WORD ACCENT

8.3.1 Nouns

The examples in [3] illustrate the possible pitch patterns for nouns of three and four short syllables. In each case I give the pattern for the noun in isolation and the pattern for the noun followed by the enclitic topic particle /wa/, since some of the distinctions do not show up in the isolation forms (section 6.2).

[3]			
a.	/sakana/	'fish'	LHH
	/sakanawa/		LHHH
b.	/mákura/	'pillow'	HLL
	/mákurawa/		HLLL
c.	/kokóro/	'heart'	LHL
	/kokórowa/		LHLL

d. /takará/	'treasure'	LHH
/takaráwa/		LHHL
e. /kamaboko/	'fish paste'	LHHH
/kamabokowa/		LHHHH
f. /kámakiri/	'mantis'	HLLL
/kámakiriwa/		HLLLL
g. /kudámono/	'fruit'	LHLL
/kudámonowa/		LHLLL
h. /kagaríbi/	'bonfire'	LHHL
/kagaríbiwa/		LHHLL
i. /kamisorí/	'razor'	LHHH
/kamisoríwa/		LHHHL

In general, a noun of n short syllables can have any of $n + 1$ possible pitch patterns (Akinaga 1966:47): there can be a fall from H to L after any syllable or no fall at all. I will call the last H syllable the "accented syllable" and indicate it with an acute accent mark in phonemic transcription (section 6.2). Words with no accented syllable, like /sakana/ [3a] and /kamaboko/ [3e], are unaccented. An initial short syllable is always low unless it is the accented syllable. Thus, the pitch pattern on a noun, as on any Japanese word, is entirely predictable once we know which syllable, if any, is accented. No word can have more than one accented syllable.

As we saw in section 7.3.2, long syllables, too, are either accented or unaccented. Thus, the number of potential accent sites in any Japanese word is equal to the number of syllables, and the number of possible pitch patterns for a noun of n syllables, long or short, is $n + 1$. When a long syllable is accented, the first mora is H and the second mora is L, at least in careful pronunciation. Martin (1970:429) says that both moras of an accented long syllable seem to be H at a faster tempo, but I will ignore this complication. When an initial long syllable of the form /(C)(y)VV/ or /(C)(y)VN/ is unaccented, some standard speakers pronounce it LH, but others pronounce it HH (Hattori 1954:246). See the examples in [4].

[4] /kóokoo/	'filial piety'	HLLL
/kookoo/	'high school'	LHHH~HHHH
/kéNdoo/	'fencing'	HLLL
/keNtóo/	'guess'	LHHL~HHHL
/keNtoo/	'examination'	LHHH~HHHH

Accent dictionaries like Hirayama (1960) and Nihon Hōsō Kyōkai (1966) consistently give LH as the pitch pattern on unaccented initial syllables of the form /(C)(y)VQ/, but Haraguchi (1977:34–35) says that LL is more accurate. See the examples in [5].

[5]		*Hirayama*	*Haraguchi*
a. /kéQsoN/	'deficit'	HLLL	HLLL
b. /keQšoo/	'crystal'	LHHH	LLHH

Since /Q/ is generally voiceless (section 5.2.3), the basis for treating it as H or L is not clear. Hirayama and Nihon Hōsō Kyōkai give LH for all unaccented initial long syllables, and it may be that they simply treat /(C)(y)VQ/ syllables like all other long syllables by analogy.

We saw in section 6.2 that according to Han (1962b:81–82), the /i/ in both /šiku/ 'spread' (LH) and /šíku/ '4 times 9' (HL) is devoiced at normal tempo. Han says that the syllable /ku/ has a rising pitch in the former and a falling pitch in the latter. If so, we may be able to determine whether /Q/ is H or L by looking at the preceding vowel. For example, if the /e/ in /keQšoo/ [5b] has a rising pitch, then presumably /Q/ is H. I will return to this question briefly in section 8.5.2.

Hamano (personal communication, 1984) has pointed out to me that there seem to be some marginal cases of an accent appearing on the second mora of a long syllable. When an unaccented word is quoted emphatically, an accent seems to appear on the last mora. For example, the word /koobaN/ 'police box' is unaccented, but if a speaker wants to say something like 'I said *police box*!', there is a fall in pitch between /N/ and the quotative particle /to/: /koobaŃ to iQta/. In addition, some onomatopoetic mimetic adverbs that appear before /to/ can be pronounced with elongated vowels and with an accent on the final mora. For example, in /piN to íto o hajíku/ 'snap a string plink', the adverb can be pronounced /piiŃ/. It might be better to attribute the fall in pitch in these examples to intonation rather than to accent, but I will leave this question unresolved.

A one-mora word, whether accented or unaccented, is apparently H in isolation (McCawley 1968:133, n. 4, Haraguchi 1977:19–20). Examples [6a] and [6b] are illustrations. In general, a short final syllable is H in the isolation forms of both unaccented words and final-accented words (Akinaga 1966:47). Consequently, the isolation forms of /haši/ 'edge' [6c] and /haší/ 'bridge' [6d] are identical (section 6.2).

[6]					
a.	/ki/	'spirit'	H	/kiwa/	LH
b.	/kí/	'tree'	H	/kíwa/	HL
c.	/haši/	'edge'	LH	/hašiwa/	LHH
d.	/haší/	'bridge'	LH	/hašíwa/	LHL

There is actually some doubt about whether the pitch patterns on the isolation forms of unaccented and final-accented words are the same. Uwano (1977:289), for example, says that they are not identical for all speakers on all occasions, but I will hereafter ignore this problem.

The various particles that can be added to nouns have different effects on the location of accent in the noun + particle combinations. Some, like the topic marker /wa/, have no effect except to bring out the distinction between final accent and no accent, as in [6]. The genitive particle /no/, on the other hand, generally removes a final accent from a noun with more than one syllable (Martin 1952:45, Akinaga 1966:58). We saw some examples of this accent loss in section 7.3.2, but there are a few exceptions. Martin notes the exceptions in [7].

[7] /yosó/   'other'   /yosóno/
     /cugí/   'next'   /cugíno/
     /ehóN/   'picture book'   /ehóNno/
     /seNséi/   'teacher'   /seNséino/

Numerals, numeral + classifier compounds, and words denoting indefinite quantities frequently occur before /no/, and they are also exempt from final-accent loss (Martin 1952:45, Hirayama 1960:891). See the examples in [8].

[8] /hyakú/   'hundred'   /hyakúno/
     /iQsacú/   'one (book)'   /iQsacúno/
     /oozéi/   'crowd (of people)'   /oozéino/
     /takusáN/   'many, much'   /takusáNno/

McCawley (1977:267) mentions an additional class of exceptions. He says that a final accent before /no/ is retained if the noun phrase before /no/ consists of more than just the noun. See the examples in [9].

[9] a. /umá/   'horse'
     b. /umano/   'horse's'
     c. /anoumá/   'that horse'
     d. /anoumáno/   'that horse's'

Martin (1970:438–440) suggests that, in general, a final accent is retained when a phrase boundary immediately follows /no/, and I suspect such a boundary is more likely after [9d] than after [9b].

Akinaga (1966:80–81) says that when an accent is shifted onto the last syllable of a word to avoid a devoiced vowel (section 6.2), it does not disappear before /no/. Examples [10a] and [10b], with the devoiced vowels in italics, illustrate this point. When a shifted final accent is no longer felt to be shifted synchronically, however, Akinaga says that it does disappear before /no/. One of his examples is [10c].

[10] a. /kikí/   'crisis'   /kikíno/
      b. /fukíN/   'vicinity'   /fukíNno/
      c. /kišá/   'train'   /kišáno/~/kišano/

Hirayama (1960) and Nihon Hōsō Kyōkai (1966) list /kikí/ and /kíki/ as alternatives for 'crisis' [10a], but they list only /fukíN/ for 'vicinity' [10b] and only /kišá/ for 'train' [10c]. It is therefore not clear what the evidence is for the earlier unshifted forms of [10b] and [10c] that Akinaga posits.

Akinaga (1966:81) also lists several deverbal nouns that end in /Vi/ and says that accent loss before /no/ is subject to variation. Deverbal nouns of three short syllables generally have final accent if they are related to accented verbs (Martin 1952:34, Akinaga 1966:48). See the examples in [11].

[11]	*Verb*		*Noun*	
a. /hanásu/	'speak'		/hanaší/	'story'
b. /hikáru/	'shine'		/hikarí/	'light'
c. /yasúmu/	'rest'		/yasumí/	'vacation'

When the citation form of a verb (i.e., the nonpast form; see section 12.1) ends in /V́u/, however, the deverbal noun ends in /V́i/, as the examples in [12] show.

[12]	/omóu/	'think'	
	/omói/	'thought'	/omoino/~/omóino/
	/nióu/	'smell'	
	/niói/	'odor'	/nioino/~/nióino/
	/negáu/	'ask'	
	/negái/	'request'	/negaino/~/negáino/

Akinaga says that the accent has been retracted in the nouns in [12], and we might try to account for this retraction by saying that the /(C)Vi/ sequences are long syllables. We saw in section 7.5, however, that the /i/ in a /Vi/ sequence can be a separate syllable, and it must be if it bears accent. In addition, there is arguably a morpheme boundary before /i/ in these examples, so there is no obvious motivation for an accent retraction.

I suggested in section 7.5 that if a polysyllabic word ends in /(C)(y)V́i/, whether or not the accent disappears before /no/ can be a test for the syllable structure of this sequence. It may be that accent retention or loss before /no/ in the examples in [12] depends on whether the speaker treats the final /(C)V́i/ sequence as one syllable or two. On the other hand, given the exceptions in [7] and [8], it may simply be that accent loss before /no/ is generally not a very reliable indicator of syllable structure.

When the particle /nado/ 'etc.' follows an accented noun, the accent of the noun appears, but when it follows an unaccented noun, an accent appears on the first syllable of the particle (Martin 1952:44, Akinaga 1966:58–59). See the examples in [13].

[13]	/mákura/	/mákuranado/
	/kokóro/	/kokóronado/
	/takará/	/takaránado/
	/sakana/	/sakananádo/

There are several other particles that contribute an accent to an unaccented noun in parallel fashion (Martin 1952:44, Akinaga 1966:58–59).

When the particle /gurai/ 'at least' follows a noun, the accent of the noun + particle combination always falls on the first syllable of the particle (Martin 1952:44), as the examples in [14] illustrate.

[14] /mákura/ /makuragúrai/
/kokóro/ /kokorogúrai/
/takará/ /takaragúrai/
/sakana/ /sakanagúrai/

There are a few other particles that behave in parallel fashion for at least some speakers (Martin 1952:44, Akinaga 1966:59).

According to Martin (1952:43–44), McCawley (1977:263–264), and Higurashi (1983:33–34), when the particle /šika/ 'only' is added to an unaccented noun with a short final syllable, an accent appears on that syllable. When /šika/ is added to an accented noun, the accent of the noun appears in the expected place. See the examples in [15].

[15] /mákura/ /mákurašika/
/kokóro/ /kokórošika/
/takará/ /takarášika/
/sakana/ /sakanášika/

If /šika/ simply contributed an accent on the final syllable of an unaccented noun, it would provide a straightforward test for determining the syllable structure of /(C)(y)VV/ and /(C)(y)VN/ sequences at the end of unaccented nouns (section 7.5). Higurashi claims, however, that in all such cases the last mora of the noun is H and the first mora of /šika/ is L. She gives examples like those in [16].

[16] /gaQkoo/ 'school' /gaQkoóšika/
*/gaQkóošika/
/koobaN/ 'police box' /koobaŃšika/
*/koobáNšika/

If Higurashi is right, noun + /šika/ combinations contradict the generalization that the second mora of a long syllable cannot bear accent (section 7.3.2). Earlier in this section I mentioned some marginal counterexamples to this generalization involving /to/, but it would be harder to dismiss examples with /šika/ as marginal.

For the standard speakers with whom I have checked, /šika/ behaves exactly like /nado/ in [13]. As the examples in [17] show, an accent appears on the first syllable of /šika/ when it follows an unaccented noun.

[17] /mákura/ /mákurašika/
/kokóro/ /kokórošika/
/takará/ /takarášika/
/sakana/ /sakanašíka/
/gaQkoo/ /gaQkoošíka/
/koobaN/ /koobaNšíka/

The /i/ in /šika/, of course, is ordinarily devoiced (section 6.1), and this is undoubtedly the cause of the difference between the pattern in [15] and [16] and the pattern in [17]. I do not know of any evidence for a shift in progress toward one or the other of these two patterns, but I would certainly expect the pattern in [17] to win out, since it conforms to the generalization about accent on long syllables. As we saw earlier in this section and in section 6.2, Han (1962b:81–82) says that a falling pitch on the following syllable signals accent on a syllable with a devoiced vowel. If this claim is correct, we would expect to find a difference in the pronunciation of speakers whose intuitions differ about the location of accent in noun + /šika/ combinations. In any case, this question clearly merits further investigation.

In addition to noun + particle combinations, many noun + particle + particle combinations are also possible. When the first particle contributes an accent to an unaccented noun, as /nado/ does [13], the second particle is L throughout. The examples in [18] illustrate this point with noun + /nado/ + /wa/ combinations.

[18] /mákura/ /mákuranado/ /mákuranadowa/
/kokóro/ /kokóronado/ /kokóronadowa/
/takará/ /takaránado/ /takaránadowa/
/sakana/ /sakananádo/ /sakananádowa/

When the first particle behaves like /wa/ [3], however, the last mora of the first particle is H and all subsequent moras are L. The examples in [19] illustrate this point with /kara/ 'from' as the first particle and the topic marker /wa/ as the second particle.

[19] a. /mákura/ /mákurakara/ /mákurakarawa/
 b. /kokóro/ /kokórokara/ /kokórokarawa/
 c. /takará/ /takarákara/ /takarákarawa/
 d. /sakana/ /sakanakara/ /sakanakaráwa/

This pattern suggests that /kara/ and all similar particles do in fact contribute an accent when added to an unaccented noun. Thus, the second phrase in [19d] should be /sakanakará/. The final accent is, of course, indistinguishable from no accent unless an additional particle follows.

8.3.2 Verbs

The possibilities for accent patterns on verb forms are much more limited than those for accent patterns on nouns. For example, the citation form of a verb, the nonpast (section 12.1), can be either accented or unaccented. No matter how many syllables the form contains, there are only two possibilities (Akinaga 1966:60), as the examples in [20] show. In general, when the nonpast is accented, the accent appears on the second mora from the end. As we saw in section 7.5, however, when the second mora from the end is the second mora of a long syllable, the accent appears on the third mora from the end (Martin 1952:33, Akinaga 1966:61). See the examples in [21].

[20]	/naru/	'cry'	LH
	/náru/	'become'	HL
	/hareru/	'swell'	LHH
	/haréru/	'clear up'	LHL
	/kuraberu/	'compare'	LHHH
	/širabéru/	'investigate'	LHHL
[21]	/tóoru/	'pass'	HLL
	/háiru/	'enter'	HLL

In addition, Martin (1952:33) and Akinaga (1966:61) note that the accent sometimes shifts to the final mora when the second-to-last mora contains a devoiced vowel. Hirayama (1960) lists the shifted and unshifted forms as alternatives. See the examples in [22] (the devoiced vowels are in italics).

[22]	/cúku/ ~ /cukú/	'arrive'
	/fúku/ ~ /fukú/	'blow'
	/kakúsu/ ~ /kakusú/ ~ /kakúsu/	'hide'

I will refer to verbs with unaccented nonpast forms as "unaccented verbs" and to verbs with accented nonpast forms as "accented verbs."

Some other verb forms show the same accented/unaccented distinction, although the location of the accent in an accented verb is not always the same as in the nonpast. The negative (section 12.1), for example, always ends /nai/, and the negative of an accented verb always has an accent on the syllable before /nai/. See the examples in [23].

[23] Nonpast		Negative
/naru/		/naranai/
/náru/		/naránai/
/hareru/		/harenai/
/haréru/		/harénai/
/okonau/	'conduct'	/okonawanai/
/tecudáu/	'help'	/tecudawánai/

In other verb forms, the distinction between accented and unaccented verbs is neutralized. The polite form, for example, always ends with /masu/ (section 12.2.5.2), and the first syllable of /masu/ always carries an accent (Akinaga 1966:67). See the examples in [24].

[24] Nonpast	Polite
/naru/	/narimásu/
/náru/	/narimásu/
/hareru/	/haremásu/
/haréru/	/haremásu/

Still other verb forms are always accented, but the location of the accent depends on whether the verb is accented or unaccented. The conditional form (section 12.1), for example, is accented on the second syllable from the end if the verb is unaccented and on the third syllable from the end if the verb is accented (Martin 1952:42, Akinaga 1966:66). See the examples in [25].

[25] *Nonpast*   *Conditional*
/naru/   /naréba/
/náru/   /náreba/
/hareru/   /hareréba/
/haréru/   /haréreba/
/okonau/   /okonaéba/
/tecudáu/   tecudáeba/

I have considered only a few representative verb forms in this section. More complete information is readily available in Hirayama (1960:918–923), Akinaga (1966:60–71), Martin (1967:251–257), and McCawley (1977:265–266).

8.3.3 Adjectives

It is widely accepted that adjective forms, like verb forms, have at most two possible accent patterns. I will refer to adjectives as "accented" or "unaccented," depending on the citation form (the nonpast). Martin (1967) argues persuasively that adjective forms show differences in accentuation that require four distinct classes of accented adjectives. I will not come to terms with these complications here, but any thorough treatment would have to take them into consideration.

All two-mora adjectives are accented, and in general, the nonpast of an accented adjective has the accent on the second mora from the end (Akinaga 1966:72), as the examples in [26] illustrate.

[26] /kói/   'thick'   HL
     /acui/   'thick'   LHH
     /acúi/   'hot'   LHL
     /cumetai/   'cold'   LHHH
     /miɟikái/   'short'   LHHL

When the second mora from the end of an accented adjective is the second mora of a long syllable, the accent appears on the third mora from the end (Akinaga 1966:72). Hirayama (1960) and Nihon Hōsō Kyōkai (1966) list /óoi/ and /oói/ as alternatives for the adjective meaning 'numerous', and the katakana spellings represent the first two moras as a single long syllable in /óoi/ and as two short syllables in /oói/.

Some other adjective forms show the same accented/unaccented distinction, although the syllable that carries the accent is not always the same as in the nonpast form. For example, the adverbial form, which Bloch (1946a:15–16) calls the "infinitive," always ends with /ku/, and the adverbial of an unaccented adjective is unaccented. For some speakers, the adverbial of an accented adjective is accented on the syllable immediately preceding /ku/ (Akinaga 1966:73). For other speakers, the accent generally falls on the second syllable preceding /ku/ (when there is one), although McCawley (1968:155–156) lists several exceptions. See the examples in [27].

[27] *Nonpast*	*Adverbial*
/kói/	/kóku/
/itái/ 'painful'	/ítaku/~/itáku/
/miǰikái/	/miǰíkaku/~/miǰikáku/

When one of the two syllables before /ku/ contains a devoiced vowel, the accent apparently always appears on the other (Akinaga 1966:73). The examples in [28] illustrate this point, with the devoiced vowels in italics.

[28] *Nonpast*	*Adverbial*
/acúi/	/ácuku/
/futói/ 'fat'	/futóku/

In other adjective forms, the distinction between accented and unaccented adjectives is neutralized. The (nonpast) presumptive (Bloch 1946a:15), for example, always ends with /karoo/, and the next-to-last mora of /karoo/ always carries the accent (Akinaga 1966:73). See the examples in [29].

[29] *Nonpast*	*Presumptive*
/acui/	/acukaróo/
/acúi/	/acukaróo/
/cumetai/	/cumetakaróo/
/miǰikái/	/miǰikakaróo/

If we consider adjective + enclitic combinations, there are clear cases in which the phrase is always accented but the location of the accent depends on whether the adjective is accented or unaccented. For example, when an accented adjective precedes /daroo/, the presumptive form of the copula, an accent appears on the same mora of the adjective as in the nonpast. When an unaccented adjective precedes /daroo/, however, an accent appears on the second-to-last mora of /daroo/ (Akinaga 1966:76). See the examples in [30].

[30] *Nonpast*	*Before* /daroo/
/acui/	/acuidaróo/
/acúi/	/acúidaroo/
/cumetai/	/cumetaidaróo/
/miǰikái/	/miǰikáidaroo/

I have considered only a few representative adjective forms in this section. More complete information is readily available in Hirayama (1960:928–930), Akinaga (1966:72–77), Martin (1967, 1968), and McCawley (1977:265–266).

8.4 McCAWLEY'S TREATMENT

McCawley (1977:261–262) gives the three rules in [31] for predicting the pitch pattern on a phrase. As they stand, the rules must apply in the order given. The two alternative versions of [31c] reflect alternative pronunciations; when an initial long syllable is unaccented, some standard speakers pronounce it LH, but others pronounce it HH (section 8.3.1).

[31] **a.** Make every mora H.
   b. Make every mora after the first mora of an accented syllable L.
   c. (i) Make the first mora L if the second mora is H.
      (ii) Make the first mora L if the second mora is H and not in the same syllable.

The examples in [32] show how these rules apply to isolated nouns.

[32]	/mákura/	/kokóro/	/takará/
[31a]	H H H	H H H	H H H
[31b]	H L L	H H L	—
[31c]	—	L H L	L H H
	/sakana/	/keNtóo/	/kookoo/
[31a]	H H H	H H H H	H H H H
[31b]	—	H H H L	—
[31c]	L H H	—	—
		(or LHHL)	(or LHHH)

McCawley (1977:263–264) treats the particle /nado/ as accented on the first syllable: /nádo/. As we saw in [13], the accent in a noun + /nado/ phrase appears on the first syllable of /nado/ when the noun is unaccented. When the noun is accented, the accent on the noun is the accent of the phrase. McCawley proposes a general rule that deletes all accents in a phrase except the first. The examples in [33] illustrate the effect of this ACCENT DELETION rule.

[33]	/mákuranádo/	/sakananádo/
Accent deletion	/mákuranado/	—

We saw in section 8.3.1 that for some speakers the particle /šika/ apparently contributes an accent to the last mora of a preceding unaccented noun. McCawley (1977:264) treats /šika/ as "preaccented," and we might represent it as / ´ šika/. The accent deletion rule will eliminate this accent except when an unaccented noun precedes.

We saw in [19] that a phrase of the form noun + /kara/ + /wa/ has an accent on the last syllable of /kara/ when the noun is unaccented. McCawley (1977:264) therefore treats /kara/ as accented on its final syllable: /kará/. The accent deletion rule produces the desired forms in this case as well.

The same accent deletion rule allows parallel treatment of many verb and adjective forms. We saw in [25] that the conditional form of an unaccented verb is accented on the second syllable from the end. The conditional of an accented verb, on the other hand, is accented on the same syllable as the nonpast. McCawley (1977:265) handles this problem by simply giving /réba/ as the underlying form of the conditional suffix. (The initial /r/ of this suffix is deleted by another rule in some cases; see section 12.4.3.) The adjective + /daroo/ phrases in [30] can be handled the same way by saying that /daroo/ is accented: /daróo/.

We saw in [14] that a noun + /gurai/ combination is always accented on the first syllable of /gurai/. McCawley (1977:267) treats /gurai/ as accented (/gúrai/) and PREDOMINATING. The accent of a predominating morpheme appears even when there is an accent earlier in the phrase, so the behavior of such morphemes violates the accent deletion rule. The polite verb suffix /masu/ [24] and the presumptive adjective suffix /karoo/ [29] can also be treated as accented (/másu/, /karóo/) and predominating.

We saw in [27] that some speakers generally have the accent on the second syllable before /ku/ in the adverbial form of an accented adjective. Since the adverbial of an unaccented adjective is unaccented, the suffix /ku/ itself is clearly unaccented. McCawley (1977:265–266) argues that the accent location in /ítaku/ and /miʝíkaku/ is basic; therefore, the nonpast forms /itái/ and /miʝikái/ involve a rightward shift of one syllable. McCawley (1977:268) proposes a rule of ACCENT ATTRACTION to account for cases of this kind. Under this proposal, morphemes like the nonpast adjective suffix /i/ are unaccented and attracting.

Verbs of a certain type show a similar alternation in accent location. The examples in [34] illustrate this alternation with past (section 12.1) and nonpast forms (Martin 1952:43).

[34]

Past	Nonpast	
/dékita/	/dekíru/	'be able'
/tábeta/	/tabéru/	'eat'
/širábeta/	/širabéru/	'investigate'
/kokorómita/	/kokoromíru/	'try'

In general, verbs in this class are accented on the syllable before the nonpast suffix /ru/ and on the second syllable before the past suffix /ta/. McCawley (1977:266) takes the stem-penultimate location as basic and treats the nonpast suffix as attracting.

On the basis of the examples we have considered so far, we might suggest that an attracting morpheme attracts an accent onto the last syllable of the preceding morpheme. There are other morphemes, however, that appear to attract accent over the morpheme boundary. McCawley (1977:268) mentions /soo/ 'looks as if', which appears as /sóo/ when added to an accented verb. See the examples in [35].

[35]

Past	Nonpast	Stem + /soo/
/hareta/	/hareru/	/haresoo/
/háreta/	/haréru/	/haresóo/

It thus appears that each attracting morpheme will have to specify the location to which it attracts the accent.

The passive and causative morphemes (section 12.2.5.2) can also be treated as attracting, although McCawley (1977:268–269) does not explicitly classify them as such. See the examples in [36] with forms of the verb /tabéru/ 'eat'.

[36] **a.** /tábe + ta/   Past
     b. /tabé + ru/   Nonpast
     c. /tabe + sáse + ta/   Past causative
     d. /tabe + sasé + ru/   Nonpast causative
     e. /tabe + sase + ráre + ta/   Past passive causative
     f. /tabe + sase + raré + ru/   Nonpast passive causative

In [36f], for example, we could say that the causative suffix /sase/ attracts the basic accent on the verb stem /tábe/ to yield /tabe + sáse/. The passive morpheme /rare/ then attracts it to yield /tabe + sase + ráre/, and finally, the nonpast suffix /ru/ attracts it to yield [36f].

We saw in [23] that the negative of an unaccented verb is unaccented, while the negative of an accented verb is accented. It is clear, therefore, that the negative suffix /nai/ itself is unaccented. Since the accent on the negative of an accented verb always falls on the syllable before /nai/, we can say that /nai/ is attracting. For example, the negative of /tabéru/ 'eat' (past /tábe + ta/) is /tabé + nai/.

As McCawley (1977:268) points out, however, the negative of a verb inflects just like an adjective, and this presumably means that /nai/ should be analyzed as /na + i/, where /i/ is the nonpast adjective suffix. As we saw above, McCawley treats this /i/ adjective suffix as attracting; therefore, the negative verb forms are exceptional. The reason is that the /i/ in /na + i/ does not attract an accent onto the immediately preceding syllable. The examples in [37] illustrate this point with forms of the adjective /miǰikái/ 'short' and the verb /tabéru/ 'eat'.

[37] *Adverbial*   *Nonpast*
     /miǰíka + ku/   /miǰiká + i/
     /tabé + na + ku/   /tabé + na + i/

We might suggest that accent attraction cannot operate across two morpheme boundaries, but this is clearly an ad hoc solution.

8.5 HARAGUCHI'S TREATMENT

8.5.1 Autosegmental Phonology

Haraguchi (1977) analyzes Japanese accent in a framework known as AUTOSEGMENTAL PHONOLOGY. This approach is based on work by Goldsmith (1976, 1979), although it has clear affinities to the SIMULTANEOUS COMPONENTS of Harris (1944) and the PROSODIC ANALYSIS of Firth (1948) and his followers. Auto-segmental phonology makes it possible to extract chosen features from the phonological representation and treat them as relatively autonomous. The most commonly extracted feature is pitch (tone), and certain tonal phenomena in African languages provide the best-known motivation for the autosegmental approach.

One relevant phenomenon is the apparent assignment of identical tone patterns to words with different numbers of syllables. Leben (1978:186) gives the examples in [38] from Mende, a language of Sierra Leone. (In these and all subsequent examples in this section, ′ represents a high tone, ‵ a low tone, ^ a falling tone, ˇ a rising tone, and ᷝ a rising-falling tone.)

[38] a. /nìkílì/　　'groundnut'
　　　 b. /nyàhâ/　　'woman'
　　　 c. /mbã̌/　　　'companion'

Leben suggests that all three words in [38] have the tone pattern LHL. Since [38a] has three syllables, each syllable has its own level tone, but the same three tones are crowded onto two syllables in [38b] and onto a single syllable in [38c].

Autosegmental phonology can represent the segmental features (consonants and vowels) and the suprasegmental features (tones) independently. In a simple case like the Mende examples in [38], associating tones with syllables is a straightforward procedure. We simply try to match the first tone with the first syllable, the second tone with the second syllable, and so on. When we run out of syllables, we assign the remaining tones to the last syllable. Using lines to represent these associations, [39] illustrates the process.

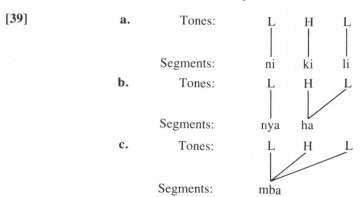

[39]　　　　　　　　　a.　　Tones:　　　L　　H　　L

　　　　　　　　　　　　　　Segments:　ni　　ki　　li

　　　　　　　　　　　　b.　　Tones:　　　L　　H　　L

　　　　　　　　　　　　　　Segments:　nya　　ha

　　　　　　　　　　　　c.　　Tones:　　　L　　H　　L

　　　　　　　　　　　　　　Segments:　mba

When the postposition /ma/ 'on' is added to /nyàhâ/ [38b], the result is /nyàhámà/. Leben (1978:195) handles this tone assignment by saying that /ma/ has no inherent tone of its own. As [40] shows, the final L in the LHL tone pattern of the noun simply moves onto the postposition, since there are now three syllables.

[40]

Tones: L H L + ∅

Segments: nya ha + ma

In addition to toneless morphemes like Mende /ma/, there appear to be morphemes that consist entirely of tones, with no segments. For example, Welmers (1973:127) argues that the third-person singular object pronoun consists only of a high tone in Yoruba, a language of Nigeria. See the sentences in [41] containing /ó/ 'she' and /wè̩/ 'bathed'.

[41] **a.** /ówè̩é̩/ 'She bathed you'
b. /ówě̩/ 'She bathed him'

In [41a] the object is /é̩/ 'you', but in [41b] the object is signaled by a rising tone (instead of a low tone) on the final vowel. As [42] shows, this is what we expect if the object morpheme in this case is just a high tone.

[42]

Tones: H + L + H

Segments: o + wè̩ + ∅

All the examples in this section illustrate the potential autonomy of tones and segments. If tones were simply properties of the segments that carry them, we would not expect this kind of independent behavior. The autosegmental approach provides a convenient notation for representing this relative independence, and it allows us to express the regularities we have considered very neatly. Features other than pitch can also be treated autosegmentally, but this possibility will not concern us here.

8.5.2 Application to Japanese Accent

Haraguchi (1977:9) argues that the accent patterns on Japanese words are all manifestations of a single HL tone pattern, or MELODY. To assign this melody to words and short phrases of the sort we considered in sections 8.3–8.4, we need to mark individual lexical items with accent marks. The observed pitch patterns result from the combined application of language-specific rules and putatively universal conventions for associating tones and segments. Haraguchi's system requires accent marks at the same locations as McCawley's system (section 8.4).

I will paraphrase the basic language-specific rule in Haraguchi's (1977:9) analysis as the TONE ASSOCIATION (TA) rule in [43].

[43] **a.** If a phrase has at least one accent mark, associate the H of the melody with the leftmost accented mora.
b. If a phrase has no accent mark, associate the H with the rightmost mora.

It might be helpful to imagine this rule scanning the phrase from left to right. It searches for an accented mora and associates H with the first one it finds. If it reaches the end of the phrase without finding an accent, it associates H with the last mora by default. The examples in [44] show the effect of the tone association rule on some of the isolated nouns in [3].

[44]

As Haraguchi (1977:10) points out, [43a] requires the association of H with the first accented mora in a phrase that contains more than one accent. The examples in [45] illustrate this point with some of the noun + /nádo/ phrases in [13]. Like McCawley, Haraguchi treats /nádo/ as accented.

[45]

Haraguchi (1977: 10–12) explains that UNIVERSAL TONE ASSOCIATION CONVENTIONS (UTAC) serve to insure that every tone is associated with a tone-bearing unit and vice versa. If we ignore the problems caused by devoiced vowels (section 6.2) and the mora obstruent /Q/ (section 5.2) for the time being, we can say that the tone-bearing units in standard Japanese are moras. I will paraphrase the universal conventions that Haraguchi proposes as [46]. A tone or tone-bearing unit is bound if it is already associated and free if it remains unassociated.

[46] a. If there is only one free tone, or only one free tone to the left or right of a bound tone, associate the free tone with every free tone-bearing unit on the same side of the bound tone.

b. If there is no free tone-bearing unit on the same side of a bound tone as a free tone, associate the free tone with the bound tone-bearing unit.

c. If, on either side of a bound tone, there is at least one tone-bearing unit and no free tone, associate the bound tone with the remaining free tone-bearing units.

The examples in [47] illustrate the application of the universal tone association conventions.

[47]

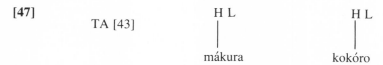

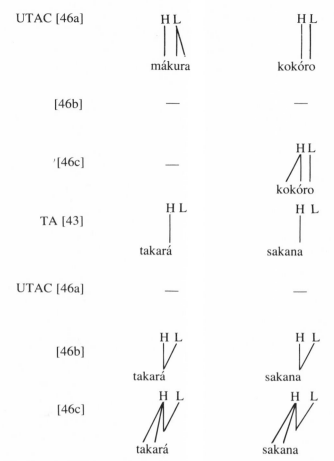

At this stage /mákura/ has the correct pitch pattern (HLL), but the other three words in [47] do not. For one thing, /kokóro/, /takará/, and /sakana/ should all begin with L, but the first mora of each is associated with H in [47]. Haraguchi (1977:17) proposes a language-specific INITIAL LOWERING (IL) rule to convert an initial H mora to L if the second mora is H. Using M to represent a mora, we could write this rule as [48].

[48]

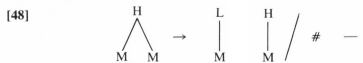

As Haraguchi (1977:33–34) notes, [48] must be modified for speakers who pronounce initial long syllables HH when unaccented. If we apply initial lowering to the outputs of the universal tone association conventions in [47], the results are as in [49].

[49]

Output of UTAC [47]

IL [48]

Output of UTAC [47]

IL [48]

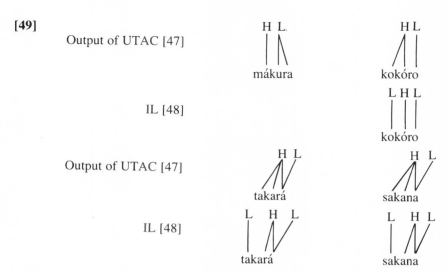

At this point /kokóro/ has the correct pitch pattern (LHL), but in both /takará/ and /sakana/ the final mora has a falling tone (H̲L̲). As Haraguchi (1977:18) notes, standard Japanese accent patterns do not involve contour tones. He therefore proposes a TONE SIMPLIFICATION (TS) rule to remove the L from a mora associated with both H and L. We could write this rule as [50].

[50]

$$\begin{array}{ccc} H & L & & H \\ \diagdown & \diagup & \rightarrow & \vert \\ & M & & M \end{array}$$

If we apply [50] to the outputs of the initial lowering rule, it affects /takará/ and /sakana/ as in [51], and we get the correct pitch pattern (LHH) in each case.

[51]

Output of IL [48]

TS [50]

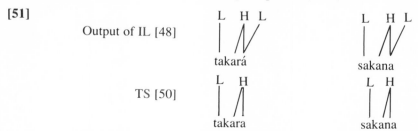

It makes no difference, of course, whether tone simplification [50] applies before or after initial lowering [48].

The tone simplification rule eliminates the final L of the basic melody from /takará/ and /sakana/ [51], but there are many other phrases containing these words in which the final L appears. For example, when the particle /nádo/ follows, the rules we have considered in this section apply as in [52].

[52]

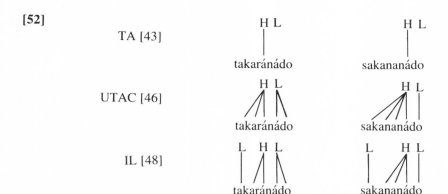

As we saw in [13], the correct pitch patterns are in fact LHHLL for /takará/ + /nádo/ and LHHHL for /sakana/ + /nádo/.

McCawley (1977:266) suggests that there is a rule shifting an accent to the right off a mora with a devoiced vowel, but he notes several exceptions. Some of these exceptions involve devoiced moras that remain accented (section 6.2), but others involve apparent leftward shifts. For example, when the topic marker /wa/ follows the adverbial form of an unaccented adjective, an accent generally appears on the syllable before the suffix /ku/. See the forms in [53].

[53] *Nonpast*   *Adverbial* + /wa/
/akai/   'red'   /akákuwa/
/cumetai/   'cold'   /cumetákuwa/

When the vowel in the syllable before /ku/ is devoiced, however, the accent appears one syllable earlier, as in [54].

[54] *Nonpast*   *Adverbial* + /wa/
/yasašii/   'easy'   /yasášikuwa/

As the first step in an attempt to provide a general account of accent shifts, Haraguchi (1977:31 – 36) argues that completely voiceless moras cannot be tone-bearing units. This statement means that when vowel devoicing applies, the mora containing the devoiced vowel can no longer be associated with a tone. Haraguchi proposes a general ERASURE CONVENTION (EC) that removes the association line between a tone and a segmental sequence that has lost its ability to bear a tone. The derivation in [55] shows how this convention applies to /yasášikuwa/, assuming that some general accent assignment rule originally assigns the accent to /ši/.

[55]

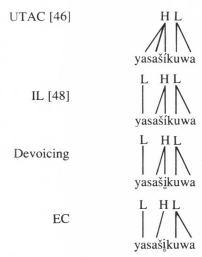

UTAC [46]	H L yasašíkuwa
IL [48]	L H L yasašíkuwa
Devoicing	L H L yasašị̆kuwa
EC	L H L yasašị̆kuwa

The erasure convention leaves /ši/ unassociated with any tone, and this leaves H associated only with /sa/. Haraguchi does not explain why speakers interpret the unassociated /ši/ as L, but presumably they simply interpret every mora after the last H as L.

Haraguchi (1977:43) also gives a derivation for the adverbial form of /acui/ 'thick' followed by /wa/. Here again, an accent placement rule applies first to make /cu/ the accented mora, and the derivation proceeds as in [56].

[56]

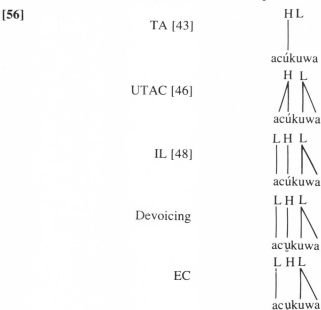

TA [43]	H L acúkuwa
UTAC [46]	H L acúkuwa
IL [48]	L H L acúkuwa
Devoicing	L H L acụ̆kuwa
EC	L H L acụ̆kuwa

At this point, we have a tone that is not associated with any tone-bearing unit, a situation that the universal tone association conventions are supposed to rule out. As these conventions are stated in [46], however, they do not tell use what to do in a case like [56]. Haraguchi (1977:44–45) suggests that the tone association rule [43] reapplies and associates the H with the rightmost available mora, that is, with /ku/. We cannot associate H with /wa/, since this operation would require association lines to cross. Autosegmental phonology rules this out in principle (Haraguchi 1977:11), because it makes no sense to say that the tones on two moras occur in a different order than the moraś that carry them. The reassociation leaves /ku/ with a contour tone (H͟L), and the tone simplification rule [50] applies. The derivation continues in [57].

[57]

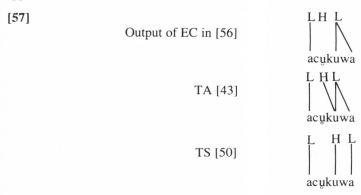

Output of EC in [56]	L H L ... acukuwa
TA [43]	L H L ... acukuwa
TS [50]	L H L ... acukuwa

The reason the accent shifts to the right in /ac*u*kúwa/ is that the combined effect of the tone association rule, the universal tone association conventions, and the initial lowering rule in [56] is to leave H associated only with /cu/. As a result, the H is stranded when the vowel in /cu/ is devoiced, and the tone association rule reassociates H with the next mora to the right. In /yasášikuwa/, on the other hand, the H is originally associated with both /sa/ and /ši/ [55]. Thus, when the vowel in /ši/ is devoiced, the H is not stranded. On the basis of examples of this kind, Haraguchi claims that his system provides a principled account of the direction of accent shifts.

I do not know of any examples of an accent shifting in the opposite direction from what Haraguchi predicts, but there are, of course, many cases of an accent remaining on a mora with a devoiced vowel (section 6.2). In fact, Hirayama (1960) lists /ac*ú*kuwa/ rather than Haraguchi's /ac*u*kúwa/ in the entry for /acui/. In any case, Haraguchi's application of the erasure convention to all moras with devoiced vowels is surely an oversimplification.

Haraguchi (1977:47–48) points out that for his account of accent shifts to work, vowel devoicing must apply after initial lowering. The derivation in [58] illustrates what would happen to /acúkuwa/ if the order of application were reversed.

[58]

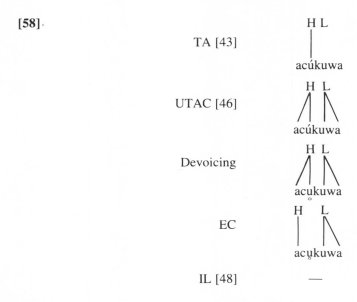

TA [43]

UTAC [46]

Devoicing

EC

IL [48] —

The result in [58] is /ácukuwa/, with the accent shifted in the wrong direction.

I mentioned in section 8.3.1 that the pitch pattern on unaccented initial /(C)(y)VQ/ sequences like those in [5] is unclear. Haraguchi (1977:34–36) says it is LL, and this means that an unaccented word like /haQpa/ 'leaf' has the pitch pattern LLH. Haraguchi also says that the mora containing the devoiced vowel in a word like /ašikake/ 'foothold' is L. In this case, the pitch pattern on the word is LLHH. Since /Q/ is voiceless in /haQpa/, it cannot be a tone-bearing unit in Haraguchi's system, and he argues that it is never associated with a tone in the course of a derivation. Since vowel devoicing must follow initial lowering in Haraguchi's system, we first associate the /ši/ in /ašikake/ with a tone and later erase the association line. See the derivations in [59].

[59]

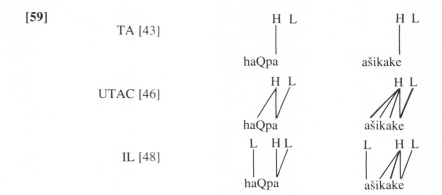

TA [43]

UTAC [46]

IL [48]

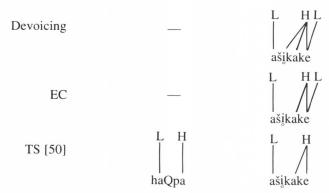

Haraguchi does not explain why speakers interpret the unassociated moras as L in cases like this, but presumably they interpret any mora before the first H as L.

As I mentioned in section 8.3.1, accent dictionaries such as Hirayama (1960) and Nihon Hōsō Kyōkai (1966) consistently represent unaccented initial /(C)(y)VQ/ sequences as LH. I suggested that a phonetic rising pitch on the vowel before /Q/ might be responsible for this representation. These dictionaries also represent the first two moras in a word like /ašikake/ as LH rather than LL, and here again, rising pitch on the first mora may be involved. Haraguchi (1977:36–38) considers this possibility and suggests a special rule for speakers who pronounce the moras in question with a rising pitch. We could write this rule as [60].

[60]

$$
\begin{array}{ccc}
\text{L} & & \text{H} \\
| & & | \\
\text{M} & \text{M} & \text{M} \\
& \text{[-vce]} &
\end{array}
\rightarrow
\begin{array}{ccc}
\text{L} & & \text{H} \\
| & & | \\
\text{M} & \text{M} & \text{M} \\
& \text{[-vce]} &
\end{array}
$$

This rule produces exceptions to the generalization that moras cannot carry contour tones in standard Japanese. We must keep in mind, however, that speakers interpret the first two moras in the words in question as L and then H, and not as LH followed by Ø. In other words, [60] is what Haraguchi calls a "low-level phonetic rule." Something similar is surely necessary to account for moras with devoiced vowels that retain accent.

8.5.3 A Comparison with McCawley's Treatment

On the basis of the brief summaries of McCawley's treatment (section 8.4) and Haraguchi's treatment (section 8.5.2), it is clear that the two are very nearly equivalent. In many cases, they have identical rules. For example, Haraguchi (1977:23–25) proposes a rule just like McCawley's (1977:267) for removing a final accent from a polysyllabic noun before the genitive particle /no/. In addition, Haraguchi's treatment clearly requires mechanisms equivalent to McCawley's for handling attracting and predominating morphemes.

McCawley's pitch assignment rules [31] differ somewhat from Haraguchi's. The combined effect of McCawley's [31a] ("Make every mora H.") and [31b] ("Make every mora after the first mora of an accented syllable L.") is equivalent to applying Haraguchi's tone association rule [43] and the universal tone association conventions [46]. The latter, of course, are supposed to apply in any language and need not be part of a description of Japanese. Assuming these conventions are correct as Haraguchi states them, his analysis requires only a rule to associate H with a single mora; everything else follows automatically. On the other hand, Haraguchi's treatment requires the existence of a melody for Japanese. McCawley's treatment incorporates the melody into the pitch assignment rules. Haraguchi's initial lowering rule [48] is equivalent to McCawley's [31c].

McCawley proposes an accent deletion rule to eliminate all accents but the first in a phrase. For example, this rule converts /mákura + nádo/ 'pillow, etc.' into /mákura + nado/, and the pitch assignment rules [31] then assign the correct pitch pattern. Haraguchi's treatment does not require an accent deletion rule, since the tone association rule [43] associates H with the leftmost accented mora. As [61] shows, however, a simple revision of McCawley's pitch assignment rule [31b] will eliminate the need for the accent deletion rule in his treatment as well. Shibatani (1972:589–590) makes essentially the same suggestion.

[61] Original [31b]:   Make every mora after the first mora of an accented syllable L.

Revision: Make every mora after the first mora of the leftmost accented syllable L.

On the other hand, McCawley's treatment requires no analog to Haraguchi's tone simplification rule [50].

In what we have seen so far, the only substantial difference between the two treatments is their handling of accent shifts off moras with devoiced vowels. Haraguchi's analysis accounts for the leftward shift in examples like /yasáš-ikuwa/, whereas McCawley treats it as an exception to his rightward shift rule. On the other hand, the rightward shift in Haraguchi's treatment of examples like /acukúwa/ does not conform to the entries in accent dictionaries. In sum, it seems fair to say that neither treatment is obviously superior to the other in handling the phenomena we have considered so far.

8.6   LONGER PHRASES

8.6.1   Major and Minor Phrases

So far in this chapter I have limited my attention to short phrases with at most a single rise and at most a single fall in pitch. McCawley (1968:137–138) and Shibatani (1972) use the term MINOR PHRASE to refer to phrases of this kind. The division of a phrase into minor phrases is not fixed, and in general, the slower the tempo, the more minor phrases there are. McCawley (1977:272–273) says that a phrase containing more than one word often allows three possible pronunciations. The first is to pronounce each word as its own independent phrase. I will refer to such an independent phrase as MAJOR PHRASE. The second is to pronounce the words as "a single group of phrases," that is, as a single major phrase divided into minor phrases. The third is to pronounce the words as a single minor phrase.

Following McCawley (1977:272–273) and Shibatani (1972), I will use % to mark minor phrase boundaries and @ to mark major phrase boundaries. (These boundaries seem to correspond to Martin's (1967:246, 1970:429) major and minor junctures.) The examples in [62] illustrate the three possibilities for the phrase /táko + nádo tábeta/ 'ate octopus, etc.', which consists of /táko + nádo/ 'octopus, etc.' and /tábeta/ 'ate'. I also provide the pitch patterns that McCawley and Shibatani would give, using M to represent a mid pitch.

[**62**] **a.** Separate major phrases   /@táko + nádo@tábeta@/
                                          H L L L H L L

b. Single major phrase   /@táko + nádo%tábeta@/
                              H L L L M L L

c. Single minor phrase   /%táko + nádo tábeta%/
                              H L L L L L L

[62a] is a very unnatural pronunciation and almost certainly requires a pause between the two phrases. Japanese language teachers occasionally speak this way in the classroom. In [62c], of course, only the first accent is realized.

Shibatani (1972:587) and McCawley (1977:272–273) both say that in a sequence of minor phrases within a single major phrase, only the first minor phrase contains H; all subsequent minor phrases contain M instead. [62b] illustrates this principle, and [63] provides a longer example.

[**63**] /@há ya ku %na ra N da hó o + ga %í i @/   'It's better to get
         H L L   L MM M ML   L ML   in line early.'

Haraguchi (1977:316) challenges this claim about the distribution of M, and I will illustrate the problem using Kawakami's (1962) phrase /are + wa úmakaQta/ 'That was good'. Haraguchi would say that the pitch pattern on this phrase is never LHH MLLLL, and I agree. When a pause intervenes and there are two major phrases, we naturally get @LHH@HLLLL@. Because of downdrift (section 8.2) in each major phrase, the actual pitch of /wa/ is naturally lower than that of /ú/. If this whole sequence is treated as a single minor phrase, we expect the pattern %LHHHLLLL%. In this case, as Kawakami's (1962:120–123) measurements show, the actual pitch of /ú/ is lower than that of /wa/, but no more than we would expect from downdrift.

It appears that when /are + wa úmakaQta/ is treated as two minor phrases, there is a substantial rise in actual pitch from /wa/ to /ú/. Kawakami (1962:120) gives a pitchgram showing this rise, even though no pause intervenes between /wa/ and /ú/ and there is no special emphasis on /úmakaQta/. If we represent the pitch pattern in this last case as @LHH%HLLLL@, we cannot distinguish it from the pattern that occurs when the sequence is treated as a single minor phrase. Kawakami uses examples of this kind to argue that representing Japanese accent patterns in terms of H and L is fundamentally wrong. I am sympathetic to this view, but I will not pursue the problem any further here.

We might suggest at this point that a minor phrase can be defined as "the domain of downdrift." When /are + wa úmakaQta/ is treated as a single minor phrase, there is a rise in pitch after the first mora and a sharp fall in pitch after the accented mora. Elsewhere there is a gradual fall in pitch from one mora to the next. When the sequence is treated as two minor phrases, the pitch jumps up at the beginning of the second phrase. Recall, however, that the phonetic explanation I suggested in section 8.2 identifies the domain of downdrift as a breath group. Since there is no pause between minor phrases, they presumably are not separate breath groups. This problem certainly deserves more careful attention than I can give it here.

Haraguchi (1977:29–33) also challenges other pitch patterns that McCawley and Shibatani would give for certain phrases. Haraguchi claims, for example, that when no pause intervenes, the normal pattern on /úmi + de oyógi/ 'swimming in the ocean' is not @HLL%LML@ [64a] but @HLL%LLD@ [64b], where D is a lower tone than L.

[64] /@ú mi + de %o yó gi @/
   a.   H L   L L M L
   b.   H L   L L L D

Haraguchi says that [64a] is possible only when a pause intervenes. In general, he claims that a sequence LM is impossible unless a pause occurs somewhere before M.

The experimental results that Higurashi (1983:81–130) reports indicate that even when no pause intervenes, a pitch pattern that could reasonably be described as HLL LML sometimes occurs on /úmi + de oyógi/. A pattern that could be described as HLL LLL also occurs, and in this case, the speakers presumably treated the whole phrase as a single minor phrase. In assigning these descriptions, of course, we must take the effect of downdrift into account. There is no good evidence in Higurashi's data for the HLL LLD pattern that Haraguchi suggests.

8.6.2 Contour Tones

Haraguchi (1977:50–53) claims that contour tones occur on single moras in some phrases. He says that when a phrase with final accent is followed by another phrase, the final mora of the first phrase has the contour tone H̰L. See the example in [65].

[65] /nečá/ 'slept, and then'   /ókita/ 'got up'
/nečá ókita/ 'slept, and then got up'

Haraguchi says that /nečá/ is LH in isolation but L<u>HL</u> before /ókita/. Examples like this lead him to propose that his tone simplification rule [50] must be blocked when a phrase follows a final accent. See the derivation in [66].

[66]

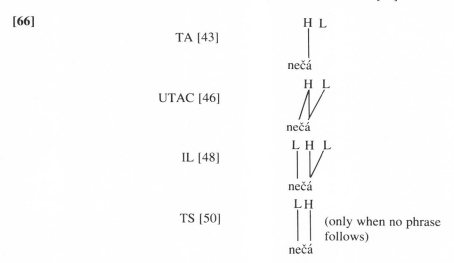

The form /nečá/ is a contraction of /neté + wa/, and as Higurashi (1983: 131–136) points out, the contraction /nečáa/ is also possible. Higurashi reports an experiment in which speakers read both /nečá ókita/ and /nečáa ókita/ spelled out in kana. The results clearly indicate that when speakers say /nečáa/, with a long final vowel, the pitch pattern in LHL, but when they say /nečá/, with a short final vowel, the pitch pattern is LH. There is no evidence for contour tones on single moras in this case.

As we saw in section 8.5.2, there is reason to believe that phonetic contour tones may occur next to completely voiceless moras. This problem clearly requires more careful experimental investigation, but even if experiments confirm such contour tones, it is clear that the contours are spread over two moras phonologically.

The lack of evidence for phonological contour tones in standard Japanese casts a certain amount of doubt on the appropriateness of an autosegmental treatment of the accent system. As we saw in section 8.5.1, one of the characteristics of African languages that motivates the autosegmental approach is the crowding of *n* tones onto a word with fewer than *n* syllables. In standard Japanese, however, whenever the H and L of the melody are crowded onto a single mora, Haraguchi's tone simplification rule [50] eliminates the contour tone. In other words, Japanese does not work the way we expect a language with relatively autonomous tones to work. This does not mean that an autosegmental treatment of the accent system is impossible. It simply means that there is no obvious advantage to such a treatment. As I noted in section 8.5.3, McCawley's treatment does not require any analog to Haraguchi's tone simplification rule.

8.7   PITCH ACCENT AND TONE

Stress in English has what is sometimes called a CULMINATIVE FUNCTION (Sloat, Taylor, and Hoard 1978:72). As we saw in section 7.2.1, the number of stresses in an English utterance tells us how many feet it contains. Pitch patterns in Japanese have the same kind of culminative function; they tell us the number of minor phrases in an utterance (section 8.6.1). Since the culminative mark in Japanese is pitch rather than stress, Japanese is commonly described as having PITCH ACCENT (Hyman 1975:230–231).

It is well known that stressed syllables in English generally have higher pitch than unstressed syllables (Ladefoged 1982:225), but auditorily, Japanese accent is quite strikingly different. Jinbō (1927:15) and Kindaichi (1965:43–44) suggest that this is because Japanese minor phrases can have sequences of two or more H moras, whereas English feet cannot contain sequences of stressed syllables.

Lehiste (1970:83) defines TONE as "contrastive function of fundamental frequency at word level." According to this definition, a language is a TONE LANGUAGE if it uses pitch patterns to differentiate individual words. Standard Japanese clearly fits this definition, but most linguists define tone languages more narrowly. Pike (1948:2), for example, says that each syllable in a tone language has a significant pitch. If Japanese is a tone language with two tones, H and L, Pike's definition implies that a word of n syllables could have any of 2^n possible pitch patterns. As we saw in section 8.3, however, the possibilities are much more limited in Japanese. Nouns allow the greatest number of possibilities, but a noun of n syllables must have one of only $n + 1$ patterns (section 8.3.1).

Hyman (1975:213) points out that many tone languages have restrictions on the possible tone patterns, but we would still expect more than $n + 1$ possibilities for n-syllable words. McCawley (1978) argues that languages are tonal to varying degrees and puts pitch accent at one end of a continuum.

8.8   OTHER TOPICS

One question I have not considered at all is whether the accent of a compound word can be predicted from the accents of its members. There seem to be relatively straightforward regularities in verb + verb and adjective + adjective compounds, but noun + noun compounds do not show any simple pattern. Akinaga (1966:50–54), Okuda (1971:183–277), McCawley (1977:268–272), and Higurashi (1983:59–77) all devote considerable attention to this problem.

I have also neglected the interaction between accent and intonation, aside from the suggestion about the fall in pitch before /to/ in section 8.3.1. Kawakami (1977:116) says that strong emotional emphasis can obliterate accent patterns, and Haraguchi (1977:317) claims that a kind of "peevish" intonation puts the same pitch pattern on any phrase it applies to, regardless of accent. This is an important and interesting topic, but I have nothing to contribute.

I will close this chapter by briefly considering the notion of FUNCTIONAL LOAD. Hockett (1958:398) characterizes the functional load of a distinction as the frequency with which two utterances, both possible in the same situation, differ only by that distinction. There is little doubt that the functional load of accent distinctions in standard Japanese is very low, and there are nonstandard dialects that have no accent distinctions at all (Hirayama 1960:16, McCawley 1977:273). Accent is probably the most difficult aspect of standard pronunciation for nonstandard speakers to master, but incorrect accent patterns very seldom cause any confusion for listeners. The primary importance of accent patterns is social rather than linguistic. Incorrect patterns mark a speaker as a nonnative of the Tokyo area.

In subsequent chapters I will not indicate accent in phonemic transcriptions unless it is directly relevant to the discussion.

Chapter 9

THE VELAR NASAL

9.1 HISTORICAL BACKGROUND

There is good reason to believe that voiced obstruents were "prenasalized" in Old Japanese (Vance 1982:335–337), and some modern dialects, notably those of southern Shikoku and northern Honshū, have retained prenasalization to some extent. Old Japanese apparently did not permit word-initial voiced obstruents except in mimetic adverbs (Okumura 1972:111), but this restriction was soon relaxed as loans from Chinese began to have a major impact (Miller 1967:194). Because of stringent limitations on syllable structure (section 7.1), any noninitial obstruent was intervocalic (or perhaps preceded by a vowel and followed by a glide; see section 11.1.1), and [1] shows some of the phonetic sequences inferred for the standard language at that time.

[1] *Some Old Japanese Phonetic Sequences*
[VtV]	[VsV]	[VkV]
[ṼdV]	[ṼzV]	[ṼgV](?)

    I have had the opportunity to listen at some length to speakers from two northern Honshū locations (Aomori City, Aomori Prefecture, and Ōdate City, Akita Prefecture), and [2] shows the corresponding sequences in these dialects.

[2] *Corresponding Northern Honshū Phonetic Sequences*
[VdV]	[VsV]	[VgV]
[ṼdV]	[ṼzV]	[ṼŋV]

In these northern Honshū dialects, there is a contrast in initial position between simple voiced and voiceless obstruents. For example, [t] and [d] contrast initially in [togo] 'bed' versus [dogo] 'where'. Once initial voiced obstruents were permitted at the stage just after Old Japanese, they probably were not prenasalized (although Hattori (1957:341–347) disagrees). If this surmise is correct, Japanese at this stage had the same initial voiced/voiceless contrast as the modern standard, but voiced obstruents had prenasalized allophones in intervocalic position.

I have chosen to transcribe prenasalization as nasalization on the preceding vowel, but some writers prefer to describe it as a nasal onglide preceding a medial voiced obstruent, and one often sees transcriptions like [ⁿd]. In any case, the preceding vowel is phonetically nasalized regardless of whether there is a perceptible onglide of this sort.

Original voiceless stops in the northern Honshū dialects have become voiced in medial position, and prenasalization is often distinctive, as in [mado] 'target' (cf. modern standard /mato/) versus [mãdo] 'window' (cf. modern standard /mado/). The result is a textbook case of PARTIAL OVERLAPPING in the sense of Bloch (1941) (Hattori 1957:346).

Another important feature of the northern Honshū dialects is that they have [ṼŋV] rather than [ṼgV]. According to Inoue (1971), other prenasalizing dialects have [ṼgV], but there seems to be a tendency for [g] to absorb the nasality and become [ŋ] in this environment. Kamei (1956) argues that this sequence was already [ṼŋV] in the eighth century, and Lange's (1973) reconstructions can be interpreted as supporting this view. This is the reason for the question mark in [1]. The majority view, however, seems to be that older [ṼgV] became [ṼŋV], while [ṼbV] and [ṼdV] remained unchanged (Hattori 1957:345, n. 11).

I am not aware of any reason why a velar stop should be more likely to absorb nasality than a labial or an alveolar. Japanese has had phonemic contrasts between /b/ and /m/ and between /d/ and /n/ all along, of course, but there does not seem to be any general constraint on language change to prevent the loss of contrast.

In many dialects, including that of Tokyo, prenasalization has been lost. Medial [ŋ], however, has remained as a residue, although it seems to be losing out to medial [g] in modern Tokyo. This explanation for the occurrence of medial [ŋ] in standard Tokyo Japanese is due to Hashimoto (1966b:126–129), and [3] shows the modern Tokyo sequences corresponding to those in [1] and [2]. In section 9.2 I will consider the shift from [ŋ] to [g] apparently now in progress; [3] simply lists [ṼŋV] and [VgV] as alternatives.

[3] *Corresponding Tokyo Standard Phonetic Sequences*

[VtV]	[VsV]	[VkV]
[VdV]	[VzV]	[ṼŋV] ~ [VgV]

There has never been an orthographic distinction between [ŋ] and [g].

9.2 MODERN STANDARD JAPANESE

As we saw in section 1.1, modern standard Japanese is based on the Yamanote dialect. Within this relatively homogeneous dialect, however, there are differences among speakers with regard to medial [ŋ]. Because noninitial voiced obstruents can occur after the mora nasal /N/ as well as intervocalically in modern Japanese, [4] will serve as a first approximation to the situation for speakers with consistent medial [ŋ]. I will treat exceptions to rule [4] in sections 9.4–9.5.

[4] /g/ → [ŋ]/ $\left\{ {N \atop V} \right\}$ —V

It is well known that the pronunciation with consistent medial [ŋ] has a kind of official status. According to Nakazawa (1955), the Japanese Ministry of Education made a real effort to have [ŋ] taught as the standard in elementary schools before World War II. Maeda (1977a) mentions that some people still hold the view that [ŋ] should be taught to children in language and music education. Since [ŋ] is more sonorant than [g], music teachers have a preference for [ŋ] in singing. Jōo (1977:139) mentions a prominent figure in the Japanese musical world who laments the increase in young singers who pronounce [ŋ] "dirtily" as [g]. It is also common knowledge that, for example, news broadcasters on the government television network use [ŋ]. In spite of this official recognition, however, Nakazawa, Maeda, Jōo, Sakurai (1966), and Kindaichi (1942) all agree that younger speakers are less likely to use [ŋ] than their elders and that the velar nasal is dying out.

According to Kamei (1956), some standard speakers consistently use [ŋ] medially, some consistently use [g], and some are inconsistent. I know several speakers in the 20–40 age range who are inconsistent or consistently use [g], but none who consistently uses [ŋ]. If [ŋ] is in fact dying out, we would not really expect to find consistent [ŋ] except in older speakers. Arisaka (1940:47–48), who grew up in Tokyo, describes Tokyo pronunciation as having [ŋ] in the relevant items no matter how carefully they are pronounced. This description suggests that Arisaka himself was probably a consistent [ŋ] speaker.

Kindaichi (1942) reports a survey he carried out among middle-school students in Tokyo in 1941. Although he gathered no data from older speakers, he says that Yamanote speakers over 30 at that time would probably use [ŋ] consistently. Seventy students, all born and raised in Tokyo, participated in the survey, and most were 14 or 15 years old. Each student pronounced the same thirteen items by reading them from a list. About 30 percent of the students consistently used [ŋ], and about 30 percent consistently used [g]. This result does not mean that only 40 percent were inconsistent speakers, however, since pronunciation varies not only from item to item but also from occasion to occasion, often depending on style. In any case, if Kindaichi is correct about the consistent [ŋ] of older speakers, these figures do suggest that a shift to [g] was in progress.

When the locations of the students' homes and schools are taken into account, Kindaichi's results indicate that the shift to [g] was characteristic of students from the Yamanote area. The results of a recent survey by Inoue et al. (1983) suggest that modern Tokyo speakers in the 12–24 age range use [g] almost exclusively. According to Hibiya (to appear), however, tape recordings of actual conversations among such speakers show that [ŋ] is still rather frequent. I agree with Maeda (1977a) that more surveys by age and social class are called for.

I have had the opportunity to observe rather closely one inconsistent speaker (KH) from the Yamanote area over the past several years, and for this speaker, [ŋ] occurs frequently in unguarded speech. When reading a word list as part of an interview with a tape recorder running, however, KH consistently used [g]. A survey like Kindaichi's would probably have put KH in the consistent [g] category. Labov (1972:70–109) says that word lists of this kind will elicit "careful speech," and the expectation is that careful speech will be closer to the prestige norm than casual speech. Labov's remarks suggest that for KH the prestige norm is [g], in spite of the official status of [ŋ]. This preference is really not very surprising, since Kindaichi's survey results indicate that [g] is a Yamanote innovation. Yamanote residents generally do not hold the Shitamachi area (section 1.1) in very high regard, and the fact that Shitamachi speakers, including the students in Kindaichi's survey, generally retain [ŋ] is not likely to lend it any prestige. It may also be relevant that the northern Honshū area, where [ŋ] is strong, is one of the lowest prestige areas in all of Japan.

9.3 PHONETIC MOTIVATION

Rule [4] does not look very natural. The appearance of [ŋ] in the context N—V (which was phonotactically impossible in Old Japanese) seems to be an assimilation, but here again there is an asymmetry, since the sequences /NbV/ and /NdV/ show no signs of changing in parallel fashion. The real problem, however, is nasalization intervocalically.

As Stampe (1973:1) points out, there is an obvious difficulty in pronouncing voiced stops: the complete oral and nasal closure makes it hard to maintain the outward airflow necessary for phonation. Donegan and Stampe (1979:141) suggest that a velar voiced stop is more difficult than one articulated farther forward, because the air chamber between the glottis and the obstruction is smaller and therefore fills up more quickly. While it is true that nasalization overcomes this difficulty by allowing air to escape through the nose, I am not aware of any evidence that it is a natural way to overcome it. In fact, this difficulty is probably not even relevant in intervocalic position; voiceless stops tend to become voiced in this environment. Hattori (1957:338–341) argues at length that there is no phonetic reason for [g] to become [ŋ] intervocalically.

In any case, as far as I know, children acquiring a language do not spontaneously nasalize intervocalic voiced obstruents. What we do find again and again is spirantization (i.e., change to a fricative), as in [5].

[5] /g/ → [γ]/V—V

Kamei (1956:7), Hattori (1956:306, n. 6), and Kindaichi (1942:187) all suggest that speakers who do not have [ŋ] frequently produce [γ]. Kawakami (1977:32–37) says that some young people use [γ] instead of [ŋ], and we saw in section 4.2.3 that intervocalic /b/ is also sometimes spirantized, although intervocalic /d/ apparently is not. My guess is that the natural weakening in [5] is likely in rapid speech unless preempted by the unnatural weakening in [4]. As we have seen (section 9.1), the historical origin of [ŋ] in Tokyo was not an intervocalic weakening at all.

9.4 MEDIAL VOICED VELAR STOPS

9.4.1 Background

Trubetzkoy (1969:292), whose book first appeared in 1939, tells his readers that "in Japanese, where 'g' initially is realized as the voiced obstruent g, and medially as a nasal ŋ, g is a positive and ŋ a negative nonphonemic boundary signal." If there were no exceptions to rule [4], Trubetzkoy's statement would be correct for consistent [ŋ] speakers. In fact, however, exceptions to rule [4] have become widely known, and Jōo (1977:140) justifiably takes Koizumi (1971: 97–98) to task for uncritically repeating Trubetzkoy's account.

Aside from some marginal phenomena that I will discuss in section 9.5, the exceptions to rule [4] are cases where, even for consistent [ŋ] speakers, medial [g] appears. To the best of my knowledge, the first person to cite such exceptions was Sakuma (1929:159). Many more putative examples have since been discovered, and the remainder of this section will treat these exceptions in detail. I will continue to write /g/ in all phonemic transcriptions, but the phonemic status of [ŋ] remains open.

9.4.2 Compounds

9.4.2.1 Sino-Japanese Compounds

Arisaka (1940:58) notes that /niQpoN giNkoo/ 'Bank of Japan' (from /niQpoN/ 'Japan' and /giNkoo/ 'bank') is pronounced [ɲip:ˆpõŋ:ˆg, ĩŋ:ˆko:]. This particular item is a proper name, but it is clearly a single word in terms of accent (i.e., it cannot be two phrases; see section 8.6.1), and it is representative of a class of compounds, most of which are common nouns.

The notion of a compound in Japanese is complicated by the existence of a huge class of words composed of two morphemes of Chinese origin. For example, /gaku.ša/ 'scholar' consists of /gaku/ 'learning' and /ša/ 'person'. (I will hereafter use a dot rather than a plus sign to indicate the morpheme boundary in combinations of this kind.) Many of these Sino-Japanese morphemes cannot occur free, but some can. Thus, while /ša/ cannot occur as an independent word, /gaku/ sometimes does, and the /giN/ of /giN.koo/ frequently occurs as a word meaning 'silver'. For consistent [ŋ] speakers, two-morpheme combinations of this kind apparently always have [ŋ]. Kindaichi (1967a) lists /doku.ga/ 'poison moth' (from /doku/ 'poison' and /ga/ 'moth') as an example with [g], but Hirayama (1960) and Nihon Hōsō Kyōkai (NHK) (1966), two pronunciation dictionaries, list it only with [ŋ]. (According to the entry in Masuda (1974), this word refers to a particular species called the "Oriental tussock moth" [*Euproctis subflava*].)

In more complex formations, the situation is not so simple. In /oN.gaku + gaQ.koo/ 'music school', for example, there are four Sino-Japanese morphemes, and /oN.gaku/ 'music' and /gaQ.koo/ 'school' are both well-established words. According to Nakazawa (1955), /oN.gaku + gaQ.koo/ is pronounced [oŋ:ˆŋakɯgak:ˆko:], and Nihon Onsei Gakkai (1976:201) agrees. This is also the only pronunciation listed in Hirayama (1960) and NHK (1966).

McCawley (1968:87) says that "long" Sino-Japanese compounds of this kind often have [g] and [ŋ] in free variation immediately following the major division, and Sakurai (1966:39–40) agrees. As Labov (1972:9) points out, however, labelling variation "free" is tantamount to abandoning the search for social significance. I will not come to terms with this issue here, but it is clear that this is why we need the sociolinguistic studies suggested in section 9.2.

When I checked the examples of [g] ~ [ŋ] variation from McCawley (1968: 87) and Sakurai (1966:39–40) in the two pronunciation dictionaries, only McCawley's /koo.too + gaQ.koo/ 'high school' turned up, and while Hirayama (1960) says it can have either [g] or [ŋ], NHK (1966) says it has [g]. An unsystematic search of my own suggests that four-morpheme examples listed with variation are quite rare.

One consistent [ŋ] speaker I contacted (SK), whose judgments provided much of the data in this chapter, can have either [g] or [ŋ] in /koo.too + gaQ.koo/ and also in /ǰo.ši + gaku.sei/ 'female student'. In general, however, [g] seems to be the norm after the major division in four-morpheme Sino-Japanese compounds, even for consistent [ŋ] speakers. Since we can analyze /niQ.poN + giN.koo/ 'Bank of Japan' as a compound of this type, the [g] is expected.

It is interesting to compare three-morpheme Sino-Japanese words at this point, because we find an asymmetry. In words of the form X + Y.Z, we seem to get [g] after the major division. Thus, for example, SK has [g] in /dai + geN.soku/ 'major principle' and /šiN + gi.ǰucu/ 'new technology'. In words of the form X.Y + Z, on the other hand, we seem to get [ŋ] after the major division. For example, both Hirayama (1960) and Nihon Hōsō Kyōkai (1966) list /geN.go + gaku/ 'linguistics' and /ǰi.dai + geki/ 'period drama' only with [ŋ].

Since Sino-Japanese morphemes are often bound, as I mentioned above, words of the form X.Y + Z will often have a bound morpheme after the major break. This fact suggests that [g] tends to appear at the beginning of a second element that can occur as an independent word. The bound morpheme /geN/ 'limit', for example, occurs in the word /geN.do/ 'limit', and NHK (1966) lists /sai. šoo + geN/ 'minimum limit' with [ŋ] but /sai.šoo + geN.do/ 'minimum limit' with [g]. On the other hand, the final morphemes in /geN.go + gaku/ 'linguistics' and /ji.dai + geki/ 'period drama' both occur as independent words: /gaku/ 'learning' and /geki/ 'drama' (Masuda 1974).

One exception to the generalization that [g] appears after the major division in words of the form X + Y.Z is /iči + gaQ.ki/ 'one term' (from /iči/ 'one' and /gaQ.ki/ '(academic) term'). Kamei (1956:12) says that this word always has [ŋ], and Hirayama (1960) lists it only with [ŋ]; SK can have either [g] or [ŋ]. Another possible exception is /fu + gi.kai/ 'prefectural assembly' (from /fu/ 'prefecture' and /gi.kai/ 'council'), which NHK (1966) lists with either [g] or [ŋ]. The word /neN.gaQ.pi/ 'date' (from /neN/ 'year', /gaQ/ 'month', and /pi/ 'day') also consists of three morphemes (the last of which is not Sino-Japanese), but it does not have an obvious major division. Sakurai (1966:38) says it can have either [g] or [ŋ], and the entries in Hirayama and NHK agree.

Momoi (personal communication, 1984) has brought some four-morpheme Sino-Japanese examples to my attention that strongly favor [ŋ] for consistent [ŋ] speakers. Two of these are /kei.zai + gaku.bu/ 'school of economics', which Hirayama (1960) lists only with [ŋ], and /teN.moN + gaku.ša/ 'astronomer', which NHK (1966) lists only with [ŋ]. In each case, there are well-established words consisting of the first three morphemes (/kei.zai + gaku/ 'economics' and /teN.moN + gaku/ 'astronomy') and the last two morphemes (/gaku.bu/ 'school' and /gaku.ša/ 'scholar'). As a result, the location of the major division in the four-morpheme words is not entirely clear, and speakers may analyze them as /kei.zai + gaku/ + /bu/ and /teN.moN + gaku/ + /ša/. As we have seen, [ŋ] is expected after the major division in a three-morpheme Sino-Japanese word of the form X.Y + Z. Momoi says that for him, /keizaigakubu/ sounds all right with [g] but /teNmoNgakuša/ does not. He suggests that this is because /kei.zai/ 'economy' is a well-established independent word, whereas /teN.moN/ 'astronomy' is not.

9.4.2.2   Native Second Elements

When we come to native Japanese morphemes, it is much more difficult to find appropriate examples. Aside from mimetic adverbs, which I will consider in section 9.4.5, native Japanese words generally do not begin with voiced obstruents. There is a phenomenon known as "sequential voicing" (Chapter 10) that frequently produces medial voiced obstruents (as in /hoši + zora/ 'starry sky' from /hoši/ 'star' and /sora/ 'sky'), but as Kamei (1956:12) and McCawley (1968: 86–87) point out, when a /k/ undergoes sequential voicing, the result is apparently always [ŋ] for consistent [ŋ] speakers. Thus, Sino-Japanese /fuu.fu + geN.ka/ 'domestic quarrel' (from /fuu.fu/ 'husband and wife' and /keN.ka/ 'quarrel') and native Japanese /yama + gawa/ 'mountain river' (from /yama/ 'mountain' and /kawa/ 'river') both have [ŋ].

According to the entries in *Nihon Kokugo Daijiten*, the native words /gawa/ 'side' and /gara/ 'pattern, build, character' derive from older /kawa/ and /kara/. Apparently these items have been used as second elements in longer formations so much that speakers have interpreted them as starting with a voiced velar even in isolation. When consistent [ŋ] speakers use compounds containing these words as second elements, they generally have [ŋ]. For example, /migi + gawa/ 'right side' (cf. /migi/ 'right'), /roo.doo + ša + gawa/ 'the workers' side' (cf. /roo.doo + ša/ 'worker'), /aida + gara/ 'relation' (cf. /aida/ 'between'), and /koto + gara/ 'matter' (cf. /koto/ 'fact') all have [ŋ].

The only exception I know of is /šiN + gara/ 'new pattern'. This word contains the Sino-Japanese morpheme /šiN/ 'new', which cannot occur free. Nihon Hōsō Kyōkai (1966) lists it only with [ŋ], but Hirayama (1960) lists it with either [g] or [ŋ], and SK has [g]. Nonetheless, it seems fair to say that those native words with initial /g/ that exist generally behave like Sino-Japanese morphemes in two-morpheme words, that is, we expect [ŋ].

9.4.2.3 Recent Borrowings as Second Elements

In addition to Sino-Japanese and native words, some relatively recent loanwords from European languages also occur in compounds, and some of these begin with /g/ in isolation. According to Kamei (1956:12), some compounds of this type have [g] and some have either [g] or [ŋ]. For example, Kamei says that /suri + garasu/ 'frosted glass' (from /suri/ 'grinding' and /garasu/ 'glass') has [g]. The word /garasu/ was borrowed from Dutch, and according to Umegaki (1966), the first attestation is 1713. Kindaichi (1967a) gives /ita + garasu/ 'plate glass' (cf. /ita/ 'board') as an example of a compound with [g], and Nihon Onsei Gakkai (1976:201) gives /nyuu.haku + garasu/ 'milky white glass' (cf. /nyuu/ 'milk' and /haku/ 'white'). Another common compound with /garasu/ is /mado + garasu/ 'window glass' (cf. /mado/ 'window').

Kamei (1956:12) says that /doku + gasu/ 'poison gas' (from /doku/ 'poison' and /gasu/ 'gas'), /keši + gomu/ 'eraser' (from /keši/ 'erasing' and /gomu/ 'rubber'), and /wa + gomu/ 'rubber band' (cf. /wa/ 'circle') can all have either [g] or [ŋ]. The words /gasu/ and /gomu/, like /garasu/, are old Dutch loans, and Umegaki (1966) gives the earliest attestations as 1822 and 1820, respectively. Nihon Onsei Gakkai (1976:201) gives /to.ši + gasu/ 'city gas' (cf. /to.ši/ 'city') and /teN.neN + gomu/ 'natural rubber' (cf. /teN.neN/ 'natural') as examples with [g], and another common compound with /gasu/ is /teN.neN + gasu/ 'natural gas'.

I list the examples in this section in [6], along with the pronunciations given by Hirayama (1960), NHK (1966), and SK. It appears that in compounds with native or Sino-Japanese first elements, second elements borrowed from European languages behave much like two-morpheme Sino-Japanese second elements: we generally find [g], but there are a few exceptions.

[6]	*Hirayama*	*NHK*	*SK*
/ita + garasu/	g	g	g
/mado + garasu/	g	g	g(?)
/nyuu.haku + garasu/	—	—	(?)
/suri + garasu/	g	g	g
/doku + gasu/	g	g ~ ŋ	g ~ ŋ
/teN.neN + gasu/	g	g	g
/to.ši + gasu/	—	—	g
/keši + gomu/	g	g	g
/teN.neN + gomu/	—	—	g
/wa + gomu/	g ~ ŋ	g	g

There are also a few apparent compounds in which both elements are of relatively recent foreign origin. SK has [g] in /basu + gaido/ 'bus guide' and /gaadeN + gorufu/ 'miniature golf', and my guess is that consistent [ŋ] speakers generally have [g] in the few items of this kind. Neither Hirayama (1960) nor NHK (1966) lists either of these two examples.

9.4.2.4 Native + Sino-Japanese Compounds

There are a few compounds consisting of a single native morpheme followed by a single Sino-Japanese morpheme that begins with /g/ in isolation. Kamei (1956:12) says that /zaru + go/ 'a game of go between poor players' (from /zaru/ 'basket' and /go/ '(the game of) go') can have either [g] or [ŋ], and Kindaichi (1967a) gives /ai + go/ 'go players of equal skill' (cf. /ai/ 'mutual') as an example with [g]. Other examples of this kind with /go/ are /kake + go/ 'go for money' (cf. /kake/ 'betting') and /oki + go/ 'go with a handicap' (cf. /oki/ 'accepting a handicap' from /oki/ 'placing', that is, placing extra stones on the go board).

Kindaichi (1967a) also gives /ko + gaN/ 'gosling' (from /ko/ 'child' and /gaN/ 'goose') as an example with [g]. Another relevant example with /gaN/ is /kuro + gaN/ 'brant' (cf. /kuro/ 'black').

Sakurai (1966:38) gives /atari + gei/ 'successful performance' (from /atari/ 'succeeding' and /gei/ 'performance, art') and /omote + gei/ 'principal accomplishment' (cf. /omote/ 'front') and says that they can have either [g] or [ŋ], although they favor [ŋ]. Another example with /gei/ is /hara + gei/ 'gut interpretation' (cf. /hara/ 'belly').

One other Sino-Japanese element that occurs in words of the relevant kind is /gu/ 'tool, means', as in /kawa + gu/ 'leather articles' (cf. /kawa/ 'leather') and /ama + gu/ 'rain gear' (cf. /ama/, an allomorph of /ame/ 'rain'; see section 11.1.2).

I list the examples mentioned so far in this section in [7], along with the pronunciations given by Hirayama (1960), NHK (1966), and SK. The two dictionaries suggest that [ŋ] is favored in examples of this kind, but SK apparently has [g] in /gaN/ and /go/.

[7]	*Hirayama*	*NHK*	*SK*
/ko + gaN/	—	—	g
/kuro + gaN/	—	—	g
/atari + gei/	ŋ	g~ŋ	g~ŋ
/hara + gei/	ŋ	ŋ	g~ŋ
/omote + gei/	—	g~ŋ	g~ŋ
/ai + go/	—	—	g
/kake + go/	—	ŋ	g
/oki + go/	g~ŋ	ŋ	g
/zaru + go/	ŋ	ŋ	g
/ama + gu/	ŋ	ŋ	ŋ
/kawa + gu/	—	ŋ	ŋ(?)

There are also a few examples of compounds consisting of a native morpheme followed by a two-morpheme Sino-Japanese word. Arisaka (1940:171) gives /yama + go.boo/ 'pokeweed' (from /yama/ 'mountain' and /go.boo/ 'burdock') as an example of a word with medial [g]. Kamei (1956:12) says that /širo + go.ma/ 'white sesame' (from /širo/ 'white' and /go.ma/ 'sesame'), /kuro + go.ma/ 'black sesame' (cf. /kuro/ 'black'), and /asa + go.haN/ 'breakfast' (from /asa/ 'morning' and /go.haN/ 'meal') all have [g]. Martin (1952:22) also gives /asa + go.haN/, and another example with /go.haN/ is /hiru + go.haN/ 'lunch' (cf. /hiru/ 'noon').

Kamei (1956:12) also mentions /hiyori + ge.ta/ 'dry weather clogs' (from /hiyori/ 'fair weather' and /ge.ta/ 'clogs') and says that it can only have [ŋ]. One could easily argue, however, that I have put this word in the wrong category. The first element should probably be analyzed as two morphemes (/hi + yori/), but the real point is that the analysis of /ge.ta/ as two Sino-Japanese morphemes is questionable. Although /ge.ta/ is written like an ordinary Sino-Japanese word of this kind, that is, with two kanji, *Nihon Kokugo Daijiten* says that the etymology is obscure. It is relatively easy to find words in which /ge.ta/ is preceded by what is clearly a single native morpheme. Two examples are /niwa + ge.ta/ 'garden clogs' (cf. /niwa/ 'garden') and /taka + ge.ta/ 'high clogs' (cf. /taka/ 'high').

Sakurai (1966:39) gives /ne + go.za/ 'sleeping mat' (from /ne/ 'sleeping' and /go.za/ 'mat') as an example which can have either [g] or [ŋ]. Kindaichi (1967a) gives /ki + gu.mi/ 'yellow oleaster' (from /ki/ 'yellow' and /gu.mi/ 'oleaster') as an example with [g].

I list the examples in this section with two-morpheme Sino-Japanese second elements in [8], along with the pronunciations given by Hirayama (1960), NHK (1966), and SK. These examples suggest that [g] is strongly favored in compounds consisting of a single native morpheme followed by a two-morpheme Sino-Japanese word.

[8]	*Hirayama*	*NHK*	*SK*
/hiyori + ge.ta/	ŋ	ŋ	g~ŋ(?)
/niwa + ge.ta/	ŋ	g~ŋ	g

/taka + ge.ta/	ŋ	ŋ	g
/yama + go.boo/	—	g	g
/kuro + go.ma/	—	—	g
/širo + go.ma/	—	g	g
/asa + go.haN/	g	g	g
/hiru + go.haN/	g	g	g
/ne + go.za/	—	g~ŋ	g
/ki + gu.mi/	—	—	g

9.4.2.5 Summary

On the basis of the data presented in this section, it appears that even for consistent [ŋ] speakers, there is a very strong tendency for medial [g] to appear in compounds with European second elements or second elements consisting of two Sino-Japanese morphemes. In compounds with a single native or Sino-Japanese morpheme as the second element, [ŋ] is favored, although this tendency does not seem so strong.

9.4.3 Prefixes

Kamei (1956:12) asks his readers to suppose that the prefix /oo/ 'big' were added to /karasu/ 'crow' and /garasu/ 'glass'. The results, he says, would be [o:ŋɑrɑsɯ] 'big crow', with sequential voicing (section 9.4.2.2) having applied, and [o:gɑrɑsɯ] 'big glass'. Kindaichi (1967a) adds this prefix to /kama/ 'sickle', /kama/ 'kettle', and /gama/ 'toad' and says that the first two undergo sequential voicing to give [o:ŋɑmɑ] 'scythe/cauldron', while the result in the latter case is [o:gɑmɑ] 'big toad'. McCawley (1968:85–88) says that the behavior after the prefix /ko/ 'small' is the same, and he proposes a solution to preserve original /g/ while sequential voicing converts original /k/ into [ŋ]. This solution is tantamount to a GLOBAL RULE (Hyman 1975:131–132), but McCawley himself (personal communication, 1979) now repudiates this anlaysis, and it will not work anyway, since, according to Hirayama (1960) and Nihon Hōsō Kyōkai (1966), adding these prefixes to /gara/ 'build' gives [o:ŋɑrɑ] 'big build' and [koŋɑrɑ] 'small build'.

Martin (1952:22) says that [g] is usual after the honorific prefix /o/ and gives /o + gyoo.gi/ 'manners' and /o + geN.ki/ 'health' as examples. Sakurai (1966:38) gives /o + geN.ki/ and /o + gi.ri/ 'duty'. McCawley (1968:86) says that we find [g] after the honorific prefix /go/ as well, and I have no reason to doubt this. All the examples mentioned here have two-morpheme Sino-Japanese stems, but I do not think this fact is significant. As mentioned in section 9.4.2.2, native morphemes with initial /g/ are rare, and honorific prefixes are not commonly added to European borrowings. If an honorific prefix were added to a /g/-initial native or European stem, however, I am quite certain that the result would have [g].

Since sequential voicing generally does not apply after the honorific prefixes, we do not find [g]/[ŋ] minimal pairs in words of this type. The only example of sequential voicing after an honorific prefix that I know of is in /o + guši/ 'hair', which both Hirayama (1960) and NHK (1966) list with [ŋ]. This word is not very common, however, and the stem /kuši/ 'hair' is apparently obsolete. (Masuda [1974], for example, does not list /kuši/ and marks /o + guši/ as 'elegant', which is defined on page ix as 'poetic or very polite'.)

Sakurai (1966:38) says that prefixes other than the honorific ones are often followed by either [g] or [ŋ]. The only example he gives is /fu + gi.ri/ 'dishonesty' (from /fu/ 'not' and /gi.ri/ 'honesty, duty'). Since all three morphemes in this word are Sino-Japanese, however, there is some question whether /fu/ ought to be singled out as a prefix if this means treating it differently from other Sino-Japanese morphemes. (Recall that many morphemes in this class cannot occur free; see section 9.4.2.1.) In other words, perhaps we should simply treat /fu + gi.ri/ as another compound of Sino-Japanese morphemes with the major division after /fu/. As we saw in section 9.4.2.1, words of this kind, such as /šiN + gi.jucu/ 'new technology', generally seem to have [g]. Hirayama (1960) and NHK (1966) list /fu + gi.ri/ as having either [g] or [ŋ].

I list several three-morpheme words beginning with /fu/ 'not' in [9], along with the pronunciations given by Hirayama (1960), NHK (1966), and SK.

[9]

	Hirayama	*NHK*	*SK*
/fu + gi.ri/ 'dishonesty'	g~ŋ	g~ŋ	g
/fu + gyoo.gi/ 'bad manners'	—	g	g
/fu + gyoo.ǰoo/ 'misconduct'	—	g	g
/fu + gyoo.seki/ 'misconduct'	g~ŋ	g	g
/fu + goo.kaku/ 'disqualification'	g~ŋ	g~ŋ	g
/fu + goo.ri/ 'irrationality'	g~ŋ	g~ŋ	g~ ŋ(?)

Since the tendency in three-morpheme Sino-Japanese words with the major division after the first morpheme is to have [g], there does not appear to be any reason to treat /fu/ differently from any other Sino-Japanese morpheme.

The closest I can come to a generalization for compounds and prefix-stem formations is to recall a proposal by Ōtsu (1980) that in certain kinds of compounds, sequential voicing applies when the affected morpheme is on a right branch in constituent structure (section 10.2.1). Consider the suggestion that [ŋ] appears at the beginning of a morpheme on a right branch. This proposal would account for the behavior of three-morpheme Sino-Japanese words like /šiN + gi.jucu/ 'new technology' (with [g]) and /ǰi.dai + geki/ 'period drama' (with [ŋ]) as in [10]. (Ōtsu's proposal actually treats two-morpheme Sino-Japanese words as nonbranching, but I will assume the structure shown.)

[10]

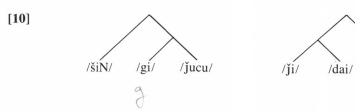

/šiN/   /gi/   /ǰucu/   /ǰi/   /dai/   /geki/

This principle will also account for [g] in four-morpheme Sino-Japanese words like /oN.gaku + gaQ.koo/ 'music school'. On the other hand, it also makes many wrong predictions. It fails in one direction for a speaker who has [ŋ] in /koo.too + gaQ.koo/ 'high school' or /fu + gi.ri/ 'dishonesty', and it fails in the other direction for a speaker who has [g] in /keši + gomu/ 'eraser' or /oo + gama/ 'big toad'.

9.4.4   The Morpheme /go/ 'five'

Perhaps the best-known examples of medial [g] are words containing the Sino-Japanese morpheme /go/ 'five'. Sakuma (1929:159) notes that /go.juu + go/ 'fifty-five' (cf. /juu/ 'ten') has [g] both initially and medially, and we saw in section 9.4.2.1 that [ŋ] is expected after the major division in Sino-Japanese words of the form X.Y + Z. Arisaka (1940:58) cites two minimal pairs: /juu.go/ 'fifteen' and /dai.go/ 'fifth' with [g] versus /juu.go/ 'homefront' (from /juu/ 'gun' and /go/ 'behind') and /dai.go/ 'zest for life' (from /dai/ 'whey' and /go/ 'a kind of cream') with [ŋ]. When Kindaichi (1942:180) did his survey in the Tokyo schools (section 9.2), he had the students pronounce /juu.go/ 'fifteen', but since they all pronounced it with [g], he excluded this item from his statistics. Martin (1952:22) gives the minimal pair /seN.go/ 'one thousand five' (cf. /seN/ 'thousand') with [g] versus /seN.go/ 'after the war' (from /seN/ 'war' and /go/ 'after') with [ŋ].

Martin (1952:22) says that /go/ 'five' always has [g] except in "fossilized compounds," which he lists. The examples on this list are /juu.go + ya/ 'full-moon night' (i.e., 'fifteenth night (of the lunar month)'; cf. /ya/ 'night'), /šiči.go.saN/ 'Seven Five Three' (a holiday for children aged 7, 5, or 3; cf. /šiči/ 'seven' and /saN/ 'three'), and /saN.saN + go.go/ 'by three's and five's' (i.e., 'in small groups'). According to Nihon Hōsō Kyōkai (1966), these words are all pronounced with medial [ŋ]; /saN.saN + go.go/ ends [goŋo]. Martin also points out that in reciting the multiplication tables, /go/ appears with [ŋ] in cases such as /go.go ni.juu + go/ '5 times 5 is 25' (cf. /ni/ 'two'), which begins [goŋo]. Sakurai (1966:38) mentions /šiči.go + čoo/ '7–5 meter' (in Japanese poetry; cf. /čoo/ 'meter'), which also has [ŋ].

Hattori (1939–40:231, n. 1) notes the /juu.go/ 'homefront/fifteen' minimal pair, but he goes on to make an important observation about the accent on these two words. He says that the pitch pattern on 'homefront' is HLL and that 'fifteen' is often pronounced with the same pattern. When /go/ 'five' is emphasized, however, it is on a higher pitch than the preceding mora. This means that there are, at least potentially, two accent phrases (section 8.6.1), and Hattori suggests that we get [g] at the beginning of an accent phrase. A parallel argument applies to /dai.go/ 'fifth', which can be either HLL or HLM. In general, numerals ending with /go/ are potentially two accent phrases.

Kuroda (personal communication, 1984) has brought another example to my attention. Consistent [ŋ] speakers have [g] in /juu.go + oku/ 'one billion five hundred million' (cf. /oku/ 'hundred million'), and the melody is HL.M + LL, with /go/ at the beginning of an accent phrase. Note that in this case the division into accent phrases does not coincide with the major semantic division. The word means 'fifteen hundred-millions' and not 'ten five-hundred-millions'. This example clearly supports the claim that [g] occurs at the beginning of an accent phrase.

In the so-called fossilized compounds and in the multiplication tables, however, /go/ is not at the beginning of a potential accent phrase. The first /go/ in /saN.saN + go.go/ 'by threes and fives' has [g], but it is after the major division in a four-morpheme Sino-Japanese word. We have already seen that [g] is expected in such cases (section 9.4.2.1).

It thus appears that accentual behavior provides an independent reason for saying that the boundary in words like /ǰuu.go/ 'fifteen' is different from the boundary in words like /ǰuu.go/ 'homefront'. There is, however, at least one problematical example. In /dai.go + kyoo.wa + koku/ 'The Fifth Republic' (cf. /kyoo.wa + koku/ 'republic'), there does not seem to be any potential for division into two accent phrases with /go/ at the beginning of the second. Nevertheless, Nihon Hōsō Kyōkai (1966) lists this word only with [g].

9.4.5 Reduplicated Mimetic Adverbs

The other example of medial [g] that Sakuma (1929:159) cites is /gara + gara/ 'rattle-rattle', and it is now well known that reduplicated mimetic adverbs never have [ŋ] after the morpheme division. Martin (1952:22), Sakurai (1966:38), and Nihon Onsei Gakkai (1976:201) all state explicitly that words in this class have [g]. (In an example like /mogu + mogu/ 'mumblingly', of course, consistent [ŋ] speakers have [ŋ], since the velars are not morpheme-initial.)

Kamei (1956:12) says that we find medial [g] in "words in which alliteration has expressive value," and he lists three examples. The first is /geǰi + geǰi/ 'millipede', which presumably started out as mimetic, and the second is /gara + gara + seN.bei/ 'crispy rice cracker', which obviously has /gara + gara/ as its first element. Kamei's third example is /gyoo.gyoo + šii/ 'grandiose', which consists of the Sino-Japanese morpheme /gyoo/ 'looking up' reduplicated, with the adjective-forming suffix /šii/ added. Hirayama (1960) lists this word only with [g], but NHK (1966) lists it only with [ŋ].

There are certainly some problems in determining whether a given morpheme belongs in the mimetic class, but it seems quite clear that /gyoo/ does not. For one thing, as far as I know, the suffix /šii/ is not added to mimetic morphemes. In addition, it is common for the same mimetic morpheme to occur reduplicated to indicate something repeated or continuous and unreduplicated to indicate something that happens only once or that is closer to instantaneous. The mimetic morpheme /gyuu/, for example, occurs in /gyuu + gyuu/ 'creak-creak' and also in /gyuu + to/ 'with a creak', but /gyoo/ does not occur in any formation of this second kind.

For consistent [ŋ] speakers who have [g] in /gyoo.gyoo + šii/, perhaps Kamei's (1956:12) statement about alliteration is accurate. For speakers with [ŋ], medial [g] is perhaps restricted to morphemes which those speakers identify as mimetic.

I have found five additional examples of reduplicated /g/-initial Sino-Japanese morphemes listed in NHK (1966): /ga.ga + taru/ 'rugged' (from /ga/ 'high mountain' and /taru/, which converts a noun into an adjective), /gai.gai + taru/ 'silver white' (cf. /gai/ 'white'), /geN.geN/ 'gunwale to gunwale' (cf. /geN/ 'gunwale'), /geN.geN + ku.ku/ 'every word and phrase' (from /geN/ 'word' and /ku/ 'phrase'), and /goo.goo + taru/ 'noisy' (cf. /goo/ 'noise'). NHK lists /ga.ga + taru/ only with [ŋ] and all the others only with [g].

Hattori (1957:338) gives /sei.ji + goro/ 'politician's henchman' (from /sei.ji/ 'politics' and /goro/ 'ruffian, vagabond') as an example with medial [g]. Etymologically, /goro/ is apparently a mimetic morpheme, and the entry in *Nihon Kokugo Daijiten* says that this use derives from the fact that a /goro/ "lives like pebbles lying around." The reduplicated mimetic adverb /goro + goro/ can be used to describe pebbles lying around and people being idle.

Kindaichi (1967a) gives /boN + goro/ 'routine grounder' (from /boN/ 'common' and /goro/ 'grounder') as an example with medial [g]. According to Umegaki (1966), /goro/ may derive from English *grounder*, but it may also derive from the mimetic morpheme /goro/, since /goro + goro/ can describe rolling.

When Kamei (1956:12) says that alliteration has expressive value in reduplicated items, he probably means that the exact repetition of the morpheme is ICONIC, since a part of the meaning of such words is repetition or continuation. This is certainly the case for mimetic adverbs. Sequential voicing never occurs in reduplicated mimetic adverbs either (section 10.2.3), and perhaps the reason is the same: to preserve this iconicity. Thus, we find mimetic adverbs like /kera + kera/ 'cackle-cackle' but not like */kera + gera/. This appeal to iconicity is not relevant, of course, in /sei.ji + goro/ or /boN + goro/, and there is perhaps some question whether it is relevant in all the reduplicated Sino-Japanese morphemes.

9.4.6 Morpheme-Internal [g] in Recent Borrowings

All the examples of medial [g] we have considered so far have been immediately after a morpheme boundary. I have never encountered an example of a native morpheme in which consistent [ŋ] speakers have medial [g], and there are no Sino-Japanese morphemes with a noninitial voiced velar.

The situation is not so simple, however, in loanwords from European languages. Martin (1952:22) says that some relatively recent borrowings have medial [g], whereas older borrowings tend to have [ŋ]. He gives the following monomorphemic examples: /doguma/ 'dogma' and /harogeN/ 'halogen' with [g] versus /igirisu/ 'England', /berugii/ 'Belgium', and /orugaN/ '(musical) organ' with [ŋ].

Sakurai (1966:40) says that some European loanwords have only [ŋ], some have only [g], and some can have either. Among his examples are /taNgo/ 'tango' and /ɟaNguru/ 'jungle' with [ŋ], /baNgaroo/ 'bungalow' with [g], and /aNguru/ '(photographic) angle' and /kategorii/ 'category' with either.

Other relevant European borrowings are /egoisuto/ 'egoist', /maagariN/ 'margarine', and /nega/ '(photographic) negative'. I list the examples in this section in [11], along with the pronunciations given by Hirayama (1960), NHK (1966), and SK. It seems fair to conclude from these examples that consistent [ŋ] speakers favor [ŋ] in morpheme-internal position in European borrowings, but NHK lists several words with either [g] or [ŋ], and SK can have [g] or [ŋ] in all of them. This suggests that for at least some consistent [ŋ] speakers, at least some items in this class can occur with medial [g].

[11]	*Hirayama*	*NHK*	*SK*
/aNguru/	ŋ	g~ŋ	g~ŋ
/baNgaroo/	ŋ	ŋ	g~ŋ
/berugii/	ŋ	g~ŋ	g~ŋ
/doguma/	g	g~ŋ	g~ŋ
/egoisuto/	ŋ	g~ŋ	g~ŋ
/harogeN/	—	—	g~ŋ
/igirisu/	ŋ	ŋ	g~ŋ
/ɟaNguru/	ŋ	ŋ	g~ŋ
/kategorii/	ŋ	g~ŋ	g~ŋ
/maagariN/	ŋ	ŋ	g~ŋ
/nega/	ŋ	ŋ	g~ŋ
/orugaN/	ŋ	ŋ	g~ŋ
/taNgo/	ŋ	ŋ	g~ŋ

9.4.7   The ga-Line of the Syllabary

Martin (1952:22) points out that when consistent [ŋ] speakers recite the relevant line of the Japanese kana syllabary, they pronounce [g] throughout. Accentually, the line is treated as a single word: /gagigúgego/ (section 7.3.2).

9.4.8   Summary

We have seen in this section that most of the examples of medial [g] for consistent [ŋ] speakers are immediately after morpheme boundaries. The suggestion that we get [ŋ] on a right branch in constituent structure and [g] elsewhere (section 9.4.3) accounts for many of the compound and prefix-stem examples, although there is still a substantial residue of exceptions.

The examples involving /go/ 'five' are generally accounted for if we posit a different boundary on the basis of accentual behavior (section 9.4.4). This analysis raises the possibility of simply assigning this different boundary whenever we have a medial [g], but unless there is some independent reason for the boundary, this solution is tantamount to saying that the occurrence of medial [g] is unpredictable.

Nakazawa (1955) says that when the second element of a compound has a feeling of independence or when there is a consciousness of a pronunciation break between the two elements, [g] occurs. His examples are /oN.gaku + gaQ.ko/ 'music school', which presumably illustrates a feeling of independence, and /juu.go/ 'fifteen', which presumably illustrates a consciousness of a pronunciation break. Sakurai (1966:38–39) says that when the degree of composition is weak and there is a consciousness of two original words in a compound, we get either [g] or [ŋ]. When the degree of composition is even weaker, he says, we get only [g].

These accounts are not very helpful, of course, unless there is some independent way of determining when speakers feel that the elements in a compound are relatively independent. In other words, if the only way of knowing that the degree of composition is weak is by whether or not [g] occurs, the account is circular. I cannot help being reminded of Bloomfield's (1933:38) remarks on the so-called compound stress pattern in English.

> To say, for instance, that combinations of words which are "felt to be" compounds have only a single high stress (e.g., *blackbird* as opposed to *black bird*), is to tell exactly nothing, since we have no way of determining what the speakers may "feel": the observer's task was to tell us, by some tangible criterion, or, if he found none, by a list, which combinations of words are pronounced with a single high stress.

I am not quite so pessimistic about being able to find out what people feel, and I would substitute the word *independent* for the word *tangible*, but I think Bloomfield's point is well taken.

The occurrence of morpheme-internal [g] in some loanwords (section 9.4.6) and the consistent [g] in reduplicated mimetic adverbs (section 9.4.5) pose additional difficulties. The iconicity explanation for the latter is seriously compromised by the [g] in items like /boN + goro/ 'routine grounder'.

9.5 INITIAL VELAR NASALS

Sakuma (1929:159) remarks that even when there is a pause before it, the conjunction /ga/ 'but' is pronounced with [ŋ] if there is a feeling of continuation in terms of meaning. Martin (1952:22) says that this word /ga/ and the literary word /gotoši/ have initial [ŋ], and Nihon Onsei Gakkai (1976:201) also mentions utterance-initial /ga/.

The conjunction /ga/ is ordinarily an enclitic and so does not occur utterance-initially nearly as often as utterance-medially. Another enclitic with an initial voiced velar is /gurai/ 'about', which is commonly added to words denoting quantities. For example, /ičijikaN + gurai/ means 'about one hour' (cf. /ičijikaN/ 'one hour'). I have heard a speaker begin an utterance with /gurai/ as a response to a quantity suggested by the other party in the conversation. It was a case of one speaker finishing another's sentence, and this /gurai/ began with [ŋ].

We could perhaps dismiss utterance-initial /ga/ and /gurai/ as marginal, but /gotoši/ presents a more serious problem. Typical uses of this word involve a noun followed by /no gotoši/ to mean 'like [noun]'. Since /no/ is a genitive particle, /gotoši/ is clearly not an ordinary enclitic.

Another problematical word of this kind, first brought to my attention by Imai (personal communication, 1977), is /gawa/ 'side'. This word often occurs as the second element in compounds, as we saw in section 9.4.2.2. The example in [12] is from Kuroda (personal communication, 1984), and he has [ŋ] in /gawa/.

[12] /kumiai ni haiQte iru roodooša no   gawa wa/
     union in enter   be worker GEN side   TOP
     'As for the side of the workers in unions . . .'

Kuroda points out, however, that the accent pattern on /roodooša no gawa/ must be as in [13a] and not as in [13b].

[13] **a.** /roodóoša no gawa wa/
     b. /roodóoša no % gawa wa/

In [13a] /gawa wa/ is accentually subordinated to the preceding phrase, whereas in [13b] it forms its own accent phrase (section 8.6.1). Kuroda says that if the accent is as in [13b], then /gawa/ has [g]. This is not surprising, perhaps, in view of what we have seen in connection with /go/ 'five' (section 9.4.4), but it is not clear why /gawa/ should ever have [ŋ]. Although /gotoši/ is not a colloquial word, I suspect that is always accentually subordinated to the preceding phrase.

Another marginal example of initial [ŋ] occurs when a speaker wants to describe the kind of pronunciation that has [ŋ] as opposed to the kind that has [g] everywhere. I have heard speakers describe the [ŋ] pronunciation by saying that it has [ŋaŋiŋɯŋeŋo], that is, by pronouncing the **ga**-line of the syllabary with [ŋ] throughout. In any event, consistent [ŋ] speakers seem to have no trouble pronouncing initial [ŋ] when they want to.

9.6   NATURAL PROCESS versus LEARNED RULE

9.6.1   Background

In the kind of NATURAL PHONOLOGY advocated by Stampe (1973) and Donegan and Stampe (1979), there is a distinction between NATURAL PROCESSES and LEARNED RULES. Natural processes, it is claimed, are phonetically motivated and innate, and phonological acquisition is understood to be largely a matter of limiting or suppressing the application of those processes that do not apply freely or do not apply at all in adult speech.

This approach offers a very attractive account of the fact that as a child's pronunciation gets better and better, the "distance" between the target adult pronunciation and the child's pronunciation decreases. It is widely accepted that a child's mental representations are essentially identical to adult pronunciations (Clark and Clark 1977:384–387), although this view almost certainly involves some oversimplification (Linell 1979:216–220). Assuming that this idea is not too far from the truth, it is possible to write a set of rules to derive the child's forms from the adult ones (Smith 1973). Since fewer and fewer rules are necessary as a child progresses, however, it seems absurd to say that acquisition involves learning these rules. If what the child learns is to selectively limit or suppress natural processes that all apply freely at first, the progression seems perfectly reasonable.

Learned rules, unlike natural processes, lack synchronic phonetic motivation, and Donegan and Stampe (1979:127–128) consider them outside the scope of natural phonology. Stampe (1973:47) says the following:

> The distinction between [natural] processes and [learned] rules, as I understand it, is an absolute one, a distinction between constraints which the speaker brings to the language and constraints which the language brings to the speaker, whose distinct origins are reflected in their distinct roles in speech production.

I will now consider some of the properties that are supposed to differentiate these two kinds of constraints. Bjarkman (1975) provides a list of distinguishing properties, and Sommerstein (1977:235–237) reviews this list.

9.6.2 Optionality

Bjarkman (1975:68–69) says the following: "Processes are often optionally retained, relative to style and speed of articulation. Rules apparently never have this property." On the other hand, Bjarkman says that learned rules can be "suppressed," but only by conscious effort. To illustrate, he notes that the rule of VE-LAR SOFTENING (Hyman 1975:197–198), which is supposed to account for the alternation in *electri*[k] and *electri*[s]*ity*, is not sensitive to tempo or style. At the same time, speakers find it easy to pronounce *electri*[k]*ity* if they want to.

We have already seen (section 9.2) that for inconsistent speakers, [ŋ] is more likely to appear as the style becomes more casual. KH pronounced only [g] when reading a list of words but pronounces [ŋ] frequently in ordinary conversation. I am quite sure that KH is also more likely to pronounce [ŋ] at faster tempos, but I have no hard evidence on this point. In any event, the behavior relative to stylistic shifts suggests that /g/ → [ŋ] is an optional natural process.

9.6.3 Minimal Substitutions

Bjarkman (1975:69) also says, "Processes make only minimal substitutions while rules make more radical substitutions." Donegan and Stampe (1979:137) say that "a process normally changes only one feature." Whether or not all learned rules make radical substitutions, this criterion does not provide any reason for saying that the /g/ → [ŋ] phenomenon is not a natural process.

9.6.4 Nonphonetic Environments

Another of Bjarkman's (1975:70) criteria is that learned rules "have abstract or nonphonetic environments requiring reference to, say, some specific morphemes, lexical items, or nonphonetic boundaries." Sommerstein (1977:236, n. 44) expresses doubt that every learned rule will involve nonphonetic elements, but certainly any substitution that does have such elements would be classified as a learned rule.

The examples we have seen (section 9.4) indicate that for consistent [ŋ] speakers, various nonphonetic elements are involved in the /g/ → [ŋ] phenomenon. Even if we allow for the fact that the two pronunciation dictionaries (Hirayama [1960] and NHK [1966]) are not based on any single person's pronunciation, the data from SK make it clear that we cannot tell when [ŋ] will appear unless we have some nonphonetic information.

For inconsistent speakers, if /g/ → [ŋ] is a natural process, then we expect the percentage of [ŋ] in any particular item to increase as the style becomes more casual and the tempo increases. In addition, as Donegan and Stampe (1979:140) suggest, the input class may expand, that is, [ŋ] may appear in items that always have [g] in more careful speech. If both the minimal input class and the additions to it can be characterized phonetically, there is no problem in saying that by the criterion under consideration, /g/ → [ŋ] is a natural process. I doubt very much, however, that this is the case. There is good reason to suspect that the items which consistent [ŋ] speakers pronounce with medial [g] never shift into the input class, no matter how casual the style. If these and only these items are barred from having [ŋ] under any circumstances, the inconsistent speaker has the same kind of nonphonetic environments as the consistent [ŋ] speaker.

It would be a time-consuming but worthwhile project to record inconsistent speakers in a variety of settings and find out just how they do behave. I am certain, in any case, that KH never pronounces reduplicated mimetic adverbs with [ŋ], and I have never heard any other speaker do so either. This observation alone is enough to show that for inconsistent speakers like KH, the environment for /g/ → [ŋ] cannot be strictly phonetic.

It is worth pointing out that the iconicity of reduplicated mimetic adverbs (section 9.4.5) is no impediment to the operation of genuinely automatic substitutions. For example, as we saw in section 4.4.2.3, /z/ generally appears as [dz] word-initially and after the mora nasal, and as [z] elsewhere (i.e., intervocalically). KH consistently pronounces reduplicated mimetic adverbs like /zoro + zoro/ 'in droves' as [dzoɾozoɾo].

We might try to maintain the status us /g/ → [ŋ] as a natural process by relaxing the phonetic environment criterion. Perhaps natural processes can tolerate some exceptions involving certain semantic or lexical categories, or even certain individual items. Donegan and Stampe (1979:171, n. 23) seem to be allowing for this possibility, although the intent of their statement is not really clear.

By way of comparison, it might be helpful to consider two apparent exceptions to English FLAPPING (section 4.7), which figures crucially in much of Stampe (1973) and Donegan and Stampe (1979). On the one hand, I usually flap the medial consonant in *today*. On the other hand, I do not flap the medial consonant in *Hittite*. According to Stampe (1973:56), flapping affects syllable-final [t d n] (producing [ř] in the last case), and we might be tempted to argue that *today* and *Hittite* are syllabified *tod.ay* and *Hi.ttite*. In that case, however, these words are exceptions to Stampe's (1973:56) natural process of "syllabication," which "attaches a nonsyllabic to the syllable to its right; but if the syllable to its right is unstressed and the syllable to its left is stressed, the nonsyllabic is instead attached to the syllable to its left."

If we do in fact accept the idea that natural processes can tolerate exceptions of this kind, however, the phonetic environment criterion is no longer relevant to distinguishing natural processes from learned rules unless there is some clear difference between the nonphonetic environments in the two cases. To maintain the criterion as Bjarkman gives it would, I think, force us to classify not only Japanese velar nasalization but also English flapping as learned.

9.6.5 Counterfeeding Order

Sommerstein (1977:236) interprets another of Bjarkman's (1975) criteria to mean that "no natural process is ever crucially ordered before any rule or process." If we consider examples like /juu.go/ 'fifteen', we find that the two accent phrases of careful speech are replaced by a single accent phrase at faster tempos (section 9.4.4). This accentual subordination is presumably one of what Donegan and Stampe (1979:142) call "prosodic processes." If we attribute the medial [g] in this word to the fact that it is potentially two accent phrases, we are saying in effect that /g/ → [ŋ] is ordered before the accentual subordination process, that is, that the relationship between the two is COUNTERFEEDING (Sloat, Taylor, and Hoard 1978:148). Donegan and Stampe (1979:145−151), however, allow for this kind of restricted application as a learned constraint on a natural process, that is, as a kind of limitation. As a result, this ordering relationship is not an obstacle to classifying /g/ → [ŋ] as a natural process.

9.6.6 Productivity

Another of Bjarkman's (1975:68) criteria is that learned rules "are not productive in the language synchronically (i.e., they do not apply to nativize loanwords)." Obligatory natural processes presumably do apply to nativize loanwords, but as Sommerstein (1977:236) points out, "the more careful the style, the more closely the loanword is likely to approximate its pronunciation in the source language."

The fact that consistent [ŋ] speakers apparently can have [ŋ] in recent loanwords (section 9.4.6) thus suggests that /g/ → [ŋ] is a natural process. KH frequently pronounces loanwords with medial [ŋ], so this criterion points the same way for inconsistent speakers.

Even more striking than [ŋ] in loanwords is the fact that even inconsistent speakers often substitute [ŋ] for [g] when speaking English. Pronunciations like [ɕuŋɑ:] for *sugar* and [mɑ:ŋɑɾɛt] for *Margaret* are common in KH's English, and they often impair communication with monolingual English speakers. Donegan and Stampe (1979:127) say that natural processes "impose a 'substratum' accent on languages we learn as adults," and /g/ → [ŋ] clearly does this.

It seems remarkable that a Japanese speaker could produce medial [g] in Japanese and yet be unable to do so consistently when speaking a foreign language, but I cannot recall ever hearing a morpheme-initial English /g/ replaced by [ŋ]. Since the only putative examples of morpheme-internal [ŋ] in Japanese are in relatively recent borrowings (section 9.4.6), and since KH seems to be able to pronounce any of these words that she knows with [ŋ], the situation is perhaps not quite as paradoxical as it first appears.

A consistent [ŋ] speaker who has morpheme-internal [g] in some loanwords and yet pronounces English /g/ as [ŋ] would be more of a paradox, but I would not be surprised to find such a person. It seems reasonable to suppose that some kind of special effort is required to produce a sequence ([VgV] in this case) that deviates from the typical pattern in a speaker's native language. The added problems of operating in a foreign language presumably make it much harder to pay attention to details of pronunciation, and the typical native sequence ([V̄ŋV] in this case) is likely to result.

9.6.7 Phonetic Motivation

The last of Bjarkman's (1975:68) criteria that I will consider is the requirement that processes "have an obvious phonetic function." We have already seen that /g/ → [ŋ] does not have any clear phonetic motivation (section 9.3), and that this fact is not surprising in view of what we know about its history (section 9.1).

This point brings up what is perhaps the most serious difficulty with the phonological theory under scrutiny here. Miller (1975) argues on the basis of an example from Ancient Greek that automatic substitutions are not necessarily natural processes, and he also adduces the case of aspiration. In his words, "if aspiration of initial voiceless stops in English is a natural process (i.e., an innate restriction on speech capacity), as suggested by Stampe . . . , then why is it as difficult for a speaker of Spanish to aspirate stops in English as it is for an English speaker not to do so in Spanish?"

Manaster-Ramer (1981:27–30) mentions this problem with aspiration and also gives examples of automatic insertions whith are quite clearly learned in the languages that have them and not suppressed in the languages that lack them. One example is the intrusive /r/ that appears in some dialects of English to break up vowel sequences (as in *Cuba-r-is*). HIATUS rules like this are good examples of what Vennemann (1972:212–216) calls RULE INVERSION.

clearly the idea of p. 124 is right.

Hiatus rules are motivated only to the extent that they create the preferred syllable structure (C)VCV by introducing some consonant(s) in certain (C)VV combinations; but the particular identity of the introduced consonant(s) is synchronically unmotivable. The particular consonant(s) introduced by a hiatus rule can only be explained historically.

Bjarkman (1975:70) answers Miller by saying, "To argue that the aspiration of **r** [in Ancient Greek] or indeed any other process is completely automatic and unexceptional is precisely to say that it is a natural process." Bjarkman's position, however, clearly undercuts what is most appealing about natural phonology, namely, that the natural processes are the unsuppressed innate processes that children bring to language acquisition.

9.6.8 Summary

The Japanese velar nasalization phenomenon has some of the properties of a natural process and some of the properties of a learned rule. Sommerstein (1977: 235) says the following:

> It may be noted that a theory of phonology incorporating [Bjarkman's] criteria makes a very strong empirical claim about language: the theory will be falsified by a single example of a substitution which has at least one feature which the theory assigns uniquely to natural processes and at least one feature which the theory assigns uniquely to learnt rules.

I am very sympathetic to the natural phonology approach, but I am skeptical that any revision of Bjarkman's criteria can save the theory without eviscerating it.

9.7 CONSEQUENCES FOR NATURAL PHONOLOGY

The natural phonology approach has been criticized as circular because the natural processes themselves are the only evidence for the phonetic causes that are supposed to account for those very processes. Thus, whenever a substitution is observed to occur in a language, it can be attributed to an innate natural process. Ohala (1974:268) argues that "this hypothesis is too powerful: there is almost no data that couldn't be explained in this way."

Donegan and Stampe (1979:169, n. 4) protest that although we do not yet have adequate phonetic explanations for the perceptual and articulatory difficulties that natural processes overcome, the approach is not circular because the evidence for these difficulties comes from independent sources. The example they give, however, is that "the greater difficulty of perceptibly rounding low as against high vowels is independently attested by their consistently different behavior in a wide variety of substitutions." I frankly do not see how this reply refutes the charge of circularity.

There is, however, an obvious way to try to establish independently that a given substitution is a natural process. Such processes are, after all, those that children are supposed to apply spontaneously in language acquisition. Although it would be a prodigious task, independent evidence could in principle come from careful observation of children acquiring a wide variety of languages. Stampe (1973) does, of course, cite evidence of this kind for some substitutions, such as final obstruent devoicing, but clearly a great deal remains to be done.

The objection raised in this chapter is, I think, even more serious. I have used data on the nasalization of voiced velar stops in Japanese to support the claim that a substitution can be learned and yet show some of the putative criterial attributes of a natural process. Since children do not apply such learned substitutions spontaneously, they cannot be classified as natural processes on independent grounds. They apparently do sometimes act to constrain speech production, however, and this means that natural phonology does not explain what it was devised to explain.

Rhodes (personal communication, 1983) has suggested that a possible way out in the case of the Japanese velar nasal would be to claim that there is a marginal phonemic distinction between [g] and [ŋ], and that the distinction is neutralized initially. The substitution would then be as in [14].

[14] /ŋ/ → /g/ / # —

For a consistent [ŋ] speaker, then, morphemes that never occur with [ŋ] (i.e., mimetic morphemes [section 9.4.5] and perhaps some loanwords [section 9.4.6]) would have /g/, and any morpheme that ever appears with [ŋ] would have /ŋ/. All the examples of medial [g] other than mimetic adverbs and loanwords involve morphemes that sometimes appear with [ŋ], so these examples would be exceptions. The advantage of rule [14] is that there is at least some evidence that children spontaneously denasalize initial nasals (Rhodes, personal communication, 1983).

There are two objections to rule [14]. First, it makes it difficult to understand the substitution of [ŋ] for [g] in speaking English (section 9.6.6). If the distinction between [g] and [ŋ] is phonemic in Japanese, why would a speaker mistakenly lexicalize English *sugar* with /ŋ/, even though no English speaker pronounces it that way? Second, we would not expect an inconsistent speaker like KH to neutralize a phonemic distinction between /g/ and /ŋ/ in careful speech while maintaining it in more casual speech (section 9.2). The marginal phonemic distinction in English between *witch* and *which* is, as expected, maintained best in careful speech.

We might try to argue that KH used [g] in reading a word list because a sharpening process neutralizes the distinction between /g/ and /ŋ/ in elaborated pronunciation (section 3.2.2). Kindaichi (1942:195) mentions that he caught himself pronouncing the Sino-Japanese word /ki.gu/ 'misgivings' with [g] when he wanted to make sure that students taking a vocabulary test would hear it. It seems reasonable to expect elaborated pronunciation under such circumstances, but we would also expect [g] in elaborated pronunciation if the process involved is /g/ → [ŋ]. I argued in section 3.2.2 that vowel rearticulation in the middle of a long vowel is a sharpening process, and it is clear that it makes the second mora of a long-vowel syllable more like a postpausal mora, since we get something like the glottal stop that we expect before an utterance-initial vowel (section 4.10). It should come as no surprise, therefore, that an elaborated pronunciation of /ki.gu/ would make the second mora more like it would be utterance-initially, and we would expect [g], even if [ŋ] is due to a /g/ → [ŋ] process. In addition, I do not think it would be accurate to describe KH's pronunciation during the interview reported in section 9.2 as elaborated.

It thus appears that the process involved in Japanese is nasalization and not denasalization, and, as we have seen, it poses a serious problem for natural phonology.

Chapter 10

SEQUENTIAL VOICING

10.1 HISTORICAL BACKGROUND

The term SEQUENTIAL VOICING is Martin's (1952:48) translation of the Japanese word **rendaku**, a technical term that refers to the replacement of a morpheme-initial voiceless obstruent with a voiced obstruent. A morpheme must be noninitial in a compound or a stem-and-affix formation for sequential voicing to apply. The resulting alternations are /k/~/g/, /t/~/d/, /s c/~/z/, /š č/~/ǰ/, and /f h/~/b/. The examples in [1] are illustrations.

[1] /iro/   /kami/   /iro + gami/
      'color'   'paper'   'colored paper'

      /iši/   /tooroo/   /iši + dooroo/
      'stone'   'lantern'   'stone lantern'

      /take/   /sao/   /take + zao/
      'bamboo'   'pole'   'bamboo pole'

      /inoči/   /cuna/   /inoči + zuna/
      'life'   'rope'   'lifeline'

      /hoši/   /širuši/   /hoši + ǰiruši/
      'star'   'mark'   'asterisk'

/hana/	/či/	/hana + ǰi/
'nose'	'blood'	'nosebleed'
/asa/	/furo/	/asa + buro/
'morning'	'bath'	'morning bath'
/se/	/hone/	/se + bone/
'back'	'bone'	'backbone'

The alternation of /b/ with /f h/ rather than with /p/ is the result of a historical change. There is little doubt that initial /f h/ in native Japanese words are descended from /p/, although I will assume that Old Japanese already had /ɸ/, as I did in section 7.1 (As we saw in section 4.3.2.1, the conservative variety does not have separate /f/ and /h/ phonemes.) The /s c/~/z/ and /š č/~/ǰ/ alternations reflect the merger of /d/ and /z/ before high vowels (sections 4.4.2.3 and 4.4.2.5). As I noted in section 9.4.2.2, sequential voicing converts /k/ into [ŋ] for consistent [ŋ] speakers, but the [g]/[ŋ] problem is not directly relevant here. Throughout this chapter I will simply write /g/ and include it among the voiced obstruents.

The kana syllabary uses a diacritic known as **dakuten** (Nakata and Tsukishima 1955) to mark voicing. For example, to write the syllable /da/, the diacritic is added to the symbol for /ta/. The same is true not only for /t/-/d/, /k/-/g/, and /s/-/z/, but for /f h/-/b/ as well. In most cases, the diacritic is added to the symbols for /su ši ša šo šu/ to represent /zu ǰi ǰa ǰo ǰu/. However, when a morpheme that begins with one of /cu či ča čo ču/ undergoes sequential voicing, the orthographic practice is simply to add the diacritic to the symbol for that syllable to represent /zu ǰi ǰa ǰo ǰu/. In general, we can characterize sequential voicing orthographically as the addition of the diacritic to the first kana letter of a morpheme.

In some cases, spelling can provide a clear indication that an etymological compound is no longer recognized as a compound. For example, Maeda (1977b) points out that /sakazuki/ 'wine glass' is etymologically a compound of /sake/ 'rice wine' and /cuki/ 'bowl'. But the first element appears with a different final vowel (section 11.1), and the second element is obsolete. Furthermore, when /sakazuki/ is written in kanji rather than spelled out in kana, a single character is used. All these factors have probably contributed to the loss of recognition as a compound, and the modern kana spelling of /sakazuki/ represents the syllable /zu/ with the symbol for /su/ (not /cu/) plus the diacritic.

A segment affected by sequential voicing is always in the environment V—(y)V or N—(y)V, and Kindaichi (1938:154) describes the change as an assimilation to the surrounding voiced segments. As Sakurai (1972:2) points out, however, this is clearly an inadequate account of the situation in modern standard Japanese. There is a voiced/voiceless contrast both word-initially and in the environments V—(y)V and N—(y)V. It is generally agreed that Old Japanese had no word-initial voiced obstruents in native words (Hashimoto 1938:75,

Miller 1967:194–195). In intervocalic position, however, it is clear that there were two contrasting obstruent series corresponding to the modern voiced and voiceless series. Sequential voicing was already in operation in Old Japanese, and this fact leads Kamei, Yamada, and Ōtō (1963:298–299) to conclude that its origin lies hidden in the distant, unrecorded past. In any event, there have been two contrasting obstruent series throughout the recorded history of Japanese.

As we saw in section 9.1, Old Japanese voiced obstruents were probably prenasalized. Hashimoto (1932:5–6) cites several Old Japanese words for which the existence of prenasalization helps to provide plausible etymologies. In each case, an inferred older sequence of nasal-plus-vowel-plus-voiceless-obstruent has developed into a voiced obstruent. One of Hashimoto's examples appears in [2].

[2] /yuge/ 'bow whittling' < /yumike/
    cf. /yumi/ 'bow', /ke/ < /kezuru/ 'whittle'

Hashimoto suggests that if /yuge/ was [jūge] in Old Japanese, the development from /yumike/ is fairly straightforward. We need only assume that the vowel /i/ was deleted. This deletion alone would have left the sequence /mk/, but since there was no mora nasal at this stage (section 7.1), nasalization on the preceding vowel /u/ is a plausible development. Since only voiced obstruents were prenasalized (i.e., preceded by a nasal vowel), the pronunciation [jūge] would have been a natural result of the vowel loss.

Unger (1975:8–9) suggests that the same kind of vowel deletion after a nasal was the original source of sequential voicing. This account requires that we posit a prehistoric sequence of the form nasal-plus-vowel between the morphemes of Old Japanese words that show sequential voicing. It implies, for example, that the Old Japanese word /ki+do/ 'wooden gate' (from /ki/ 'wood' and /to/ 'door') derives from some prehistoric form of the shape /ki/+NV+/to/. As Unger points out, the obvious source for this NV sequence in noun+noun compounds is the genitive particle /no/. The dative/locative particle /ni/ may have been involved in some other formations. This is the most satisfactory explanation yet proposed for the origin of sequential voicing.

There is little doubt that sequential voicing is largely unpredictable in modern standard Japanese. I will consider the situation in detail in the remainder of this chapter. Martin (1952:48–57) surveys proposed conditioning factors and comes to this same conclusion. McCawley (1968:87) says the following: "I am unable to state the environment in which the 'voicing rule' applies. The relevant data are completely bewildering." Miller (1967:194–195) agrees, but speculates that sequential voicing may have been regular at some time in the distant past.

> Probably there were Old Japanese dialects where such voicing was completely regular or at least predictable in terms of pitch, juncture, or other features which the script does not record and which are therefore largely beyond our grasp. Later dialect borrowing between such Old Japanese dialects and others in which the phenomenon did not occur resulted in the irregular and unpredictable situation which is already present in the older texts and which remains a feature of the modern language.

There is, however, an alternative explanation for the irregularity that I find much more plausible.

There is good reason to believe that not all Old Japanese noun + noun compounds derived from phrases of the form noun + /no/ + noun, and that not all such phrases underwent vowel deletion when the second noun began with a voiceless obstruent. The examples in [3] are all attested in Old Japanese, and each contains the first element /ɸuna/, an allomorph of /ɸune/ 'boat' (section 11.1).

[3] **a.** /ɸunaɸasi/ 'pontoon bridge'
       cf. /ɸasi/ 'bridge'
    b. /ɸunanoɸe/ 'bow of a boat'
       cf. /ɸe/ 'bow'
    c. /ɸunagi/ 'wood for boat building'
       cf. /ki/ 'wood'

Forms like [3a] presumably derived from simple juxtaposition of the two nouns and therefore did not show sequential voicing. Forms like [3b] retained the genitive particle and naturally did not show sequential voicing either. Forms like [3c] presumably derived from earlier phrases like /ɸuna no ki/ by vowel deletion. If this is correct, the irregularity of sequential voicing in Old Japanese is due to the fact that noun + noun compounds did not all develop in the same way. On this account, sequential voicing has never been regular.

10.2 CONDITIONING FACTORS

10.2.1 Lyman's Law

Nearly every treatment of sequential voicing mentions that a voiced obstruent in a morpheme has an inhibiting effect. For example, Okumura (1955) compares /oo + kaze/ 'strong wind' and /oo + zora/ 'open sky', both of which contain the prefix /oo/ 'big'. He says that sequential voicing does not apply to give */oo + gaze/ for 'strong wind' because /kaze/ 'wind', unlike /sora/ 'sky', already contains a voiced obstruent. The first non-Japanese to write about this inhibiting effect was Lyman (1894), and it is sometimes called LYMAN'S LAW. According to Miyake (1932:136), however, the Japanese scholar Norinaga Motoori (1730–1801) stated categorically that if the second element of a compound contains a voiced obstruent, its initial consonant does not voice.

Motoori's statement applies to an Old Japanese text, and there are considerable differences among writers as to how strongly they state the constraint for modern standard Japanese. Martin (1952:48) says that sequential voicing never occurs if the affected morpheme already contains a voiced obstruent. Nakagawa (1966:302), on the other hand, says that a voiced obstruent in the second mora of a morpheme prevents sequential voicing. Others claim only that a voiced obstruent in the second mora makes sequential voicing unlikely (Okumura 1955,

Sakurai 1966:41, Maeda 1977b). Monomorphemic words with a voiced obstruent in the third mora are not very common, but /tokage/ 'lizard' and /hicuɟi/ 'sheep' certainly qualify. As the examples in [4] show, these words do not undergo sequential voicing in compounds, and this behavior is typical.

[4] /doku + tokage/ 'poisonous lizard, Gila monster'
      cf. /doku/ 'poison'
   /eri + maki + tokage/ 'frilled lizard'
      cf. /eri + maki/ 'collar'
   /ko + hicuɟi/ 'lamb'
      cf. /ko/ 'child'
   /merino + hicuɟi/ 'merino sheep'

It thus appears that Martin's stronger version of Lyman's Law is essentially correct.

In a systematic search through a Japanese-English dictionary (Masuda 1974), I discovered only ten counterexamples to this strong version of Lyman's Law. Nine of these are compounds with the second element /hašigo/ 'ladder', as in /nawa + bašigo/ 'rope ladder' (cf. /nawa/ 'rope'). Apparently the word /hašigo/ always shows sequential voicing when it appears as the second element in a compound. The other example is /waka + ɟiraga/ 'prematurely gray hair' (from /waka + i/ 'young' and /širaga/ 'gray hair'), but this form is doubtful. Masuda lists /waka + širaga/ as the preferred pronunciation, and this is the only pronunciation in Shinmura (1969).

Kindaichi (1976) cites three additional examples that violate Lyman's Law. The first is /fuN + ɟibaru/ 'tie up', in which an unproductive emphatic prefix /fuN/ is added to the verb /šibaru/ 'tie'. The second is the masculine name /šoo + zaburoo/. The common name /saburoo/ occurs frequently as the second element in longer names, and sequential voicing often applies. Kindaichi's third example is /rei + degami/ 'letter of thanks' (from /rei/ 'thanks' and /tegami/ 'letter'), but native speakers I checked with had never heard this word, and neither Masuda (1974) nor Shinmura (1969) lists it.

Etymologically, /hašigo/ 'ladder' and /širaga/ 'gray hair' are probably compounds, and /tegami/ 'letter' is a synchronically obvious compound of /te/ 'hand' and /kami/ 'paper'. As we will now see, however, compound structure does not explain why sequential voicing applies (to the extent that it really does).

Compounds with more than two elements, like those in [5], suggest that Lyman's Law is sensitive to constituent structure.

[5] **a.** /to/ 'door'
      /tana/ 'shelf'
      /to + dana/ 'cupboard'
      /fukuro/ 'bag'
      /fukuro + to + dana/ 'small cupboard'   /fukuro/   /to/   /dana/

b. /se/ 'back'
/to/ 'door'
/se + do/ 'back door'
/kuči/ 'mouth'
/se + do + guči/ 'back entrance'

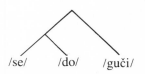

/se/   /do/   /guči/

As a second element in two-element compounds, /to/ 'door' usually undergoes sequential voicing, but its initial consonant does not voice in /fukuro + to + dana/ [5a]. Lyman's Law will account for this if it applies to each layer of compounding. As the constituent diagram in [5a] shows, /to + dana/ is the second element of the longer compound, and it contains a voiced obstruent. In /se + do + guči/, on the other hand, /do + guči/ is not a constituent, as the diagram in [5b] shows.

Ōtsu (1980:217–222) proposes a more stringent condition that he calls the RIGHT-BRANCH CONDITION. I think Ōtsu's version of this proposal is unworkable (Vance 1980a), but I will consider a modified version here. According to this version, sequential voicing can occur only if the affected morpheme is on a right branch in the constituent structure. Thus, in a compound of the form in [6] (where X, Y, and Z are morphemes), the morpheme Y cannot undergo sequential voicing even if the entire sequence Y + Z contains no voiced obstruents.

[6]

X   Y   Z

For this proposal to work at all, we must require that Y + Z is itself a compound. Two-morpheme Sino-Japanese words are commonly called "compounds," but as we saw in section 9.4.2.1, it is often the case that both morphemes are bound. For example, /hyoo.ši/ 'cover' consists of the two bound Sino-Japanese morphemes /hyoo/ 'exterior' and /ši/ 'paper'. There are several examples of sequential voicing in compounds with /hyoo.ši/ as the second element, as in /ura + byoo.ši/ 'back cover' (cf. /ura/ 'back'). Many other two-morpheme Sino-Japanese words behave in similar fashion. It does not seem too unreasonable to solve this problem by defining compounds in a way that includes /ura + byoo.ši/ but excludes /hyoo.ši/. Ōtsu would give the constituent structure of /ura + byoo.ši/ as [7], with /byoo.ši/ on a right branch.

[7]

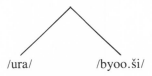

/ura/   /byoo.ši/

It is rather difficult to think of natural examples to test the right-branch condition, but the word /hacu + kao + awase/ 'first meeting' will serve as an illustration. As a second element in two-element compounds, /kao/ 'face' generally undergoes sequential voicing, as in /yoko + gao/ 'profile' (cf. /yoko/ 'side'). The word /kao + awase/ means 'meeting' (cf. /awase/ 'bringing together'), and /hacu/ is a prefix meaning 'first'. Thus, /kao/ is not on a right branch in the constituent structure of /hacu + kao + awase/, as [8] shows. The prefix does not seem to inhibit sequential voicing, since there are examples like /hacu + gacuo/ 'first bonito of the season' (cf. /kacuo/ 'bonito').

[8]

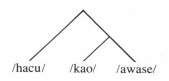

/hacu/   /kao/   /awase/

The right-branch condition predicts the absence of sequential voicing in this case, even though there is no voiced obstruent in /kao + awase/.

There are a few apparent exceptions to the right-branch condition, but they seem to be words that most speakers are not likely to know. For example, the kabuki term /oo + date + mono/ 'principal actor' consists of the prefix /oo/ 'big' and the compound /tate + mono/ 'important actor' (from /tate/ 'leading role' and /mono/ 'person'). Although /tate/ is clearly not on a right branch in the constituent structure, as [9] shows, it undergoes sequential voicing and appears as /date/.

[9]

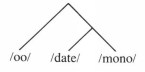

/oo/   /date/   /mono/

It may be, however, that something like the right-branch condition constrains new formations.

The results of a detailed experimental investigation of Lyman's Law are available in Vance (1979:82–114) and Vance (1980b).

10.2.2 Preceding Nasals

Okumura (1955) and Sakurai (1966:41) claim that sequential voicing is most likely when the preceding morpheme ends with /N/. Neither cites any real evidence for this assertion, but there is one small area of the vocabulary that provides some support. Martin (1952:49–52) discusses a tendency for sequential voicing to occur in compounds of the form Sino-Japanese-morpheme-plus-/suru/ 'do' when the Sino-Japanese morpheme ends with /N/. For example, /kiN + zuru/ 'forbid' begins with the Sino-Japanese /kiN/ 'prohibition'. (As Martin notes, many of these compounds have colloquial pronunciations that end /jiru/ rather than /zuru/, but this fact need not concern us here.) There are many counterexamples to this tendency, such as /kaN + suru/ 'be related' (cf. /kaN/ 'gateway'), but it seems to reflect a very old pattern.

We saw in section 7.1 that some long vowels in Sino-Japanese morphemes have developed from /Vŋ/ sequences, and even in modern Japanese, /suru/ often undergoes sequential voicing after such morphemes (Miller 1967:219). For example, /šoo + zuru/ 'produce' contains the Sino-Japanese morpheme /šoo/ 'production', and the modern Cantonese cognate (ignoring tone) is /saŋ/.

If we confine our attention to two-morpheme Sino-Japanese words, it appears that there was a strong correlation between preceding nasals and sequential voicing in eighth-century pronunciations (Okumura 1952:11–13). The entries in an early seventeenth-century dictionary suggest that this correlation still held (Endō 1966:70–71). I am not aware of any thorough investigation of the situation in modern standard Japanese, but Okumura (1952:17, 1955) says that many two-morpheme Sino-Japanese words that used to show sequential voicing no longer do.

Hamada (1952:18–19) argues that this correlation is hard to explain in terms of modern phonetic values, and he offers an explanation involving prenasalization (sections 9.1 and 10.1). He says that if postvocalic voiced obstruents were prenasalized (i.e., always preceded by nasalization on the vowel), then perhaps the tendency to voice obstruents after nasals was a kind of "analogy."

10.2.3 Vocabulary Strata

Martin (1952:48) says that sequential voicing is frequent only in native Japanese morphemes. As we saw in section 10.2.2, it appears that sequential voicing in two-morpheme Sino-Japanese words was originally confined to those in which the first morpheme ended in a nasal, and many such words have subsequently lost the voicing. We saw in section 10.2.1, however, that sequential voicing is not uncommon in compounds with two-morpheme Sino-Japanese second elements. Typical examples are /uN.doo + bu.soku/ 'lack of exercise' (from Sino-Japanese /uN.doo/ 'exercise' and Sino-Japanese /fu.soku/ 'insufficiency') and /ko + gai.ša/ 'subsidiary company' (from native /ko/ 'child' and Sino-Japanese /kai.ša/ 'company').

It is well known that sequential voicing generally does not affect recent borrowings, but as Nakagawa (1966:308) points out, it does affect some old and well-assimilated loans from languages other than Chinese. My dictionary search turned up seven examples in Masuda (1974), and I list them in [10].

[10] **a.** /kaQpa/ (< Portuguese **capa**) 'raincoat'
     /ama + gaQpa/ 'raincoat'
        cf. /ama/, an allomorph of /ame/ 'rain'
     /maru + gaQpa/ 'long mantle'
        cf. /maru/ 'circle'

b. /karuta/ (< Portuguese **carta**) 'playing card'
/hana + garuta/ 'flower cards' (a card game)
    cf. /hana/ 'flower'
/uta + garuta/ 'poem cards' (a card game)
    cf. /uta/ 'poem'

c. /kiseru/ (< Cambodian **khsier**) 'pipe'
/kuwae + giseru/ 'pipe in mouth'
    cf. /kuwae/ 'holding in the mouth'
/mizu + giseru/ 'hookah'
    cf. /mizu/ 'water'

d. /keQto/ (< English (*blan*)*ket*) 'blanket'
/aka + geQto/ 'red blanket'
    cf. /aka/ 'red'

The Portuguese loans /kaQpa/ [10a] and /karuta/ [10b] were both borrowed in the sixteenth century (Umegaki 1966) and were written in kanji for a long period. In fact, as we saw in section 1.3, it is still common to write /kaQpa/ in kanji rather than in katakana, and this spelling suggests that the word is a combination of a Sino-Japanese morpheme followed by a native morpheme. Kamei, Yamada, and Ōtō (1963:374) say that only a specialist would know that this word is a European borrowing. Nakagawa also claims that forms such as /yama + gyaNpu/ 'mountain camp' (from /yama/ 'mountain' and /kyaNpu/ (English) 'camp') and /iNdo + garee/ 'Indian curry' (from /iNdo/ 'India' and /karee/ (English) 'curry') are heard, although they are not yet established.

We saw in section 9.4.5 that Japanese uses reduplicated mimetic adverbs to express repeated or continuous sounds and actions, and Martin (1952:49) notes that sequential voicing does not occur in these words. McClain (1981:206) lists the adverb /šimi + ǰimi/ as a reduplicated mimetic adverb, but according to the entry in *Nihon Kokugo Daijiten*, this word is etymologically a reduplication of /šimi/ 'permeating' (cf. /šimiru/ 'permeate'). Martin points out that sequential voicing is the rule in reduplication of native morphemes, as long as Lyman's Law (section 10.2.1) is not violated. He illustrates with examples like /hito + bito/ 'people' (cf. /hito/ 'person') and compares mimetic examples like /haki + haki/ 'briskly'.

We might try to account for this contrasting behavior in terms of the hypothesis about the origin of sequential voicing in section 10.1. It seems highly unlikely that the genitive particle /no/ or the dative/locative particle /ni/ would ever have appeared between the two repetitions of a mimetic morpheme. In cases like /hito + bito/, on the other hand, a prehistoric form /pito ni pito/, meaning something like 'person added to person', seems plausible, although I am not aware of any evidence for such a form.

Reduplicated forms like /hito + bito/, and especially adverbs like /šimi + ǰimi/, provide models for the ANALOGICAL EXTENSION (Bynon 1977:37) of sequential voicing. As I mentioned in section 9.4.5, however, sequential voicing would diminish the iconicity of reduplicated mimetic adverbs, and perhaps this is why they have been so resistant to it.

10.2.4 Prefixes

Nakagawa (1966:314) says that the native Japanese numeral prefixes /hito/ 'one', /futa/ 'two', /mi/ 'three', etc., inhibit sequential voicing, although there are exceptions after /futa/. Typical examples are /hito + koe/ 'one cry' (cf. /koe/ 'voice'), /futa + koto/ 'two words' (cf. /koto/ 'word'), and /mi + toori/ 'three ways' (cf. /toori/ 'way'). One of the exceptions Nakagawa gives is /futa + go/ 'twins' (cf. /ko/ 'child').

Sequential voicing apparently never occurs after the honorific prefixes /o/ (native) and /go/ (Sino-Japanese). Typical examples are /o + hanaši/ 'talk (honorific)' and /go + ku.roo/ 'hardship (honorific)'. These same second elements regularly undergo sequential voicing in compounds, as in /mukaši + banaši/ 'old tale' (cf. /mukaši/ 'long ago') and /ki + gu.roo/ 'anxiety' (cf. /ki/ 'spirit').

The common native prefixes /o/ 'small', /ko/ 'small', and /oo/ 'big', on the other hand, do not seem to inhibit sequential voicing. Typical examples are /o + gawa/ 'brook' (cf. /kawa/ 'river'), /ko + bune/ 'small boat' (cf. /fune/ 'boat'), and /oo + goe/ 'big voice' (cf. /koe/ 'voice').

Nakagawa (1966:309–310) also says that sequential voicing usually does not occur after the Sino-Japanese prefixes /fu/ 'not' and /bu/ 'not'. One of his examples is /bu + ki.yoo/ 'awkwardness' (cf. /ki.yoo/ 'skillfulness'), and he compares this with /ko + gi.yoo/ 'cleverness', which contains /ko/ 'small'. He points out, however, that the exceptional form /bu + zai.ku/ is now listed in dictionaries as an alternative pronunciation of /bu + sai.ku/ 'bungling'. The word /sai.ku/ 'craftsmanship' is the second element of many compounds like /ki + zai.ku/ 'woodworking' (cf. /ki/ 'wood'), and it always undergoes sequential voicing in such words. Nakagawa suggests that this is why /bu + zai.ku/ has appeared.

10.2.5 Verb and Adjective Compounds

In traditional Japanese grammar, the term INFLECTED WORD (**yōgen**) refers to adjectives (**keiyōshi**) and verbs. Okumura (1955) says that sequential voicing does not occur in compounds of inflected-word-plus-inflected-word, and he illustrates this point with /wakači + kaku/ 'write with spaces between the words' and /wakači + gaki/ 'writing with spaces between the words'. These examples derive from the verb /wakač̌u/ 'divide' and the verb /kaku/ 'write'. In both cases, the first element appears in the stem form /wakači/ (section 12.2.5.2), and this is true of all nonfinal verbal or adjectival elements in compounds. In /wakači + kaku/, the second element retains its inflectional ending, and the compound is a verb. In /wakači + gaki/, on the other hand, the second element appears in its stem form, and the compound is a noun. Okumura thus appears to be claiming that sequential voicing does not occur in a compound that consists of two inflected words and is itself an inflected word.

Sakurai (1966:41) makes the same statement about compounds of inflected-word-plus-inflected-word, but he qualifies it by saying that if the first element is used as a noun, sequential voicing can occur. He illustrates this point with the examples /iki + zumaru/ 'reach an impasse' (from /iku/ 'go' and /cumaru/ 'be blocked') and /iki + domaru/ 'reach an impasse' (cf. /tomaru/ 'stop'). But since the first element must appear in its stem form, it is not clear how to determine whether it is being used as a noun.

My dictionary search turned up a large number of compounds in Masuda (1974) that are nouns and do not show sequential voicing, even though Lyman's $\checkmark$ Law (section 10.2.1) would not be violated. Many of these are combinations of verb-stem-plus-verb-stem. In almost every case, a compound verb derived from the same two elements is also listed. Typical examples are the verb /nori + kaeru/ 'change (trains, etc.)' and the related noun /nori + kae/ 'transfer' (both from the verbs /noru/ 'board' and /kaeru/ 'change'). Pairs like /wakači + kaku/ and /wakači + gaki/, where the noun shows sequential voicing while the verb does not, are relatively rare.

Since a nonfinal verbal or adjectival element must appear in its stem form, compound nouns consisting of two verb stems can be derived in either of the two ways shown in [11].

[11] **a.** VERB1 + VERB2 → VERB3 (= VERB1stem–VERB2)

VERB3 → NOUN (= VERB3stem)
(= VERB1stem–VERB2stem)

b. VERB1 → NOUN1 (= VERB1stem)

VERB2 → NOUN2 (= VERB2stem)

NOUN1 + NOUN2 → NOUN 3 (= VERB1stem–VERB2stem)

If sequential voicing is in fact inhibited in compound verbs derived from two verbs, there is no reason to expect it in derivation [11a]. In derivation [11b], on the other hand, the final step involves forming a compound noun from two nouns. If the behavior of nouns derived from verbs is like that of ordinary underived nouns, sequential voicing would be no surprise in [11b].

My dictionary search turned up 188 examples of compounds that are themselves verbs or adjectives and show sequential voicing. In 147 of these, the first element is an underived noun, as in /ura + giru/ 'betray' (from the noun /ura/ 'back' and the verb /kiru/ 'cut'). This fact suggests that simply being an inflected word does not inhibit sequential voicing in a compound. On the other hand, I found only eleven examples of sequential voicing in compound verbs derived from two verbs, and this is a tiny fraction of the hundreds of compounds of this type listed in any Japanese dictionary. It thus appears that sequential voicing really is inhibited in such cases. My impression is that sequential voicing is proportionately much more common in adjective + adjective compound adjectives like /usu + gurai/ 'dim' (from /usui/ 'pale' and /kurai/ 'dark') and in verb + adjective compound adjectives like /mi + gurušii/ 'unsightly' (from /miru/ 'look at' and /kurušii/ 'painful'), but I have no real evidence to offer.

The lack of sequential voicing in verb + verb compound verbs appears to have been the pattern in Old Japanese as well (Vance 1982:339), and we can interpret this lack as corroborating the hypothesis about the origin of sequential voicing in section 10.1. The verb stem has been used throughout the recorded history of Japanese as a nonfinite form for conjoining clauses. Kuno (1973:195) labels this the CONTINUATIVE FORM (section 12.2.5.2), and it seems likely that most verb + verb compound verbs originated as phrases containing this form. For example, /yoi + kuruu/ 'go crazy with drink' (from /you/ 'get drunk' and /kuruu/ 'go crazy') presumably developed from a phrase /yoi kuruu/ 'get drunk and go crazy'. There is no reason to suppose that a particle like genitive /no/ or dative/ locative /ni/ ever appeared between the two elements in a construction of this kind.

10.2.6 Coordinate Compounds

In most two-element compounds, one element is a modifier of the other. In *door-knob*, for example, *door* is clearly the subordinate, modifying element. In some cases, however, the two elements have equal status. Bloomfield (1933:235) gives the English example *bittersweet*, which he defines as 'bitter and sweet at the same time'. I will refer to compounds of this second type as COORDINATE COMPOUNDS.

Okumura (1955) and Sakurai (1966:41) say that sequential voicing is unlikely in Japanese coordinate compounds, and Sakurai gives the examples in [12].

[12] **a.** /ue + šita/ 'above and below'
      cf. /ue/ 'above', /šita/ 'below'
   b. /saN + kai/ 'land and sea'
      cf. /saN/ 'mountain', /kai/ 'sea'
   c. /taka + hiku/ 'high and low'
      cf. /takai/ 'high', /hikui/ 'low'
   d. /yomi + kaki/ 'reading and writing'
      cf. /yomu/ 'read', /kaku/ 'write'
   e. /iki + kaeri/ 'round trip'
      cf. /iku/ 'go', /kaeru/ 'return'

All these examples are nouns, and of course the adjectival and verbal elements in [12c]–[12e] appear in their stem forms (section 10.2.5). To demonstrate that co-ordinate structure inhibits sequential voicing, we must show that sequential voicing applies to the second elements involved when they appear in noncoordinate compounds. This is possible for [12d] and [12e], since there are contrasting examples such as /wakači + gaki/ 'writing with spaces between the words' (cf. /wakacu/ 'divide') and /hi + gaeri/ 'day trip' (cf. /hi/ 'day'). On the other hand, the second elements /šita/, /kai/, and /hiku/ apparently never undergo sequential voicing, and this means that [12a]–[12c] are really irrelevant examples.

Occasionally the same two elements are involved in both a coordinate and a noncoordinate compound. Nakagawa (1966:310) and Maeda (1977b) cite /yama + kawa/ 'mountains and rivers' and /yama + gawa/ 'mountain river' (both from /yama/ 'mountain' and /kawa/ 'river'). Examples of this kind are strong evidence that coordinate structure inhibits sequential voicing.

My dictionary search turned up only one example of sequential voicing in a coordinate compound. The word /suji + bone/ (from /suji/ 'sinew' and /hone/ 'bone') is defined in Masuda (1974) as 'sinews and bones', and this is the first definition in Shinmura (1969) as well. On the other hand, Hamano (personal communication, 1983) tells me that she had always understood /suji + bone/ to mean something like 'bones that go through the center of the body', that is, as analogous to /suji + gane/ 'metal reinforcement' (cf. /kane/ 'metal'). Thus, for at least some speakers, /suji + bone/ is just an exception that proves the rule.

10.2.7 Direct-Object + Verb-Stem Compounds

Okumura (1955) and Sakurai (1966:41) claim that in compounds consisting of a noun followed by a verb stem, sequential voicing is less likely when the noun is grammatically the direct object of the verb than when it is an adverbial modifier. The term "adverbial modifier" in this case seems to mean that the noun has a grammatical function other than direct object. The examples in [13] are from Sakurai.

[13] /yane + fuki/ 'covering a roof'
　　　　　cf. /yane o fuku/ 'cover a roof'
　　　　　　　/yane/ 'roof', /fuku/ 'cover', /o/ direct object marker

　　　/kawara + buki/ 'tiling a roof'
　　　　　cf. /kawara de (yane o) fuku/ 'cover (a roof) with tile'
　　　　　　　/kawara/ 'tile', /de/ instrumental marker

Akinaga (1966:53) makes a similar claim but restricts it to cases where the verb stem is one or two moras long. He says that if the noun functions grammatically as the direct object in such a case, sequential voicing does not occur and the compound is accented on the last syllable of the first element. If, on the other hand, the noun functions as an "adverbial modifier," sequential voicing occurs and the compound is unaccented. The examples in [14] (with accent indicated; see Chapter 8) illustrate the suggested pattern.

[14] /mijiN + giri/ 'mincing'
  cf. /mijiN/ 'bit', /kíru/ 'cut'

/garasú + kiri/ 'glass cutter'
  cf. /garasu/ 'glass', /kíru/ 'cut'

Okuda (1971:176) lists ten counterexamples to Akinaga's generalization. In eight of these, sequential voicing occurs and the compound is unaccented, even though the noun functions as a direct object. In the other two, sequential voicing does not occur and the compound is accented on the last syllable of the first element, even though the noun does not function as a direct object. The examples in [15] (with accent indicated) illustrate these two kinds of exceptions.

[15] /zoo.ge + bori/ 'ivory carving'
  cf. /zoo.ge/ 'ivory', /hóru/ 'carve'

/teeburú + kake/ 'table cloth'
  cf. /teeburu/ 'table', /kakéru/ 'put on'

These counterexamples suggest that there may simply be a correlation between sequential voicing and no accent in compounds of this type. Neither Akinaga nor Okuda observes any parallel phenomenon in compounds with longer verb-stem second elements.

Nakagawa (1966:312–313) notes several direct-object + verb-stem compounds in which the presence or absence of sequential voicing seems to signal a semantic distinction. He claims that sequential voicing occurs in a compound referring to an action involving the direct object, and does not occur in one referring to a person whose occupation involves the direct object. The examples in [16] provide illustrations.

[16] /hito + goroši/ 'murder'
  cf. /hito/ 'person', /korosu/ 'kill'
/inu + koroši/ 'dog catcher'
  cf. /inu/ 'dog'

/fude + zukai/ 'handling a writing brush'
  cf. /fude/ 'writing brush', /cukau/ 'use'
/niN.gyoo + cukai/ 'puppeteer'
  cf. /niN.gyoo/ 'puppet'

Shinmura (1969) lists both action and actor meanings for /inu + koroši/ and /niN.gyoo + cukai/, but perhaps the notion 'as an occupation' is what really matters.

10.3 FUNDAMENTAL IRREGULARITY

Even if we take into account all the conditioning factors suggested in section 10.2, sequential voicing is obviously irregular. If we confine our attention to cases in which no suggested constraint would be violated, some native Japanese morphemes consistently undergo sequential voicing, but others just as consistently resist. This latter group includes /cuči/ 'soil', /himo/ 'string', /kemuri/ 'smoke', /saki/ 'tip', and /šio/ 'tide', and the examples in [17] are typical.

[17] /soko + cuči/ 'subsoil'
   cf. /soko/ 'bottom'
   /kucu + himo/ 'shoelace'
   cf. /kucu/ 'shoe'
   /suna + kemuri/ 'cloud of sand'
   cf. /suna/ 'sand'
   /yubi + saki/ 'fingertip'
   cf. /yubi/ 'finger'
   /asa + šio/ 'morning tide'
   cf. /asa/ 'morning'

Other native Japanese morphemes are inconsistent. In other words, even when no constraint would be violated, they sometimes undergo sequential voicing and sometimes do not. One common morpheme of this kind is /ki/ 'tree', illustrated by the examples in [18].

[18] /niwa + ki/ 'garden tree'
   cf. /niwa/ 'garden'
   /yama + gi/ 'mountain tree'
   cf. /yama/ 'mountain'

Nakagawa (1966:311–312) suggests that /saki/ 'tip' may have developed its consistent resistance to sequential voicing as an indication of a semantic distinction. The etymologically identical /saki/ 'promontory' often shows sequential voicing in place names like /miya + zaki/ 'Miyazaki'. We might offer a similar explanation for the behavior of /cuči/ 'soil' and /šio/ 'tide'. The word /cuči/ 'hammer' usually undergoes sequential voicing as the second element of a compound, as in /ki + zuči/ 'wooden mallet' (cf. /ki/ 'wood'). The word /šio/ 'salt' shows sequential voicing in /usu + Jio/ 'light salt' (cf. the adjective /usui/ 'light'), but I am not sure whether this example is typical.

Nakagawa (1966:313–314) says that the symbol used to write the second syllable of /himo/ 'string' in an Old Japanese text could have stood for /bo/ rather than /mo/. As Miller (1967:199) observes, /m/~/b/ variation seems to have been common in Old Japanese, and in a few cases (e.g., /samišii/~/sabišii/ 'sad') this variation continues in the modern language. Since Lyman's Law (section 10.2.1) would have prevented sequential voicing in a morpheme containing a voiced obstruent, Nakagawa suggests that consistent resistance may have developed and persisted, even though only the form /himo/ survives. The form /keburi/ is listed in Masuda (1974) as a literary equivalent of /kemuri/ 'smoke', and this variant suggests a parallel explanation.

In spite of the conditioning factors discussed in section 10.2 and the plausible historical explanations considered in this section, the fundamental irregularity of sequential voicing remains a fact of modern standard Japanese.

10.4 VARIATION

Some compounds have alternative pronunciations, one with and one without sequential voicing. My dictionary search turned up thirty-six words with both variants listed in Masuda (1974). For example, both /haya + kuči/ and /haya + guči/ are listed for 'fast talking' (from /hayai/ 'fast' and /kuči/ 'mouth'). In the vast majority of cases, however, only one pronunciation is listed.

There is actually a third possibility in addition to simple concatenation and sequential voicing. In several compounds, the mora obstruent /Q/ appears before a second element that begins with a voiceless obstruent. Typical examples are /sueQko/ 'youngest child' (from /sue/ 'end' and /ko/ 'child') and /šišiQpana/ 'pug nose' (from /šiši/ 'lion' and /hana/ 'nose'). As this second example illustrates, when the initial segment of the second element is /h/ or /f/, the result is /Qp/. In general, /Q/ does not appear before /h/ or /f/ except in recent loanwords (such as /waQfuru/ 'waffle') and mimetic adverbs (such as /heQheQ/ 'heh-heh'). This alternation with /Qp/ is one of the reasons for believing that /h f/ derived from a /p/ via Old Japanese /ɸ/ (section 10.1).

My dictionary search turned up fifty-five compounds with /Q/ addition in Masuda (1974), and many of these have variants with simple concatenation or sequential voicing. In a few cases, all three pronunciations are listed. For example, /yoko + cura/, /yoko + zura/, and /yokoQcura/ are all listed for 'side of the face' (from /yoko/ 'side' and /cura/ 'face').

This addition of /Q/ in a compound tends to give the word a very colloquial flavor, and Masuda (1974) marks many of these forms as slang or vulgarisms. Miller (1967:154) says that the dialects of eastern Japan (which includes Tokyo) are often described as favoring /Q/ insertion for emphasis, and that this is characteristic of colloquial speech in these dialects. I touched on this point briefly in sections 5.2.3–5.2.4, and /Q/ addition in compounds is apparently a part of this more general phenomenon.

Chapter 11

OTHER
ALTERNATIONS

11.1 MORPHEME-FINAL VOWEL ALTERNATIONS

11.1.1 Historical Background

Martin (1952:85–86) lists several pairs of words in which it appears that a single morpheme has two allomorphs with different final vowels. See the examples in [1].

[1] **a.** /e/~/a/
      /fune/ 'ship'   /ita/ 'board'
      /funa + ita/ 'ship plank'
  b. /i/~/o/
      /ki/ 'tree'   /kage/ 'shade'
      /ko + kage/ 'shade of a tree'
  c. /o/~/a/
      /širo/ 'white'   /sagi/ 'heron'
      /šira + sagi/ 'white heron'

In each of these examples, one vowel, /V$_1$/, appears when the morpheme is used as an independent word, and another vowel, /V$_2$/, appears when the morpheme is used as the first element in a compound. We will see in section 11.1.2 that these alternations are not regular, but they are very interesting as historical residues.

Martin (1952:85–86) lists a total of ten $/V_1/\!\!\sim\!\!/V_2/$ alternations, but in some cases, modern speakers almost certainly do not recognize the two forms as allomorphs of a single morpheme. For example, Martin analyzes the verb /somuku/ 'turn one's back' as consisting of /muku/ 'turn' preceded by /so/, which he identifies as an allomorph of /se/ 'back'. Historically, this identification is undoubtedly correct, but it is unlikely that modern speakers make the connection. For one thing, the /e/~/o/ alternation is very rare. In addition, orthography obscures the etymological connection. The kanji for /se/ is used to write the /somu/ of /somuku/, and a different kanji is used to write the /mu/ of /muku/. (The /ku/ is written in kana in both cases.) The spelling /so/ (kanji for /se/) + /mu/ (kanji for the /mu/ of /muku/) + /ku/ (kana) would be transparent, but it is not used (although Shinmura [1969] uses it to explain the etymology of the word).

There is room for argument about the morpheme identifications in several of Martin's other examples. Experiments of the sort that McCawley (1984) proposes would perhaps help resolve the question in such cases. I will not pursue this matter any further, but there is undoubtedly a good deal of individual variation as far as which relationships speakers recognize.

Only the /e/~/a/ alternation [1a] is at all common in modern standard Japanese, but Miller (1967:185–188), following Marchand (1956), argues that the /i/~/o/ [1b] and /o/~/a/ [1c] alternations are also frequent enough to use as evidence for INTERNAL RECONSTRUCTION (Bynon 1977:89–98) of the vowel system. If we accept Miller's argument and ignore the less frequent alternations, we can construe the three "common" alternations as evidence for an eight-vowel system at some earlier stage of Japanese. To see why, consider the /e/~/a/ alternation. Some morphemes, like /fune/~/funa/ [1a], have two allomorphs, one ending /e/ and the other ending /a/. Other morphemes, however, always end /e/, and still others always end /a/. A possible explanation for this difference is to surmise that invariable /e/ is descended from an older /e/, invariable /a/ from an older /a/, and alternating /e/~/a/ from some third older vowel. If we offer a parallel explanation for /i/~/o/ and /o/~/a/, the upshot is that at some point in the past, Japanese had three more vowels than the five it has now.

As it turns out, there is strong independent evidence that Old Japanese did in fact have an eight-way distinction of some kind after many consonants. Old Japanese texts were written in Chinese characters used for their phonetic values; the meanings of the characters were irrelevant. This system is known in Japanese as **man'yōgana**, and it was the forerunner of the modern kana syllabary. I will refer to the characters used in this system as PHONOGRAMS. Each phonogram represented one Japanese syllable, but a given syllable could be written with any of several alternative phonograms.

Kana came into general use early in the tenth century (Miller 1967:125). It is now well known that the number of distinct syllables represented in early kana is not as large as the number represented in the eighth-century Old Japanese phonograms. In other words, eighth-century Japanese had more distinct syllables than tenth-century Japanese.

The Japanese scholar Norinaga Motoori (1730–1801) laid the foundation for this discovery when he noticed some peculiarities in the distribution of some of the phonograms in Old Japanese texts. For example, modern Japanese /sode/ 'sleeve' and /sono/ 'that' both begin with the syllable /so/. In tenth-century kana spelling, as in modern Japanese, the /so/ in both words was written with the same letter. In Old Japanese, however, the initial syllables of these two words were written with two mutually exclusive sets of phonograms. It was Motoori who first discovered that /so/ and several other tenth-century syllables correspond to two distinct sets of phonograms in this way (Furuta and Tsukishima 1972:288, Lange 1973:22).

Motoori's disciple, Tatsumaro Ishizuka (1764–1823), took up this problem and wrote a detailed work on these distinctions among Old Japanese phonograms (Furuta and Tsukishima 1972:288–289, Lange 1973:22–23). This research by Motoori and Ishizuka was the basis for the work in this area by Shinkichi Hashimoto (1882–1945). Although he may have taken a hint from a nineteenth-century commentary on Ishizuka's work (Lange 1973:23, n. 11), Hashimoto (1917) is generally credited with first proposing that the mutually exclusive sets of phonograms represented distinct sounds in Old Japanese (Furuta and Tsukishima 1972:289, Lange 1973:23).

For each case in which there were two mutually exclusive sets of phonograms, Hashimoto (1917:173–186) labels one set TYPE A (**kō-rui**) and the other set TYPE B (**otsu-rui**). For example, the first syllable of the Old Japanese word for /sode/ 'sleeve' was written with type A phonograms, and the first syllable of the Old Japanese word for /sono/ 'that' was written with type B phonograms. The assignments to type A and type B are based on distribution in grammatical and functional morphemes. The type A phonograms corresponding to a given modern syllable occur in the same kind of grammatical and functional morphemes as the type A phonograms corresponding to other modern syllables, and the same is true for type B. This leads Hashimoto to infer that the same phonetic property distinguished the type A and type B syllables in each case (Lange 1973:24–25).

The A-B distinctions are found only for Old Japanese syllables corresponding to modern syllables with the vowels /i/, /e/, or /o/. It is widely accepted that the pronunciation differences between A and B syllables in Old Japanese were distinctions in the vowels (Miller 1967: 175–177), but this view is not universal (Lange 1973:28–32). In fact, there are several competing hypotheses about the pronunciation of the A and B syllables (Lange 1973:34–98), and it seems quite likely that the distinctions were between syllables of the form CV and syllables of the form CGV, where G is a glide (Lange 1973:34–98). Most of these hypotheses depend on inferences about how Chinese was pronounced at the time, and such inferences vary from scholar to scholar. Thus, even though Old Japanese writers presumably chose characters with Chinese pronunciations as close as possible to the Japanese syllables they wanted to render, the exact phonetic values are uncertain.

It is also widely accepted that the vowels in type A syllables were more or less identical to modern Japanese /i e o/, whereas those in type B syllables differed (Lange 1973:29), but this is by no means certain (Lange 1973:126). For convenience, I will refer to the A-B distinctions hereafter as "vowel distinctions," and I will write the type A syllables with /i e o/ and the type B syllables with /I E O/.

We are now in a position to see how the modern /e~a/, /i~o/, and /o~a/ alternations [1] fit in. The same three alternations were already present in Old Japanese, but as Hashimoto (1942:183–184) points out, only type B syllables were involved. In other words, the Old Japanese alternations were /E~a/, /I~o/ (sometimes /I~O/ or /I~u/; see Nakata 1972b:24), and /O~a/. These alternations clearly corroborate the internal reconstruction suggested above, although it is not clear when or why the type B vowels began to alternate this way.

11.1.2 Current Status

As I mentioned in section 11.1.1, only the /e~a/ alternation is common in modern standard Japanese. I know of fifteen morphemes that show this alternation in words listed in Masuda (1974), and there may be a few more. The examples in [2] illustrate this alternation, and several of the compounds show sequential voicing (Chapter 10) in addition to the vowel alternation.

[2] **a.** /ame/ 'rain'   /mizu/ 'water'
        /ama + mizu/ 'rain water'
  b. /cume/ 'finger/toe-nail'   /beni/ 'red'
        /cuma + beni/ 'red nail polish'
  c. /fune/ 'ship'   /yoi/ 'sickness'
        /funa + yoi/ 'seasickness'
  d. /ine/ 'rice plant'   /taba/ 'bundle'
        /ina + taba/ 'bundle of rice plants'
  e. /kane/ 'metal'   /mono/ 'thing'
        /kana + mono/ 'hardware'
  f. /kaze/ 'wind'   /mado/ 'window'
        /kaza + mado/ 'air vent'
  g. /koe/ 'voice'   /iro/ 'color'
        /kowa + iro/ 'tone of voice'
  h. /me/ 'eye'   /futa/ 'lid'
        /ma + buta/ 'eyelid'
  i. /mune/ 'chest'   /ke/ 'hair'
        /muna + ge/ 'chest hair'
  j. /nae/ 'seedling'   /širo/ 'substitution'
        /nawa + širo/ 'rice seedling bed'
  k. /sake/ 'liquor'   /ba/ 'place'
        /saka + ba/ 'tavern'

l. /suge/ 'sedge'   /muširo/ 'mat'
/suga + muširo/ 'sedge mat'
m. /take/ 'bamboo'   /mura/ 'crowd'
/taka + mura/ 'bamboo grove'
n. /te/ 'hand'   /cuna/ 'rope'
/ta + zuna/ 'reins'
o. /ue/ 'above'   /obi/ 'sash'
/uwa + obi/ 'outer sash'

The /e/~/wa/ alternation in [2g] (/koe/~/kowa/), [2j] (/nae/~/nawa/), and [2o] (/ue/~/uwa/) reflects the change of Old Japanese /ɸ/ to /w/ and the subsequent loss of /w/ everywhere except before /a/ (section 7.1). The modern forms developed as in [3].

[3]	Old Japanese	/kOwE/	/kOwa/	/uɸE/	/uɸa/
	A-B merger	/kowe/	/kowa/	/uɸe/	/uɸa/
	ɸ → w	—	—	/uwe/	/uwa/
	w → ∅	/koe/	—	/ue/	—

None of the twelve morphemes in [2] consistently appears with final /a/ as the first element in a compound. For some, such as /fune/~/funa/ [2c], final /a/ is much more frequent than final /e/ in the compound environment. For others, such as /te/~/ta/ [2n], final /e/ is the norm and final /a/ the exception.

The number of compounds with /a/ is roughly equal to the number with /e/ only for /kane/~/kana/ [2e], and in this case, the distinction appears to be largely semantic. The word /kane/ is frequently used to mean 'money' as well as 'metal', and in the great majority of compounds, the /kane/ allomorph means 'money' while the /kana/ allomorph means 'metal'. There are a few exceptions, such as /kane + noko/ 'hacksaw' (cf. /noko/ 'saw') and /kana + guri/ 'financing' (cf. /kuri/ 'reeling in'), but the trend is clear.

There are also several cases of variation, that is, of compounds in which the first element can end in either /e/ or /a/. This variation is especially common in compounds with the first element /kaze/~/kaza/ [2f]. The examples in [4] are a few of those for which Masuda (1974) lists both pronunciations.

[4] /ame + cubu/~/ama + cubu/ 'raindrop'
cf. /cubu/ 'drop'
/kaze + mači/~/kaza + mači/ 'waiting for a wind'
cf. /mači/ 'waiting'
/mune + yake/~/muna + yake/ 'heartburn'
cf. /yake/ 'burning'

I know of one case in which the difference between the two allomorphs differentiates two otherwise identical words. Masuda (1974) defines /kaze + ire/ as a nautical term meaning 'wind scooper' and /kaza + ire/ as 'airing' (cf. /ire/ 'letting in').

As far as I know, the only modern standard morphemes that show the /i/~/o/ alternation at all frequently are /hi/~/ho/ 'fire' and /ki/~/ko/ 'tree, wood'. Both appear much more frequently with final /i/ than with final /o/ in the compound environment, and there are a few cases of variation. See the examples in [5].

[5] /ho + ya/ 'lamp chimney'
    cf. /ya/ 'house'
  /hi + bana/ 'spark'
    cf. /hana/ 'flower'
  /ko + dači/ 'stand of trees'
    cf. /tači/ 'standing'
  /ki + nobori/ 'tree climbing'
    cf. /nobori/ 'climbing'

The only modern standard morpheme that shows the /o/~/a/ alternation frequently is /širo/~/šira/ 'white'. Both allomorphs are common in the compound environment; see the examples in [6].

[6] /širo + kuma/ 'polar bear'
    cf. /kuma/ 'bear'
  /šira + hama/ 'white beach'
    cf. /hama/ 'beach'
  /širo + ǰi/~/šira + ǰi/ 'white background'
    cf. /ǰi/ 'ground'

There are a few cases in which a morpheme that shows the /e/~/a/ or /i/~/o/ alternation appears with /a/ or /o/ before the genitive particle /no/. See the examples in [7].

[7] /ki/ 'tree'   /ha/ 'leaf'
    /konoha/ 'tree leaf'
  /me/ 'eye'   /atari/ 'vicinity'
    /manoatari/ 'before one's eyes'
  /ue/ 'above'   /sora/ 'sky'
    /uwanosora/ 'inattentiveness'

If examples of this kind have any syntactic structure at all, they are certainly set phrases.

I mentioned in section 11.1.1 that orthography obscures the etymological connection between /se/ 'back' and /somuku/ 'turn one's back', which involve the rare /e/~/o/ alternation. Kanji usage also obscures etymological relationships in many examples involving the three common alternations. For example, the verb /mabataku/ 'blink' is etymologically a compound of /me/~/ma/ 'eye' and /hataku/ 'hit', but a single kanji is used to write /mabata/ (with /ku/ in kana).

Another example is /honoo/ 'flame', which is etymologically a phrase meaning 'ear of fire' (from /hi/~/ho/ 'fire', genitive /no/, and /ho/ 'ear of grain', with the /φ/ > /w/ > ∅ change (section 7.1) having applied). A single kanji is used to write this word, and the entry in Hirayama (1960) gives two pronunciations that presumably indicate [hono:] and [hono?o], where [?] is vowel rearticulation. I argued in section 3.2.2 that vowel rearticulation of this kind in careful (but not elaborated) pronunciation is due to a morpheme boundary, and this treatment suggests that /honoo/ is a single morpheme for some speakers, while the /o/ is a separate morpheme for others. (How speakers who pronounce /honoo/ with vowel rearticulation analyze it semantically is a separate question.)

It is obvious at this point that even the three common alternations are irregular. Given a morpheme that ends in /e/, /i/, or /o/ as an independent word, there is no way to predict whether it has an allomorph with the alternate vowel. Furthermore, even when we know that such a morpheme alternates, we cannot predict which compounds will have which allomorph. The only apparent regularity I can suggest involves coordinate compounds (section 10.2.6). As far as I know, when an alternating morpheme occurs as the first element of a coordinate compound, the independent-word allomorph always appears. See the examples in [8].

[8] /ame/~/ama/ 'rain'   /kaze/~/kaza/ 'wind'
     /ame + kaze/ 'rain and wind'
     /me/~/ma/ 'eye'   /hana/ 'nose'
     /me + hana/ 'eyes and nose'
     /širo/~/šira/ 'white'   /kuro/ 'black'
     /širo + kuro/ 'black and white'
     /ue/~/uwa/ 'above'   /šita/ 'below'
     /ue + sita/ 'above and below'

Some dictionaries, including Masuda (1974), list /ama + kaze/ 'rainy wind' constrasting with /ame + kaze/ 'rain and wind', but this example is suspect, since *Nihon Kokugo Daijiten* lists only /ame + kaze/ and gives both meanings.

11.2 /CV/~/Q/ ALTERNATIONS IN SINO-JAPANESE MORPHEMES

11.2.1 Historical Background

We saw in section 7.1 that many Sino-Japanese morphemes had syllable-final, /p/, /t/, or /k/ in the original Chinese. In two-morpheme Sino-Japanese words, syllable-final /t/ has generally become /Q/ before all voiceless obstruents. In other environments, high vowels have been added, and modern standard Japanese has morpheme-final /cu/ or /či/. The examples in [9] illustrate this pattern with /becu/~/beQ/ 'difference'. The modern Cantonese cognate of this morpheme is /pit/. (I omit tone in this and all subsequent Cantonese examples.)

[9] /beQ.ke/ 'branch family'
     /beQ.taku/ 'secondary house'
     /beQ.soo/ 'separate mail'

/becu.iN/ 'separate temple'
/becu.doo/ 'separate building'
/becu.mei/ 'alias'
/sa.becu/ 'discrimination'

Portuguese missionary accounts indicate that morpheme-final /t/ was maintained in Sino-Japanese in all environments in the standard (Kyoto) Japanese of ca. 1600, at least as an alternative pronunciation (Toyama 1972:224–225). The transliterations in a seventeenth-century Japanese language text for Koreans suggest that this pronunciation was confined to formal speech (Toyama 1972:264).

Chinese syllable-final /k/ has generally become /Q/ before /k/ in two-morpheme Sino-Japanese words. (We will see in section 11.2.2 that there are quite a few exceptions even before /k/.) In other environments, modern standard Japanese has morpheme-final /ku/ or /ki/. The examples in [10] illustrate this pattern with /gaku~/gaQ/ 'learning' (cf. modern Cantonese /hok/).

[10] /gaQ.ki/ 'school term'
/gaku.to/ 'scholar'
/gaku.soo/ 'learned monk'
/gaku.i/ 'academic degree'
/gaku.doo/ 'school child'
/gaku.neN/ 'school year'
/dai.gaku/ 'college'

It is widely accepted that Chinese syllable-final /k/ became /ku/ or /ki/ in all environments in Sino-Japanese borrowings (Toyama 1972:224). If this claim is correct, allomorphs with /Q/ are a later development via vowel deletion and not a direct development from the original Chinese /k.k/.

Chinese syllable-final /p/ in most morphemes became /ɸu/ in Japanese. As we saw in section 7.1, the loss of intervocalic /ɸ/ and subsequent assimilations of contiguous vowels have produced long vowels in modern standard Japanese. The examples in [11] illustrate this pattern with /kyoo/ (</keu/</keɸu/) 'cooperation' (cf. modern Cantonese /hip/).

[11] /kyoo.kai/ 'association'
/kyoo.tei/ 'pact'
/kyoo.saN/ 'mutual aid'
/kyoo.doo/ 'collaboration'
/kyoo.wa/ 'harmony'
/da.kyoo/ 'compromise'

In a few morphemes, however, Chinese syllable-final /p/ has become /Q/ before all voiceless obstruents in two-morpheme Sino-Japanese words. These morphemes have modern standard allomorphs ending with /cu/ or /či/. The examples in [12] illustrate this pattern with /ricu~/riQ/ 'standing' (cf. modern Cantonese /lʌp/).

[12] /riQ.koku/ 'founding a country'
/riQ.tai/ 'solid body'
/riQ.šoo/ 'standing guard'
/ricu.zoo/ 'standing image'
/ricu.mei/ 'enlightenment'
/doku.ricu/ 'independence'

This is the pattern we expect in morphemes with final /t/ in the original Chinese, and it suggests that Japanese listeners misheard /p/ as /t/ in a few cases. Since Old Japanese did not allow syllable-final consonants (section 7.1), it was probably quite difficult for Japanese listeners to distinguish Chinese /p t k/ in this position. On the other hand, I am not aware of any cases that would suggest mishearing /k/ as /t/, /t k/ as /p/, or /p t/ as /k/. This problem certainly deserves further investigation.

In a few other cases, Chinese syllable-final /p/ has developed one way in some words and the other way in others (Martin 1952:28–29). The examples in [13] illustrate this kind of development with /šicu/~/šiQ/~/šuu/ 'holding' (cf. modern Cantonese /čʌp/).

[13] /šiQ.sei/ 'administration'
/šuu.šiN/ 'devotion'
/šicu.ǰi/ 'steward'
/šuu.ǰaku/ 'persistence'
/šicu.mu/ 'performance of official duties'
/šuu.neN/ 'tenacity'
/ko.šicu/ 'adherence'
/ga.šuu/ 'egotistical attachment'

I will argue in section 11.4.3 that /šuu/ should probably be treated as a separate morpheme from /šicu/~/šiQ/.

The morpheme meaning 'ten' (modern Cantonese /sʌp/) is unique in that the /Q/-final reflex consistently appears before voiceless obstruents and the long-vowel reflex consistently appears elsewhere. This fact means that there is no allomorph ending in /cu/ or /či/. The form /ǰiQ/ is the historically regular development of the /Q/-final allomorph, but the form /ǰuQ/ seems to be supplanting it. In NUMERAL + COUNTER combinations (McClain 1981:236–240), most modern standard speakers use /ǰuQ/, although /ǰiQ/ is still recognized as standard (Mizutani 1981:20–21). The examples in [14] illustrate this pattern with the forms judged possible by one standard speaker (KH).

[14] /ǰuu.ǰi/ 'cross'
/ǰuu.buN/ 'enough'
/ǰiQ.šu + kyoo.gi/ 'decathlon'
/ǰuQ.šiN/~/ǰiQ.šiN/ 'decimal'
/ǰuQ.ko/ 'ten (things)' (numeral + counter)

As I mentioned in section 10.4, when /Q/ is added for emphasis before /h/ or /f/, the result is /Qp/. In similar fashion, when a Sino-Japanese morpheme that usually begins with /h/ or /f/ appears in a two-morpheme word after a Sino-Japanese morpheme that shows the /cu/~/Q/ or /či/~/Q/ alternation, the result is /Q.p/. See the examples in [15].

[15] a. /niči/~/niQ/ 'day'
  /hoo/~/poo/ 'report'
  /niQ.poo/ 'daily report'
    cf. /hoo.koku/ 'report'
  b. /šucu/~/šuQ/ 'putting out'
  /hi/~/pi/ 'expense'
  /šuQ.pi/ 'outlay'
    cf. /hi.moku/ 'expense item'

As long as sequential voicing (section 10.2.2) does not apply, this /p/ generally appears after /N/ as well, but not quite so consistently (McCawley 1968:77–78).

Some Sino-Japanese morphemes with initial /h/ or /f/ probably had bilabial stops in the original Chinese, while others probably had labiodental fricatives. Karlgren (1923:9) says that sixth-century Chinese had bilabial stops and no labiodental fricatives, but he suggests that such fricatives developed shortly thereafter, and they appear in his reconstruction of early seventh-century Chinese. Heavy borrowing into Japanese apparently continued well into the eighth century (Miller 1967:103). Modern Cantonese shows this stop/fricative distinction; the cognate of /hoo/~/poo/ [15a] is /pou/, while the cognate of /hi/~/pi/ [15b] is /fʌi/. In most environments, both the stops and the fricatives eventually became /ɸ/ in Japanese, but perhaps this phoneme had a stop allophone after stops. (As I noted in section 7.1, it is not clear just when Japanese /p/ became /ɸ/, so it is not certain how these Chinese sounds were first borrowed.) In any event, as we saw in section 10.4, modern standard Japanese has /p/ and not /h/ or /f/ after /Q/, except in mimetic adverbs and recent borrowings.

11.2.2 Current Status

11.2.2.1 Two-Morpheme Sino-Japanese Words

The /cu/~/Q/ alternation is very nearly automatic in two-morpheme Sino-Japanese words in the modern standard language: /Q/ almost always appears before a voiceless obstruent. One exception is /necukaku/ 'thermonuclear' (from /necu/ 'heat' and /kaku/ 'nucleus'), as in /necukakuhaNnoo/ 'thermonuclear reaction' (cf. /haN.noo/ 'reaction'). This seems to be an abbreviation of /necugenšikaku + haNnoo/, in which /necu/ is added to /geN.ši + kaku/ 'atomic nucleus' (cf. /geN.ši/ 'atom'). The entries in *Nihon Kokugo Daijiten* and in Masuda (1974) divide /necukakuhaNnoo/ as /necu.kaku + haN.noo/, but since the word /kaku + haN.noo/ 'nuclear reaction' also exists, it is not clear that this analysis is appropriate. The entry in Shinmura (1969) indicates /necu/ + /kaku + haN.noo/ instead. As far as I have been able to determine, when speakers encounter an unfamiliar word of the relevant kind written in kanji, they consistently supply the /Q/-final allomorph for the first morpheme.

Compounds consisting of a single Sino-Japanese morpheme followed by native Japanese /suru/ 'do' are quite common, and as Martin (1952:27) notes, a morpheme that shows the /cu/~/Q/ alternation appears with /Q/ before /suru/. See the examples in [16].

[16] /bacu/~/baQ/ 'punishment' /baQ + suru/ 'punish'
/tacu/~/taQ/ 'attainment' /taQ + suru/ 'attain'

The /či/~/Q/ alternation is inconsistent. While /niči/ 'sun, day' apparently always appears as /niQ/ before voiceless obstruents in two-morpheme Sino-Japanese words (ignoring the idiosyncratic allomorph /ni/ in /ni.hoN/ 'Japan'), /šiči/ 'seven' and /hači/ 'eight' do not behave so regularly. The examples in [17] are numeral + counter combinations, and this area of the vocabulary shows many other irregularities as well (Martin 1952:91–98).

[17] /šiči.hoN/ 'seven (long things)'
/hači.hoN/~/haQ.poN/ 'eight (long things)'

/šiči.sacu/ 'seven (books)'
/haQ.sacu/ 'eight (books)'

The /ku/~/Q/ alternation, like the /cu/~/Q/ alternation, is very nearly automatic in two-morpheme Sino-Japanese words: /Q/ almost always appears before /k/. Martin (1952:31) says there are a few examples of individual words in which either the /Q/-final allomorph or the /ku/-final allomorph can appear, and any large dictionary such as Shinmura (1969) lists several two-morpheme Sino-Japanese words with /ku/ before /k/ as the only pronunciation. Most of these counterexamples, however, are obscure words that ordinary speakers are not likely to use. As with the /cu/~/Q/ alternation, when speakers encounter an unfamiliar word of the relevant kind written in kanji, they consistently supply the /Q/-final allomorph.

The Sino-Japanese morpheme /roku/~/roQ/ 'six' shows a different sort of irregularity. In Sino-Japanese numeral + counter combinations, it appears as /roQ/ not only before /k/ but also before /p/ (from /h/ or /f/). See the examples in [18].

[18] /roku.sacu/ 'six (books)'
/roku.too/ 'six (large animals)'
/roQ.ko/ 'six (things)'
/roQ.poN/ 'six (long things)'
/roQ.pai/ 'six (cupfuls)'

Sino-Japanese /hoku/~/hoQ/ 'north' shows the same irregularity, but only in the word /hoQ.poo/ 'northward' (cf. /hoo/~/poo/ 'direction').

The /ki/~/Q/ alternation is clearly irregular. Martin (1952:30) says that some Sino-Japanese morphemes of the form /(C)Vki/ always appear as /(C)VQ/ before /k/ in two-morpheme Sino-Japanese words, others often do, and others seldom do. There are also many individual words in which the first morpheme can have either shape. The forms in [19] illustrate this point with one morpheme from each of Martin's three categories.

[19] **a.** /seki/ 'stone' (always /seQ/ before /k/)
　　　　/seQ.ka/ 'petrification'
　　　　/seQ.koku/ 'stone carving'
　　b. /teki/ 'enemy' (often /teQ/ before /k/)
　　　　/teQ.ki/~/teki.ki/ 'enemy flag'
　　　　/teki.ka/ 'enemy goods'
　　c. /eki/ 'liquid' (seldom /eQ/ before /k/)
　　　　/eki.ka/ 'liquification'
　　　　/eki.kaN + deN.ki/ 'liquid potential'

In fact, I know of no examples in which 'liquid' [19c] appears as /eQ/.

There is little doubt that modern standard speakers treat the vowel-final allomorphs in all these cases as basic. Certainly one reason for this analysis is that the /Q/-final allomorphs would make terribly inconvenient citation forms. /Q/ ordinarily occurs only before voiceless obstruents (section 5.2.3), and utterance-final /Q/ has only a marginal status (section 5.2.4). Ordinary kanji dictionaries do not even list the /Q/-final allomorphs among the possible pronunciations of the characters involved, and it is not uncommon for a speaker to identify a particular kanji by saying something like "the /tecu/ ['iron'] of /teQ.poo/ ['gun']."

Another reason for treating the vowel-final allomorphs as basic is that, given a word containing the /Q/-final allomorph of some Sino-Japanese morpheme, the other allomorph is not predictable. The examples in [20] illustrate this point.

[20] /haQ.poo/ 'all directions'
　　　cf. /hači/ 'eight'
　　/haQ.poo/ 'firing a gun'
　　　cf. /hacu/ 'discharge'
　　/riQ.koo/ 'strenuous effort'
　　　cf. /riki/ 'strength'
　　/riQ.koo/ 'traveling by land'
　　　cf. /riku/ 'land'
　　/riQ.koku/ 'founding a country'
　　　cf. /ricu/ 'standing'

We saw in section 11.2.1 that the /cu/~/Q/ and /či/~/Q/ alternations are historically the result of vowel insertion and not vowel deletion. This means that the situation in modern standard Japanese is a case of rule inversion (section 9.6.7).

11.2.2.2 Longer Sino-Japanese Words

Morphemes that alternate regularly in two-morpheme Sino-Japanese words seem to behave erratically in Sino-Japanese words of three or more morphemes. As Martin (1952:31) and McCawley (1968:117–118) point out, however, constituent structure is relevant in these longer words. In general, the /Q/-final allomorphs do not appear before the major constituent break, as the examples in [21] show.

[21]   /ka/ 'addition'
       /acu/ ~ /aQ/ 'pressure'
       /sei/ 'nature'
       /ka.acu/ 'pressurization'
       /ka.acu + sei/ 'compressibility'

       /ka/   /acu/   /sei/

       /acu/ ~ /aQ/ 'pressure'
       /sei/ 'system'
       /ša/ 'person'
       /aQ.sei/ 'oppression'
       /aQ.sei + ša/ 'oppressor'

       /aQ/   /sei/   /ša/

       /zacu/ ~ /zaQ/ 'miscellany'
       /kaN/ 'perception'
       /ǰoo/ 'decision'
       /kaN.ǰoo/ 'account'
       /zacu + kaN.ǰoo/ 'miscellaneous accounts'

       /zacu/   /kaN/   /ǰoo/

       /zacu/ ~ /zaQ/ 'miscellany'
       /ka/ 'goods'
       /teN/ 'store'
       /zaQ.ka/ 'miscellaneous goods'
       /zaQ.ka + teN/ 'variety store'

       /zaQ/   /ka/   /teN/

There are, however, quite a few cases of three-morpheme words in which a /Q/-final allomorph appears before the major constituent break (McCawley 1968:118, Okuda 1970:745). I give two such counterexamples in [22].

[22] **a.** /saN/ 'three'
            /kaku/~/kaQ/ 'angle'
            /kei/ 'shape'
            /saN.kaku/ 'triangularity'
            /saN.kaQ + kei/~/saN.kaku + kei/ 'triangle'
      b. /ǰicu/~/ǰiQ/ 'reality'
            /ša/ 'association'

/kai/ 'association'
/ša.kai/ 'society'
/ʃiQ + ša.kai/ 'the real world'

The /Q/ before the major division in examples like [22a] is undoubtedly a secondary development fostered by vowel devoicing (Chapter 6). For some standard speakers, /saN.kaQ + kei/ [22a] seems to be just an optional alternative, and Shinmura (1969) and Masuda (1974) list only /saN.kaku + kei/. Other speakers, however, reject /saN.kaku + kei/ completely. Shinmura and Masuda list only /ʃiQ + ša.kai/ [22b], and I have not yet found a standard speaker who would accept /ʃicu + ša.kai/. I am not aware of any four-morpheme Sino-Japanese words of the form X.Y + Z.W (where X,Y,Z,W are morphemes) in which Y appears with a final /Q/.

11.2.2.3 Words Containing Non-Sino-Japanese Morphemes

Leaving aside the combinations with /suru/ 'do' mentioned in section 11.2.2.1, words consisting of a Sino-Japanese morpheme followed by a native Japanese morpheme are not very common. In a search through Masuda (1974), I found twelve such words in which the Sino-Japanese morpheme has a /Q/-final allomorph and the native morpheme begins with a voiceless obstruent. /Q/ actually appears in five of them, and I list these five in [23].

[23] /doQ + keši/~/doku + keši/ 'antidote'
        /doku/~/doQ/ 'poison'   (Sino-Japanese)
        /keši/ 'erasing'   (native)
      /gaQ + pi/ 'date'
        /gacu/~/gaQ/ 'month'   (Sino-Japanese)
        /hi/ 'day'   (native)
      /koQ + pai/ 'animal bone ashes'
        /kocu/~/koQ/ 'bone'   (Sino-Japanese)
        /hai/ 'ash'   (native)
      /toQ + pana/ 'tip of a headland'
        /tocu/~/toQ/ 'protrusion'   (Sino-Japanese)
        /hana/ 'end'   (native)
      /toQ + saki/ 'tip'
        /tocu/~/toQ/ 'protrusion'   (Sino-Japanese)
        /saki/ 'tip'   (native)

In many numeral + counter combinations, the counter is a recently borrowed morpheme. It is quite common for the /Q/-final allomorph of a Sino-Japanese numeral to appear in such combinations, and the examples in [24] are typical.

[24] /iQ + seNči/ 'one centimeter'
        /iči/~/iQ/ 'one'

/roQ + kiro/ 'six kilos'
/roku/~/roQ/ 'six'

As Martin (1952:89–90) points out, we also find /CV/~/Q/ alternations in one area of the native Japanese vocabulary. When a verb is used as a nonfinal element in a compound, it appears in its stem form (section 10.2.5), and the verbs in one conjugation class generally have stems ending in /VCi/ (section 12.2.5.1). The only exceptions to this pattern are verbs whose stems ended in /Vɸi/ in Old Japanese. Because of the /ɸ/>/w/>∅ changes in this environment (section 7.1), these stems now end in /Vi/. The stems of a few verbs in this conjugation class appear in some compounds with final /Q/ rather than /(C)i/, although these alternations are not regular. See the examples in [25].

[25] /hiku/ 'pull'   stem: /hiki/
      /hiQ + paru/ 'pull'
         cf. /haru/ 'stretch'
      /hiki + hanasu/ 'pull apart'
         cf. /hanasu/ 'separate'
    /kiru/ 'cut'   stem: /kiri/
      /kiQ + saki/ 'sword point'
         cf. /saki/ 'point'
      /kiri + suteru/ 'slay'
         cf. /suteru/ 'throw away'
    /bucu/ 'hit'   stem: /buči/
      /buQ + kiru/ 'hack'
         cf. /kiru/ 'cut'
      /buQ + korosu/~/buči + korosu/ 'beat to death'
         cf. /korosu/ 'kill'
    /ou/ 'chase'   stem: /oi/
      /oQ + parau/~/oi + harau/ 'chase away'
         cf. /harau/ 'get rid of'

There is obviously a different range of alternations in these examples than in the Sino-Japanese words considered in section 11.2.2.1. In addition to /či/ and /ki/, /ri/ and /i/ alternate with /Q/, and the /Q/-final allomorph of a stem that ends in /ki/ is not restricted to cases in which the following morpheme begins with /k/.

We will see in section 12.2.5.1 that verb stems ending in /či/, /ri/, or /i/ (</ɸi/) all have /Q/-final allomorphs before the past suffix /ta/ and historically related suffixes. The /CV/>/Q/ changes that produced these alternations are among the developments traditionally known as "onbin" (section 7.1), and they probably began about the ninth century (Tsukishima 1964:30). The /Q/-final allomorphs appear absolutely regularly before these suffixes in modern standard Japanese. Verb stems ending /ki/ have generally developed in a different way, but the verb /iku/ 'go' has the stem /iki/ and the irregular past form /iQ + ta/. It thus appears that examples like those in [25] reflect the sporadic extension of these /CV/>/Q/ changes into compounds.

11.3   LIAISON

11.3.1   Historical Background

Many Sino-Japanese morphemes ordinarily begin with a vowel or glide, and Martin (1952:84) notes that a few of these sometimes appear with initial /n/ as second elements in two-morpheme Sino-Japanese words. This /n/ insertion happens only when the first morpheme ends with /N/, and it is confined to a very small number of words in modern standard Japanese. One example is /haN.noo/ 'reaction' (from /haN/ 'against' and /oo/ 'response'). The Japanese technical term for this phenomenon is **renjō**, and following a suggestion by Kamei (1954: 39), I will refer to it as LIAISON.

The earliest evidence for liaison is in a tenth-century text (Toyama 1972: 230, Matsumoto 1977b), and it was once widely accepted that liaison was completely regular in standard (Kyoto) Japanese from about 1300 until about 1600 (Matsumoto 1970:11). The textual evidence is open to more than one interpretation, however, and it may well be that liaison has always been sporadic and ordinarily confined to particular words (Hamada 1960:11–14, Fukushima 1963, Matsumoto 1970). Nonetheless, there is no doubt that it was once much more widespread (at least in Kyoto Japanese) than it is in the modern standard language.

We saw in section 7.1 that Sino-Japanese morphemes with final /N/ had syllable-final /m/ or /n/ in the original Chinese. Early examples of liaison reflect this /m/-/n/ distinction, and at least two examples with /m/ have survived into the modern standard. Martin (1952:84) and Toyama (1972:231) both cite /oN.myoo + ji/ 'fortune teller' (from /oN/ 'yin', /yoo/ 'yang', and /ši/ 'teacher') and /saN.mi/ 'trinity' (from /saN/ 'three' and /i/ 'position'). The modern Cantonese cognates of the initial morphemes in these two words are /yʌm/ 'yin' and /sam/ 'three'. (The cognate of /haN/ in /haN.noo/ is /fan/.) Toyama says that /m/ liaison had disappeared except in a few fixed words by about 1500 in the standard (Kyoto) dialect. This fact suggests that the original distinction between morpheme-final /m/ and /n/ was maintained in Sino-Japanese until about that time. The form /oN.yoo + ji/ (without liaison) has almost entirely supplanted /oN.myoo + ji/ in modern standard Japanese. Masuda (1974) lists only /oN.yoo + ji/, and Shinmura (1969) gives this as the preferred pronunciation.

We saw in sections 7.1 and 11.2.1 that Sino-Japanese morphemes with allomorphs ending in /Q/ had syllable-final /p/, /t/, or /k/ in the original Chinese, and there are examples of /t/ liaison in many texts. At least two such examples have survived into the modern standard language, but the original morphemic relationships are quite obscure. One of these is /kuQ.taku/ 'worry', which consists etymologically of /kuQ/ (~/kucu/) 'submission' and /waku/ 'confusion'. (Note that /w/ disappears when liaison applies; as we saw in section 4.8.5, Japanese has never had sequences like /nw/ or /tw/.) In modern orthography, however, the second morpheme is written with the kanji for /taku/ 'entrusting'.

The other examples is /seQ.čiN/ 'toilet' (with /č/ rather than /t/ before /i/), which is written with the kanji for /seQ/ (~/secu/) 'snow' and /iN/ 'hiding'. This word is semantically opaque and apparently entered Japanese as a Zen term. According to the entry in Morohashi (1957–60), it was coined in Chinese because a Chinese Zen priest whose name began with the kanji for 'snow' attained enlightenment while cleaning a privy, possibly at a temple with the kanji for 'hiding' in its name.

We saw in section 11.2.1 that original Chinese syllable-final /t/ has become /cu/ or /či/ in modern standard Japanese, except before voiceless obstruents. The development of /t/ liaison suggests that the Sino-Japanese morphemes involved maintained final /t/ until quite late. As we saw in section 11.2.1, this idea is widely accepted because Portuguese and Korean sources provide corroboration for the standard (Kyoto) Japanese of ca. 1600.

There is evidence in many texts, however, that liaison was extended to native Japanese morphemes, especially grammatical particles. Nihon Onsei Gakkai (1976:318) cites several examples from chants in traditional Nō dramas, including those in [26]. In [26a] the morpheme preceding the particle is Sino-Japanese, but in [26b] it is native Japanese. Modern standard /hito + cu/ consists of the numeral prefix /hito/ 'one' (section 10.2.4) and the counter /cu/. The liaison in the form /hitoQta/ [26b] suggests some sort of analogy to the /t/ liaison after Sino-Japanese morphemes, but it is hard to see what basis there could be for such analogy unless the relevant Sino-Japanese morphemes were sometimes pronounced with final /tu/ (>modern standard /cu/; see section 4.4.2.1). I therefore agree with Fukushima (1963:36) that it is not clear to what extent the Sino-Japanese of 1600 still maintained original syllable-final /t/.

[26] **a.** /rašoomoNno/ 'Rashōmon (accusative)'
        cf. modern standard /rašoomoN/ (proper name)
                            /o/ (</wo/) (accusative particle)
       b. /hitoQta/ 'one (topic)'
        cf. modern standard /hito + cu/ 'one'
                            /wa/ (topic particle)

We saw in sections 3.3 and 7.1 that Old Japanese syllables with no initial consonant were generally confined to word-initial position, and Hashimoto (1937:226–227) argues that this was the motivation for liaison. The problem with this explanation is that it does not account for liaison before glides. It seems more likely that the motivation was the lack of syllable-final consonants in Old Japanese. Even after the onbin changes described in section 7.1, /N/ and /Q/ generally did not occur before vowels or glides in native Japanese words. It therefore seems reasonable to surmise that liaison developed to maintain original Chinese syllable-final consonants while eliminating sequences that were difficult to pronounce. This is essentially the explanation that Hamada (1960:12) proposes.

11.3.2 Current Status

In section 11.3.1 I mentioned only five examples of liaison in modern standard Japanese. In [27] I list all the others I know of that appear in Masuda (1974). Since all of these involve /n/ liaison, I repeat /haN.noo/ 'reaction' to make the list complete.

[27] /aN.noN/~/aN.on/ 'tranquility'
　　　/aN/ 'peace'　　/oN/ 'calm'
　/giN.naN/ 'ginkgo nut'
　　　/giN/ 'silver'　　/aN/ 'apricot'
　/haN.noo/ 'reaction'
　　　/haN/ 'against'　　/oo/ 'response'
　/iN.neN/ 'fate'
　　　/iN/ 'cause'　　/eN/ 'relation'
　/kaN.noo/~/kaN.oo/ 'sympathetic response'
　　　/kaN/ 'feeling'　　/oo/ 'response'
　/kaN.noN/ 'Kannon' (Buddhist goddess of mercy)
　　　/kaN/ 'view'　　/oN/ 'sound'
　/kiN.noo/ 'royalism'
　　　/kiN/ 'service'　　/oo/ 'king'
　/riN.ne/ 'transmigration of souls'
　　　/riN/ 'circle'　　/e/ 'rotation'
　/šiN.noo/ 'Imperial prince'
　　　/šiN/ 'relative'　　/oo/ 'king'
　/soN.noo/ 'reverence for the Emperor'
　　　/soN/ 'exaltedness'　　/oo/ 'emperor'
　/teN.noo/ 'the Emperor'
　　　/teN/ 'heaven'　　/oo/ 'emperor'
　/uN.noo/~/uN.oo/ 'esoteric doctrine'
　　　/uN/ 'amassing'　　/oo/ 'interior'
　/uN.nuN/ 'such and such'
　　　/uN/ 'saying' (reduplicated)

Martin (1952:84) says that modern standard /Ny/ sequences are frequently pronounced with liaison, and he mentions that such pronunciations are sometimes considered substandard. One of his examples is the pronunciation of /kiN.yoo+bi/ 'Friday' as /kiN.nyoo+bi/. Given the phonetic value of modern standard /N/ before vowels and glides, this kind of occasional liaison seems quite natural. We saw in section 5.1.1.4 that /N/ does not involve complete oral closure in such cases. Hattori (1930:43) argues that these allophones are difficult for children to master, and he cites some examples of incorrect pronunciations with complete oral closure. The auditory effect of complete closure in the sequence /Ny/ is [ɲ:ˆɲj], that is, /Nny/ (section 5.1.1.4).

11.4 SINO-JAPANESE DOUBLETS

11.4.1 Historical Background

Significant cultural contact between Japan and China began about the year 400 (Miller 1967:91), and there was heavy borrowing from Chinese into Japanese for several centuries thereafter. The Chinese writing system was also adapted for Japanese (Miller 1967:90–102), and loans from Chinese were generally written just as they were in China, that is, with one kanji for each morpheme. As we saw in section 1.3, Sino-Japanese words are still written this way in modern Japan.

The first important wave of Chinese loans entered Japan via Korea, and the pronunciations in Japanese were based on a variety of Chinese spoken in the Six Dynasties Period (222–589) (Miller 1967:91, 102, Tōdō 1977:129–130). These Japanese pronunciations are known as the GO-ON ('Wu pronunciations') of the kanji involved. Since there had once been an independent kingdom of Wu centered on the lower Yangtze River, it is widely believed that the go-on were based on the Chinese spoken in this area (Tōdō 1977:129). According to Miller (1967:108), however, the term *go-on* originated as a pejorative label meaning 'nonstandard' and did not refer to this geographical location.

Japanese scholars and monks began traveling to China about 600, and they introduced the second important wave of Chinese loans into Japan. The pronunciations in Japanese were based on the standard Chinese spoken in the Tang capital of Changan (Miller 1967:103–104, Tōdō 1977:129–130), and they are known as the KAN-ON ('Han pronunciations') of the kanji involved. Since ethnic Chinese are referred to as the "Han people," this label apparently meant something like '(standard) Chinese pronunciations' (Miller 1967:108). For many kanji, the kan-on and the go-on were identical, but for many others they were not.

The Japanese imperial court adopted the newer kan-on as the official pronunciations for kanji (i.e., Sino-Japanese morphemes) in the eighth century (Habein 1984:17), but they never completely displaced the older go-on (Miller 1967:108, Tōdō 1977:129–130). The older pronunciations were generally preserved in Buddhist terminology and in Chinese loans that had already become well established. As a result, many kanji in modern Japanese orthography have two distinct Sino-Japanese pronunciations. For example, a kanji meaning 'below' has the go-on /ge/, as in /ge.sui/ 'sewer', and the kan-on /ka/, as in /ka.haN/ 'lower half'. Borrowings of this kind, made at different times from the same ultimate source, are known as DOUBLETS (Lehmann 1962:225). A comparable English example is the pair *hostel/hotel*. Both of these words were borrowed from French, the former several centuries before the latter.

Buddhist monks who studied in China in later centuries brought a third wave of loans to Japan, but these loans have had only a marginal impact on the vocabulary. The pronunciations in Japanese were based largely on the fourteenth-century Chinese of the Hangzhou area (Miller 1967:108–110, Tōdō 1977: 141–142), and they are known as the TŌ-ON ('Tang pronunciations') or SŌ-ON ('Song pronunciations') of the kanji involved. These pronunciations are generally confined to Zen terminology, although they do occur in a few ordinary words. The labels refer to the Tang dynasty (618–907) and the Song dynasty (960–1279), and are thus chronologically misleading, although this wave of borrowing probably began in Song times (Suzuki et al. 1975:910).

A few Chinese loans have trickled into Japanese in more recent times as well. Two twentieth-century examples listed in Umegaki (1966) are /gyoo.za/ 'stuffed dumpling' and /maa.jaN/ 'mah jong'. In such cases, the pronunciations of the kanji involved are usually different from all the older ones. For example, the second kanji in /gyoo.za/ means 'child' (although it is simply a noun suffix in modern Chinese) and has the go-on /ši/, the kan-on /ši/, and the tō-on /su/.

Many kanji have alternative Sino-Japanese pronunciations that cannot be attributed to different layers of borrowing. In some cases, this is because a single kanji was used in China for two different morphemes with similar meanings. For example, a kanji meaning 'evil, hatred' has the two Sino-Japanese pronunciations /o/ and /aku/, and according to the entry in Suzuki et al. (1975), /o/ is both go-on and kan-on, and so is /aku/. Karlgren (1923:87) reconstructs two different Ancient Chinese morphemes corresponding to this character.

Another source of alternative Sino-Japanese pronunciations was the inconsistent development of Chinese syllable-final /p/ in Japanese. As we saw in section 11.2.1, a kanji meaning 'holding' is pronounced /šuu/ in some Sino-Japanese words and /šicu/~/šiQ/ in others. Since /šuu/ (</siu/<siɸu/; see section 7.1) is the regular kan-on development, kanji dictionaries give this as the kan-on and label /šicu/ (~/šiQ/) a POPULAR PRONUNCIATION (**kan'yōon**). In addition to pronunciations that do not follow the general rules for go-on and kan-on, the popular pronunciation category includes "mistaken" pronunciations that have caught on and pronunciations of obscure origin (Suzuki et al. 1975:910–911).

Strictly speaking, of course, alternative pronunciations not due to different layers of borrowing are not doublets, but I will consider all alternative Sino-Japanese pronunciations here. Needless to say, it makes no difference to ordinary speakers whether or not such alternatives are etymological doublets.

Ordinary kanji dictionaries like Suzuki et al. (1975) do not list allomorphs due to Japanese alternations as alternative Sino-Japanese pronunciations. For example, we saw in sections 10.2.2 and 10.2.3 that sequential voicing applies to many Sino-Japanese morphemes, but kanji dictionaries do not list the allomorphs with initial voiced obstruents. In similar fashion, they do not list allomorphs due to liaison (section 11.3), allomorphs with initial /p/ instead of /h/ or /f/ (after /Q/ or /N/; see section 11.2.1), or allomorphs with final /Q/ (section 11.2). The only exceptions are /Q/-final allomorphs that do not alternate with /CV/-final allomorphs, such as /jiQ/ 'ten' (~/juu/; see section 11.2.1). I will follow the dictionaries and define alternative Sino-Japanese pronunciations so as to exclude allomorphs due to alternations within Japanese.

11.4.2 Current Status

In 1946 the Japanese cabinet and Ministry of Education issued a list of CURRENT USE KANJI (**tōyō kanji**) to be taught in the nine years of compulsory education (Miller 1967:135). The list included 1,850 characters and also specified the pronunciations that each could have. Newspapers and official documents were limited to these 1,850 kanji and their specified pronunciations, but many other kanji have remained in general use to some extent (Pye 1971:5). In addition, many of the current use kanji are commonly used with pronunciations other than the officially recognized ones. A revised list of 1,945 characters known as the COMMON USE KANJI (**jōyō kanji**) was adopted in 1981. Nonetheless, since the approved Sino-Japanese pronunciations of the 1,850 current use kanji were taught in the schools for thirty-five years, they are reasonably representative of the doublets that modern speakers are likely to know.

To get a clear picture of the range of officially recognized Sino-Japanese pronunciations, I made a systematic search through a standard kanji dictionary (Suzuki et al. 1975). Only 246 of the 1,850 current use kanji are listed with more than one approved Sino-Japanese pronunciation, and of these 246, 170 have one go-on, one kan-on, and no others. Most of the remaining 76 have at least one popular pronunciation. Only six have officially recognized tō-on or sō-on, and 15 have two distinct go-on and/or kan-on.

Martin (1952:82–83) gives a comprehensive list of the ways that alternative Sino-Japanese pronunciations differ, but only six of these differences apply to at least 10 current use kanji. Although the pronunciations involved are not exclusively go-on and kan-on, each of these six relationships is a modern reflection of one or more of the important correspondences between go-on and kan-on that Tōdō (1977:131–138) lists.

The most widespread relationship between alternative Sino-Japanese pronunciations is initial voiced obstruent versus initial voiceless obstruent. There are 32 current use kanji with alternative pronunciations that differ only in this way. Because of the historical changes discussed in section 10.1, we find the same voiced/voiceless partners as in sequential voicing: /b/ versus /f h/, /d/ versus /t/, /z/ versus /s c/, /ǰ/ versus /š č/, and /g/ versus /k/. As I mentioned in section 11.4.1, kanji dictionaries do not treat allomorphs with initial voiced obstruents due to sequential voicing as alternative pronunciations. When a kanji is listed with two alterative pronunciations that differ in voicing, they both occur word-initially. See the examples in [28].

[28] /biN/ versus /hiN/ 'poverty'
 /biN.boo/ 'poverty'
 /hin.miN/ 'poor people'

/ǰiN/ versus /šiN/ 'spirit'
/ǰiN.ǰa/ 'shrine'
/šiN.wa/ 'myth'
/do/ versus /to/ 'soil'
/do.ki/ 'earthenware'
/to.či/ 'land'

Another widespread relationship is /Cyoo/ versus /Cei/, and there are 23 current use kanji that differ only in this way. There are also 8 current use kanji with alternative pronunciations that show both this difference and the voiced/voiceless difference, with the voiced obstruent always in the /Cyoo/ pronunciation. I argued against treating modern standard /š č ǰ/ as underlying /Cy/ sequences in section 4.8, but in Sino-Japanese doublets we find /šoo/ versus /sei/, /čoo/ versus /tei/, and /ǰoo/ versus /sei/ or /tei/, and I include these as instances of the /Cyoo/ versus /Cei/ relationships. See the examples in [29].

[29] /myoo/ versus /mei/ 'name'
      /myoo.ǰi/ 'surname'
      /mei.ši/ 'name card'
   /šoo/ versus /sei/ 'correctness'
      /šoo.ǰiki/ 'honesty'
      /sei.kai/ 'correct answer'
   /byoo/ versus /hei/ 'level'
      /byoo.doo/ 'equality'
      /hei.ya/ 'plain'

A third important relationship is initial nasal versus initial voiced obstruent, and 18 current use kanji have alternative pronunciations that differ only in this way. I include cases of initial /ni/ versus initial /ǰi/ and initial /ny/ versus initial /ǰ/ as instances of this relationship. The examples in [30] are illustrations.

[30] /mu/ versus /bu/ 'military'
      /mu.ša/ 'warrior'
      /bu.ki/ 'weapon'
   /naN/ versus /daN/ 'man'
      /čoo.naN/ 'eldest son'
      /daN.sei/ 'male'
   /niN/ versus /ǰiN/ 'person'
      /niN.geN/ 'human being'
      /ǰiN.koo/ 'population'

Another important relationship is initial /C/ versus initial /Cy/, and there are 15 current use kanji with alternative pronunciations that differ only in this way. I include cases of initial /s/ versus initial /š/ as instances of this relationship. There are also 8 current use kanji that show both this /C/ versus /Cy/ relationship and the voiced/voiceless relationship (including one case of /z/ versus /š/). The examples in [31] are illustrations.

[31] /ko/ versus /kyo/ 'basing'
/šoo.ko/ 'evidence'
/koN.kyo/ 'basis'
/roku/ versus /ryoku/ 'green'
/roku.šoo/ 'green (copper) rust'
/ryoku.ča/ 'green tea'
/goo/ versus /kyoo/ 'strength'
/goo.ǰoo/ 'obstinacy'
/kyoo.sei/ 'coercion'

Another important relationship is short vowel versus long vowel. This relationship is confined to /u/ versus /uu/ and /o/ versus /oo/, and there are 13 current use kanji with alternative pronunciations that differ only in this way. There are 2 others that show both this difference and the voiced/voiceless difference. There are also 5 cases of /(C)u/ versus /(C)yuu/, and we could include these as instances of both the short/long difference and the /C/ versus /Cy/ difference. See the examples in [32].

[32] /yu/ versus /yuu/ 'amusement'
/yu.saN/ 'outing'
/yuu.raN/ 'sightseeing'
/to/ versus /too/ 'climbing'
/to.zaN/ 'mountain climbing'
/too.daN/ 'going on the platform'
/go/ versus /koo/ 'after'
/go.sai/ 'second wife'
/koo.haN/ 'second half'
/ru/ versus /ryuu/ 'staying'
/ru.su/ 'absence from home'
/ryuu.gaku/ 'study abroad'

The last relationship I will mention is /e/ versus /a/. There are 13 current use kanji with alternative pronunciations that differ only in this way, and there are 3 more that show the voiced/voiceless relationship in addition. There is also 1 that shows both the /e/ versus /a/ relationship and the nasal/obstruent relationship. The examples in [33] are illustrations.

[33] /ke/ versus /ka/ 'house'
/ke.rai/ 'servant'
/ka.ǰi/ 'housework'
/geN/ versus /gaN/ 'origin'
/geN.so/ '(chemical) element'
/gaN.so/ 'founder'
/gecu/ versus /gacu/ 'month'
/rai.gecu/ 'next month'
/iči.gacu/ 'January'

/sei/ versus /sai/ 'year'
/sei.bo/ 'year-end'
/sai.macu/ 'year-end'
/bei/ versus /mai/ 'rice'
/bei.ka/ 'rice price'
/haku.mai/ 'polished rice'

11.4.3 Morphemic Relationships

I now turn to the question of whether alternative Sino-Japanese pronunciations of a kanji should be treated as allomorphs of a single morpheme. I will first consider the four criteria that Martin (1952:72–73) gives for assigning such pronunciations to separate morphemes. I will use the following abbreviations: G = go-on, K = kan-on, P = popular pronunciation (section 11.4.1).

The first of Martin's criteria is the occurrence of both of two alternative pronunciations as independent words. In some cases, there is an obvious semantic distinction between such words. For example, the same kanji is used for /goku/ (G), an adverb meaning 'extremely, very', and for /kyoku/ (K), a noun meaning 'extreme, pole'. The semantic distinction between /ji/ (G) 'earth, ground' and /či/ (K) 'earth, ground' is not so clear, but each has a range of extended meanings quite different from the other. According to the entries in Shinmura (1969), /ji/ has extended meanings such as 'background' and 'actuality', whereas /či/ has extended meanings such as 'place' and 'territory'. To qualify as allomorphs of the same morpheme, two forms must be in noncontrastive distribution. When alternative pronunciations of a kanji occur as semantically distinct, independent words, they obviously contrast.

Martin's second criterion is the occurrence of two alternative pronunciations as elements of longer words that are HOMOGRAPHS (Lyons 1968:39–40). Semantically distinct two-morpheme Sino-Japanese homographs in which the pronunciation of only one of the two kanji differs would be clear cases of contrast, but such examples are very difficult to find. Martin (1952:72) cites /iči.niči/ (G.G) versus /iči.ǰicu/ (G.K) 'one day' and /šo.geN/ (K.K) versus /čo.geN/ (P.K) 'preface', but according to the definitions in Shinmura (1969), there is no clear semantic difference in either pair.

Cases in which the pronunciations of both kanji differ are relatively common, and some of these involve obvious semantic distinctions. For example, the same two kanji are used for /niN.tei/ (G.K) 'personal appearance' and for /ǰiN.tai/ (K.G) 'human body'. As Martin (1952:72) points out, it is possible in cases like this to say that the alternative pronunciations of one kanji contrast while those of the other kanji are allomorphs, but the choice is completely arbitrary. In his words, "the burden of distributional contrast falls equally on each pair [of pronunciations]."

In other homographs of this kind, there is no apparent semantic distinction. For example, /naN.nyo/ (G.G) 'male and female' and /daN.jo/ (K.K) 'male and female' seem to be synonymous. These two words are not interchangeable in compounds, such as /roo.nyaku + naN.nyo/ 'young and old, male and female' and /daN.jo + doo.keN/ 'equal rights for both sexes', and Masuda (1974) marks /naN.nyo/ as "literary," but they do not seem to contrast.

Martin's third criterion is a consistent semantic difference between alternative pronunciations. In some cases, two pronunciations that show such a consistent difference never actually contrast. For example, there is a kanji with the two Sino-Japanese pronunciations /i/ (G/K) and /eki/ (K). This character is used for the independent word /eki/ 'divination' but not for any independent word /i/. There do not seem to be any examples of contrast in two-morpheme Sino-Japanese words either, but /eki/ consistently means 'change, exchange, divination', while /i/ consistently means 'ease'. See the examples in [34].

[34] /eki.ša/ 'fortune teller'
/fu.eki/ 'immutability'
/boo.eki/ 'trade'
/yoo.i/ 'ease'
/aN.i/ 'easygoing'
/kaN.i/ 'simplicity'

We saw in section 11.4.1 that some alternative pronunciations go back to separate morphemes in the original Chinese, and this is the case with /i/ versus /eki/ (Karlgren 1923:82). According to the entry in Suzuki et al. (1975), the original meaning of the kanji was 'chameleon'. Since chameleons were used in divination, and since they change color, the meanings of /eki/ are plausible developments. The meaning of /i/ is ascribed to the fact that chameleons change color easily.

I should mention that alternative Sino-Japanese pronunciations that contrast in some examples do not necessarily show the semantic difference consistently. In other words, it is quite possible for alternative pronunciations to satisfy either or both of Martin's first two criteria without satisfying the third. For example, we saw above that /goku/ 'extremely, very' and /kyoku/ 'extreme, pole' contrast as independent words, but they are synonymous in /goku.šo/ 'extreme heat' and /kyoku.roN/ 'extreme argument'.

The last of Martin's criteria is a phonological similarity between one alternative Sino-Japanese pronunciation of a kanji and a semantically similar but orthographically distinct morpheme. For example, a kanji meaning 'emperor' has the alternative Sino-Japanese pronunciations /oo/ (G), as in /oo.ji/ 'Imperial prince', and /koo/ (K), as in /koo.kyo/ 'Imperial Palace'. There is also a kanji meaning 'king' with the Sino-Japanese pronunciation /oo/ (G/K), and Martin (1952:76, n. 36) suggests that speakers may identify /oo/ 'emperor' with /oo/ 'king' rather than with /koo/ 'emperor'. This is certainly possible, although I know of no real evidence. Another point of resemblance in this particular case is that both /oo/ 'emperor' and /oo/ 'king' occur with liaison (section 11.3). For example, as we saw in [27], /teN.noo/ 'Emperor' is written with the kanji for 'emperor', and /šiN.noo/ 'Imperial prince' is written with the kanji for 'king'.

When none of these four criteria applies, Martin (1952:72) treats alternative Sino-Japanese pronunciations of a kanji as allomorphs. The problem with this treatment is that the alternations are completely unsystematic. On the one hand, the phonological relationships between the allomorphs are unpredictable. I considered some of the more common patterns in section 11.4.2, but the fact remains that given a Sino-Japanese pronunication of a kanji, there is no way to predict what other Sino-Japanese pronunciations, if any, it may have. On the other hand, even if we know what the alternative pronunciations are, there is no way to predict which will occur in any given case. As Martin puts it, "no alternant is predictable from another, except by a specific list of words in which each morph occurs."

Alternative Sino-Japanese pronunciations are orthographically identical, of course, but so are other pronunciations. For example, the kanji meaning 'outside' that is used for /ge/ (G), as in /ge.ka/ 'surgery', and for /gai/ (K), as in /gai.koku/ 'foreign country', is also used to write native Japanese /soto/ 'outside' and /hoka/ 'other'. There is an understandable temptation to identify all these pronunciations as allomorphs of a single morpheme (Martin 1972:89), but in general, orthographic identity is not a sufficient reason for doing so.

Thus, in spite of the fact that I have included this discussion of alternative Sino-Japanese pronunciations in a chapter on alternations, I find it more reasonable to treat all such pronunciations as separate morphemes. In some cases, of course, the morphemes will be virtually synonymous. This treatment applies even to examples like /šicu/~/šiQ/ versus /šuu/ (section 11.2.1), where the alternative pronunciations are due to inconsistent development of Chinese syllable-final /p/. As the examples in [13] show, there is no way to predict whether any given word will have /šicu/~/šiQ/ or /šuu/.

My feeling is that liaison alternants (section 11.3) are also better treated as separate morphemes, but all of these questions deserve more careful study.

Chapter *12*

VERB MORPHOLOGY

12.1 BACKGROUND

Japanese is sometimes described as an AGGLUTINATIVE or AGGLUTINATING language (Hughes 1962:96, Lehmann 1983:79, 151). According to Lehmann (1962:51), it was August von Schlegel who in 1818 first proposed the familiar morphology-based classification in which agglutinative languages are one type. The traditional definition, however, includes two distinct properties that do not necessarily go together (Lyons 1968:188–189). One of these is that each morph represents only one semantic unit. In other words, ideally, we do not find cases of what Hockett (1947:333) labels a PORTMANTEAU MORPH. A portmanteau morph is a phonological sequence that cannot be analyzed into smaller units in terms of form but nonetheless has two or more distinct components in terms of semantics. Matthews (1972:66) illustrates with Latin **fer** + **a** + **r** 'I will be carried', the final **r** of which can be analyzed as containing three morphemes: first person, singular, and passive.

The other property of agglutinative languages is that morphs are simply stuck together ("agglutinated"); ideally, the boundaries between morphs are clear, and there is no allomorphy (Lounsbury 1953:379). Sapir (1921:137–138) calls this kind of word formation JUXTAPOSING and contrasts it with FUSING. He gives *good* + *ness* as an example of juxtaposing and *dep* + *th* as an example of fusing. The fusion in *dep* + *th*, of course, involves only allomorphy (/dip/~/dɛp/).

Matthews (1974:103–104) gives examples of fusion from Turkish in which the boundaries between morphs are obscure. The form /alaǰa:z/ 'we will take', for instance, contains the verb root /al/, a future suffix, and a first-person plural suffix. In other contexts, the future suffix appears as /aǰak/ (cf. /al + aǰak + sɨn/ 'you (singular) will take'), and the first-person plural suffix appears as /ɨz/ (cf. /al + ɨr + ɨz/ 'we take'). In /alaǰa:z/, however, no division will yield either /aǰak/ or /ɨz/, and it is not clear just where the future suffix ends and the first-person plural suffix begins. Anttila (1972:310–315) provides a good, concise history of this kind of morphological typology.

While no language is exclusively any one type in terms of this traditional classification, Japanese morphology certainly tends to be agglutinative. The two properties involved in agglutination, however, do not correlate very well. Portmanteau morphs are rare, and the only examples in the data we will consider here are the negative volitional suffix /mai/ (Martin 1952:63, n. 28) and the negative imperative suffix /na/. Allomorphy, on the other hand, is not at all uncommon, and it is particularly characteristic of verb morphology. There are very few irregular verb forms, and this chapter will deal only with regular verbs. The discussion will concentrate on the eleven formations listed in [1], and I will use these labels throughout.

[1] a. NEGATIVE (informal nonpast negative)
     b. CAUSATIVE (informal nonpast affirmative causative)
     c. VOLITIONAL (can also be hortative)
     d. NEGATIVE VOLITIONAL (can also be negative probability)
     e. CONTINUATIVE
     f. PAST (informal past affirmative)
     g. NONPAST (informal nonpast affirmative; the citation form)
     h. NEGATIVE IMPERATIVE
     i. CONDITIONAL
     j. POTENTIAL (informal nonpast affirmative potential)
     k. IMPERATIVE

I give the forms of eleven verbs in [2]–[12] and these examples illustrate the full range of allomorphy.

[2]	'look at'				
	a. /minai/	d. /mimai/	h. /miruna/
	b. /misaseru/	e. /mi/	i. /mireba/
	c. /miyoo/	f. /mita/	j. /mirareru/
		g. /miru/	k. /miro/

[3]	'eat'				
	a. /tabenai/	d. /tabemai/	h. /taberuna/
	b. /tabesaseru/	e. /tabe/	i. /tabereba/
	c. /tabeyoo/	f. /tabeta/	j. /taberareru/
		g. /taberu/	k. /tabero/

[4] *'buy'*
a. /kawanai/
b. /kawaseru/
c. /kaoo/

d. /kaumai/
e. /kai/
f. /kaQta/
g. /kau/

h. /kauna/
i. /kaeba/
j. /kaeru/
k. /kae/

[5] *'write'*
a. /kakanai/
b. /kakaseru/
c. /kakoo/

d. /kakumai/
e. /kaki/
f. /kaita/
g. /kaku/

h. /kakuna/
i. /kakeba/
j. /kakeru/
k. /kake/

[6] *'sniff'*
a. /kaganai/
b. /kagaseru/
c. /kagoo/

d. /kagumai/
e. /kagi/
f. /kaida/
g. /kagu/

h. /kaguna/
i. /kageba/
j. /kageru/
k. /kage/

[7] *'lend'*
a. /kasanai/
b. /kasaseru/
c. /kasoo/

d. kasumai/
e. /kaši/
f. /kašita/
g. /kasu/

h. /kasuna/
i. /kaseba/
j. /kaseru/
k. /kase/

[8] *'win'*
a. /katanai/
b. /kataseru/
c. /katoo/

d. /kacumai/
e. /kači/
f. /kaQta/
g. /kacu/

h. /kacuna/
i. /kateba/
j. /kateru/
k. /kate/

[9] *'die'*
a. /šinanai/
b. /šinaseru/
c. /šinoo/

d. /šinumai/
e. /šini/
f. /šiNda/
g. /šinu/

h. /šinuna/
i. /šineba/
j. /šineru/
k. /šine/

[10] *'call'*
a. /yobanai/
b. /yobaseru/
c. /yoboo/

d. /yobumai/
e. /yobi/
f. /yoNda/
g. /yobu/

h. /yobuna/
i. /yobeba/
j. /yoberu/
k. /yobe/

[11] *'read'*
a. /yomanai/
b. /yomaseru/
c. /yomoo/

d. /yomumai/
e. /yomi/
f. /yoNda/
g. /yomu/

h. /yomuna/
i. /yomeba/
j. /yomeru/
k. /yome/

[12] *'approach'*
a. /yoranai/
b. /yoraseru/
c. /yoroo/

d. /yorumai/
e. /yori/
f. /yoQta/
g. /yoru/

h. /yoruna/
i. /yoreba/
j. /yoreru/
k. /yore/

12.2 TRADITIONAL JAPANESE GRAMMAR

12.2.1 School Grammar

The grammatical system taught in Japanese schools treats verb forms in the modern language with categories developed for classical Japanese (Miller 1967: 308–328). Although there are disagreements among Japanese scholars over many points of detail (Tsukishima 1964:101–180), outlines produced to help secondary students study for exams present a fixed system. The description that follows is based on the relevant sections of Nichieisha (1952), a typical study aid of this type.

12.2.2 The Six-Stem System

The traditional treatment analyzes verb forms into stems and suffixes, and each verb is said to have six stems. To illustrate, I will first consider the forms of /yomu/ 'read' listed in [11].

The negative /yomanai/ [11a] is analyzed as the stem /yoma/ and the suffix /nai/. (Although /nai/ itself is analyzed as a stem /na/ and a nonpast ending /i/, /nai/ serves as the citation form and will suffice for present purposes.) The causative /yomaseru/ [11b] is also analyzed as containing the stem /yoma/, and the suffix in this case is /seru/. (Like /nai/, /seru/ is itself morphologically complex, but again, this is the citation form.) This stem is traditionally called the INDEFINITE FORM (**mizenkei**). The volitional /yomoo/ [11c] is also analyzed as containing the indefinite stem, but the phonological change /au/ > /oo/ (section 7.1) has obscured the parallel. To maintain the tradition, school grammars simply say that the indefinite stem has two different forms in the modern language. Thus, /yomoo/ consists of the stem /yomo/ and the suffix /o/.

The continuative /yomi/ [11e] is analyzed as an unsuffixed stem traditionally called the CONJUNCTIONAL FORM (**ren'yōkei**). The past /yoNda/ [11f] is also analyzed as containing the conjunctional stem, but here again a phonological change (/yomita/ > /yoNda/; see section 7.1) has destroyed the parallel. In this case, too, school grammars say that the conjunctional stem has two different shapes, and they analyze /yoNda/ as the stem /yoN/ and the suffix /da/.

The nonpast /yomu/ [11g] is the citation form and is analyzed as an unsuffixed stem traditionally called the FINAL FORM (**shūshikei**). The negative imperative /yomuna/ [11h] and the negative volitional /yomumai/ [11d] both contain the final stem, with /na/ and /mai/ as suffixes.

The fourth traditional stem is called the ATTRIBUTIVE FORM (**rentaikei**), but since the distinction between the final and attributive stems has disappeared in modern Japanese, tradition is the only reason for maintaining it.

The conditional /yomeba/ [11i] is analyzed as the stem /yome/ and the suffix /ba/. This stem is traditionally called the HYPOTHETICAL FORM (**kateikei**). The potential /yomeru/ [11j] also appears to contain the hypothetical stem, but it is not analyzed this way for reasons that will become clear below (section 12.2.5.1).

The imperative /yome/ [11k] is analyzed as an unsuffixed stem traditionally called the IMPERATIVE FORM (**meireikei**). The imperative stem of this verb is identical to the hypothetical stem, but this is not true for all verbs. The irregular honorific verb /oQšaru/ 'say', for example, has the conditional /oQšareba/ and the imperative /oQšai/. Thus, there is still motivation in the modern language for maintaining the distinction.

According to the table in Nichieisha (1952:34), each of the verb stems is itself complex, consisting of a root followed by a suffix. This analysis of the stems of /yomu/ is shown in [13].

[13]	*Root*	*Suffix*
Indefinite (1)	/yo/	/ma/
Indefinite (2)	/yo/	/mo/
Conjunctional (1)	/yo/	/mi/
Conjunctional (2)	/yo/	/N/
Final (and attributive)	/yo/	/mu/
Hypothetical	/yo/	/me/
Imperative	/yo/	/me/

12.2.3 One-Row and Five-Row Verbs

Regular verbs in modern Japanese are traditionally classified as ONE-ROW (**ichidan**) or FIVE-ROW (**godan**) verbs. These names refer to the kana syllabary, which is ordinarily displayed in the format shown in [14]. (The Japanese right-to-left orientation has been reversed, and the letters are spelled phonemically.) The other possible syllables in Japanese are written with diacritics or with digraphs. Each column in [14] is called a **gyō**, and each row is called a **dan**. Aside from /N/, which is a later addition to the original format (section 5.1.2), the syllables in each column generally have the same consonant. (Phonemic splits have altered this pattern before /i/ and /u/ in some cases.) The syllables in each row have the same vowel. The syllables /ka ki ku ke ko/ can be referred to as the "ka-column" and the syllables /o ko so to no ho mo yo ro/ as the "o-row." The syllables listed as suffixes in the stems of /yomu/ in [13] include all five syllables in the **ma**-column, that is, all five rows are represented. Thus, /yomu/ is called a "five-row verb." The verb /taberu/ 'eat', on the other hand, is a one-row verb. To see why, we must consider the forms listed in [3].

[14]	a	ka	sa	ta	na	ha	ma	ya	ra	wa	N
	i	ki	ši	či	ni	hi	mi		ri		
	u	ku	su	cu	nu	fu	mu	yu	ru		
	e	ke	se	te	ne	he	me		re		
	o	ko	so	to	no	ho	mo	yo	ro		

The negative /tabenai/ [3a], the causative /tabesaseru/ [3b], the volitional /tabeyoo/ [3c], and the negative volitional /tabemai/ [3d] are all analyzed as containing the indefinite stem /tabe/. In the traditional Japanese analysis, the suffixes added to one-row verb stems sometimes differ in shape from those added to five-row verb stems, and we have two examples here. The causative suffix is /saseru/ (cf. /seru/ in /yomaseru/), and the volitional suffix is /yoo/ (cf. /o/ in /yomoo/). Notice also that the negative volitional suffix /mai/ is added to the indefinite stem of a one-row verb as opposed to the final stem of a five-row verb. The potential /taberareru/ [3j] is also analyzed as containing the indefinite stem and the suffix /rareru/.

The continuative /tabe/ [3e] is analyzed as the unsuffixed conjunctional stem, and the past /tabeta/ [3f] contains this stem and the suffix /ta/. The indefinite and conjunctional stems are always identical for one-row verbs, and apparently the only reason for saying that the continuative and the past involve the conjunctional stem is to make one-row verbs parallel to five-row verbs. The potential /taberareru/ [3j] is analyzed as containing the indefinite stem and not the conjunctional stem because the suffix /rareru/ is also used to express the passive of a one-row verb. The passive of a five-row verb is analyzed as the indefinite stem followed by the suffix /reru/, and the passive of /yomu/ 'read', for example, is /yomareru/. The passive and the potential are distinct in five-row verbs, but since the passive involves the indefinite stem, parallelism demands that the passive, and therefore the potential, of a one-row verb be analyzed as containing the indefinite stem. The reason for analyzing the negative potential /tabemai/ [3d] as containing the indefinite stem seems to be that the irregular verb /kuru/ 'come' has distinct indefinite and conjunctional stems and adds /mai/ to the indefinite stem.

The nonpast /taberu/ [3g] is analyzed as the unsuffixed final stem, and the negative imperative /taberuna/ [3h] contains this stem and the suffix /na/. As in five-row verbs, the traditional attributive stem is always identical to the final stem.

The conditional /tabereba/ [3i] is analyzed as the hypothetical stem /tabere/ and the suffix /ba/. The imperative /tabero/ [3k] is analyzed as the unsuffixed imperative stem.

Like the five-row verbs stems, each of the one-row verb stems is itself a combination of a root and a suffix (Nichieisha 1952:34). The analysis of the stems of /taberu/ is shown in [15]. The initial syllable of each suffix in [15] contains the same vowel, that is, only one row of the syllabary is represented. All one-row verbs have either /i/ or /e/ in this position. Among the verbs whose forms are listed in [2]–[12], /miru/ 'look at' [2] and /taberu/ 'eat' [3] are one-row verbs, and all the others are five-row verbs.

[15]	*Root*	*Suffix*
Indefinite	/ta/	/be/
Conjunctional	/ta/	/be/

Final (and attributive)	/ta/	/beru/
Hypothetical	/ta/	/bere/
Imperative	/ta/	/bero/

12.2.4 The Writing System and Phonotactics

At this point it is difficult to suppress the urge to "fix" many of the morphemic segmentations in the traditional analysis. Miller (1967:314) attributes at least some of the seemingly bizarre divisions to the syllabic writing system.

> The traditional Japanese approach has limited itself to statements about syllables which can be written in the **kana** writing system, which allows no forms with syllable-final consonants other than the [mora] nasal. Hence it has been unable to arrive at a scientifically acceptable description of the language, which would require statements involving forms with final consonants.

In the case of study aids, of course, it would probably just confuse students to talk in terms of components that cannot be written in the native orthography. But what we have here is not simply a pedagogically useful description that deviates from a "correct" or "scientific" description. The kana syllabary cannot represent syllables with final consonants other than the mora nasal and the mora obstruent (which Miller forgets), because such syllables violate the phonotactic pattern of Japanese. In other words, since no word can contain such syllables, there is no reason to have letters for them. Hale (1973) presents evidence which suggests that there is at least some reason to doubt that ordinary speakers can analyze words into morphemes that are phonotactically anomalous, and I will return to this question in section 12.5.

There are some peculiarities of the traditional Japanese analysis that we cannot attribute to the writing system or the phonotactic pattern. The analysis of the stems of /yomu/ 'read' in [13] assigns the invariant portion /yo/ to the root, and the same thing happens with all five-row verbs. The analysis of the stems of /taberu/ 'eat' in [15], however, assigns only /ta/ to the root, with the result that every suffix begins with /be/. This approach seems even stranger when a shorter one-row verb like /miru/ 'look at' [2] is analyzed. In this case, every suffix begins with /mi/, and there is nothing left over for the root. The only reason I can imagine for treating one-row verbs in this fashion is to avoid having to say that the indefinite and conjunctional stems have zero suffixes.

12.2.5 Suffix Variants

12.2.5.1 Stem-Forming Suffixes

Even a cursory glance at the forms listed in [2]–[12] reveals that the suffixes in the traditional Japanese analysis do not in general have constant shapes. I will first consider the stem-forming suffixes and then other suffixes.

The analysis in [15] carries over without substantial modification to all one-row verbs. The general pattern for stem-forming suffixes is shown in [16].

[16] Indefinite   /(C)V/
Conjunctional   /(C)V/
Final   /(C)Vru/
Hypothetical   /(C)Vre/
Imperative   /(C)Vro/

As mentioned in section 12.2.3, the /V/ in these suffixes is always /i/ or /e/. The five-row verbs do not present such a simple picture, and it will be convenient to treat each stem in turn.

The indefinite (1) suffix always has the form /Ca/. As [4a]–[12a] illustrate, the consonant can be any of the following: /w k g s t n b m r/. The indefinite (2) suffix usually has the form /Co/, but if the indefinite (1) suffix is /wa/, the indefinite (2) suffix is just /o/, as in /ka + o + o/ [4c]. This is the result of phonological changes that altered /ɸ/ to /w/ intervocalically and then eliminated /w/ everywhere except before /a/ (section 7.1).

As [4e]–[12e] show, the conjunctional (1) suffix of a five-row verb usually has the form /Ci/, with the same consonant as in the indefinite (1). Because of the /ɸ/ > /w/ > ∅ changes, if the indefinite (1) suffix is /wa/, the conjunctional (1) suffix is just /i/, as in /ka + i/ [4e]. In addition, the regular changes of /s t/ to /š č/ before /i/ appear in /ka + ši/ [7e] and /ka + či/ [8e].

The conjunctional (2) suffix is more difficult to describe because it shows the effects of the onbin changes (section 7.1). The conjunctional (2) stems of the nine five-row verbs in [4]–[12] are listed in [17] along with the indefinite (1) stems. In general, if the indefinite (1) suffix is /wa/, /ta/, or /ra/, then the conjunctional (2) suffix is /Q/; if /ka/ or /ga/, then /i/; if /sa/, then /ši/; and if /na/, /ba/, or /ma/, then /N/. The only five-row verbs for which two distinct conjunctional suffixes are unnecessary are those with the indefinite (1) suffix /sa/, since these are the only ones whose past forms were left unaffected by the onbin changes.

[17]   *Indefinite (1) Stem*   *Conjunctional (2) Stem*
/ka + wa/   /ka + Q/
/ka + ka/   /ka + i/
/ka + ga/   /ka + i/
/ka + sa/   /ka + ši/
/ka + ta/   /ka + Q/
/ši + na/   /ši + N/
/yo + ba/   /yo + N/
/yo + ma/   /yo + N/
/yo + ra/   /yo + Q/

As [4g]–[12g] and [4i]–[12i] show, the final and hypothetical suffixes of a five-row verb are usually /Cu/ and /Ce/, respectively, with the same consonant as the indefinite (1) suffix. When the indefinite (1) suffix is /wa/, of course, the final and hypothetical suffixes are just /u/ and /e/, and the regular change of /t/ to /c/ before /u/ appears in /ka + cu/ [8g].

As mentioned in section 12.2.2, the potential forms of five-row verbs seem to contain the hypothetical stem, but they are not analyzed this way. We are now in a position to see why. The potential of a five-row verb is itself a one-row verb and can therefore be conjugated, although the imperative is semantically anomalous and traditionally considered nonexistent. Consider, for example, /yomeru/ 'can read' [11j], the potential of /yomu/ 'read'. The negative of this potential verb is /yomenai/, the past is /yometa/, the conditional is /yomereba/, and the nonpast is /yomeru/ itself. In terms of the traditional analysis, the indefinite and conjunctional stems are /yome/, the final stem is /yomeru/, and the hypothetical stem is /yomere/. The stem-forming suffixes are /me/, /meru/, and /mere/, and the root is /yo/. Consequently, there is nothing left over to label the "potential morpheme," and Nichieisha (1952:35) simply sidesteps the problem by giving a few examples of potentials without analyzing them into morphemes.

12.2.5.2 Other Suffixes

Some of the suffixes added to stems in the traditional Japanese analysis show allomorphy, but others have constant shapes. The negative suffix /nai/, the negative imperative suffix /na/, and the conditional suffix /ba/, for example, are all invariant. (We will see in section 12.3.3 that the negative imperative is not always treated as a morphological formation.) The negative volitional suffix /mai/ is also invariant, although it is added to the final stem of a five-row verb and the indefinite stem of a one-row verb. There are also several invariant suffixes that appear after the conjunctional (1) stem. Among these are the polite suffix /masu/ and the desiderative suffix /tai/ (both morphologically complex). Others are /kata/ (e.g., /yomi + kata/ 'way of reading'), /nagara/ (e.g., /yomi + nagara/ 'while reading'), and /soo/ (e.g., /yomi + soo/ 'looks as if [subject] will read'). In addition, the conjunctional (1) stem is used in compounding (e.g., /yomi + kiru/ 'read through') and can be used nominally. (As we saw in section 8.3.1, when the conjunctional (1) stem of an accented verb is established as a noun, there is sometimes an accent shift. For example, /hanáši/ is the conjunctional (1) stem of /hanásu/ 'speak', but the derived noun is /hanašî/ 'story'.)

Three suffixes that differ depending on verb class are listed in [18]. The allomorphy of the passive suffix is parallel to that of the causative suffix, and both are added to the indefinite (1) stem. The volitional suffix is added to the indefinite (2) stem.

[18]	*One-Row Verbs*	*Five-Row Verbs*
Causative	/saseru/	/seru/
Passive	/rareru/	/reru/
Volitional	/yoo/	/o/

The remaining suffixes with variants are all historically related to the past suffix /ta/~/da/. These include suffixes for the gerund (/te/~/de/) and the ALTER-NATIVE (Bloch 1946a:6) (/tari/~/dari/), and the voicing alternation does not depend on verb class. As [2f]–[12f] show, the alternants with /d/ occur only after a conjunctional (2) stem that ends in /N/ or /i/. In the case of /i/, the consonant in the other stem-forming suffixes must be /g/ and not /k/. Thus, /kaku/ 'write' has the past /ka + i + ta/ [5f], gerund /ka + i + te/, and alternative /ka + i + tari/, while /kagu/ 'sniff' has the past /ka + i + da/ [6f], gerund /ka + i + de/, and alternative /ka + i + dari/.

12.3   AN AMERICAN DESCRIPTIVIST ANALYSIS

12.3.1   Background

Thorough American descriptivist work on Japanese was a direct result of World War II, and the leading figure in this research was Bernard Bloch. After the war Bloch published a series of articles on Japanese, which are collected in Miller (1970). The description in this section is based on Bloch's analysis of the forms in [2]–[12]. As we have seen, some of the "suffixes" in these forms are themselves morphologically complex, but I will continue to cite them unanalyzed unless such analysis is directly relevant. As a result, my citation forms will sometimes differ from those in the references.

12.3.2   Vowel Verbs and Consonant Verbs

There are two obvious differences between the American descriptivist analysis and the traditional Japanese analysis. First, in the American descriptivist treatment, one-row verbs have vowel-final stems, and five-row verbs have consonant-final stems. Bloch (1946a:7) calls the two classes VOWEL VERBS and CONSONANT VERBS, and I will adopt these terms in this section. The second difference is that, in the American descriptivist account, each verb stem is monomorphemic, that is, it does not consist of a root plus a stem-forming suffix.

The stem of any vowel verb has a constant shape and always ends in /i/ or /e/. For example, the stem of /miru/ 'look at' is /mi/, and the stem of /taberu/ 'eat' is /tabe/. Most consonant verb stems have two allomorphs (Bloch 1946a: 9–10). One is identical to the traditional conjunctional (2) stem (section 12.2.5.1) and appears before the past suffix (and other suffixes historically related to the past; see section 12.2.5.2). The other is identical to any of the other traditional stems minus the final vowel. For example, the two stem allomorphs of /yomu/ 'read' are /yoN/, as in the past /yoN + da/ [11f], and /yom/, as in the negative /yom + anai/ [11a].

A verb with a citation form ending in /Vu/ has three stem allomorphs. For example, the stem of /kau/ 'buy' is /kaQ/ in the past /kaQ + ta/ [4f], /kaw/ in the negative /kaw + anai/ [4a], and /ka/ in the conditional /ka + eba/ [4i]. In general, a verb stem that ends in /Vw/ before /a/ ends in just /V/ before other vowels; this pattern is a reflection of the phonological change /ɸ/ > /w/ > Ø (sections 7.1 and 12.2.5.1). Verbs like /kau/ are classified as consonant verbs because even though one stem allomorph ends in a vowel, they take the same suffix allomorphs as other consonant verbs.

12.3.3 Suffixes

Since the American descriptivist treatment does not include stem-forming suffixes corresponding to those in the traditional Japanese account, the suffixes mentioned here all correspond to those labelled "other suffixes" in section 12.2.5.2. One striking feature of the American descriptivist analysis is that none of the suffixes in the forms in [2]–[12] has an invariant shape. As Bloch (1946a:7) says, vowel verb stems "are followed by one set of endings and [consonant verb stems] are followed by a different set." The suffix allomorphs in the forms in [2]–[12] are listed in [19].

[19]	*Vowel Verbs*	*Consonant Verbs*
Negative	/nai/	/anai/
Causative	/saseru/	/aseru/
Volitional	/yoo/	/oo/
Negative volitional	/mai/~/rumai/	/umai/
Continuative	Ø	/i/
Past	/ta/	/ta/~/da/
Nonpast	/ru/	/u/
Negative imperative	/runa/(?)	/una/(?)
Conditional	/reba/	/eba/
Potential	/rareru/	/eru/
Imperative	/ro/	/e/

Bloch (1946a:21) says that the negative volitional suffix has two alternants in free variation after a vowel verb stem. Thus, the negative volitional of /taberu/ 'eat' can be /tabe + rumai/ as well as /tabe + mai/ [3d]. I ignored the longer forms like /taberumai/ in my discussion of the traditional Japanese analysis (section 12.2), because prescriptive accounts like Nichieisha (1952:67) condemn them as errors.

Bloch (1946b:44) treats the negative imperative not as a morphological formation but as a syntactic construction in which /na/ is a sentence particle of prohibition following the nonpast form of a verb. The reason, presumably, is that a negative imperative can always be segmented into a sequence identical to the nonpast followed by /na/. In terms of distribution, this /na/ has no more freedom of occurrence than the affirmative imperative suffix. For any given verb, there is only one form that can precede /na/ or /ro/~/e/, and the only thing that can follow either formation is the emphatic sentence particle /yo/. The only distinction is that the stem allomorph in the affirmative imperative of a consonant verb is not identical to any word. The negative volitional could also be treated as the non-past followed by a particle if the longer form (e.g., /taberumai/) is used for vowel verbs. The existence of the shorter form (e.g., /tabemai/) apparently led Bloch to reject this analysis.

In traditional Japanese grammar, /na/ is in fact analyzed as a particle (**joshi**) (Nichieisha 1952:49), while /mai/ is analyzed as an inflected suffix (**jodōshi**) (Nichieisha 1952:80). The motivation for this distinction, however, is transparently historical. The putative cognate of /mai/ in classical Japanese was morphologically complex and inflected like an adjective (Ikeda 1975:65). The classical use of /na/, by contrast, was apparently identical to the modern use (Ikeda 1975:233). In the modern language, of course, /mai/ does not inflect any more than /na/ does.

I should mention in this connection that the final syllable /ba/ of conditionals is also traditionally classified as a particle, but this would certainly not have influenced Bloch to treat conditionals as syntactic constructions. In any event, I will continue to treat the negative imperative as a morphological formation, while acknowledging that its status is debatable. Semantically, there is no more reason to say that the negative imperative contains the nonpast than to say that the affirmative imperative does. It seems reasonable, therefore, to suggest /runa/ and /una/ as suffix allomorphs in the descriptivist framework.

12.3.4   The Past

As the forms in [19] show, the past morpheme always appears as /ta/ after a vowel verb stem. After a consonant verb stem, however, it is sometimes /ta/ and sometimes /da/. We have already seen in section 12.3.2 that in consonant verbs, the past suffix and historically related suffixes are added to a different stem allomorph than other suffixes. The negative and the past of each consonant stem verb in [4]−[12] are listed in [20] to illustrate the allomorphy. In general, if the stem allomorph in the negative ends in /w/, /t/, or /r/, then the stem allomorph in the past ends in /Q/ instead; if /k/ or /g/, then /i/; if /s/, then /ši/; and if /n/, /b/, or /m/, then /N/.

[20]   *Negative*   *Past*
       /kaw + anai/   /kaQ + ta/
       /kak + anai/   /kai + ta/
       /kag + anai/   /kai + da/
       /kas + anai/   /kaši + ta/
       /kat + anai/   /kaQ + ta/
       /šin + anai/   /šiN + da/
       /yob + anai/   /yoN + da/
       /yom + anai/   /yoN + da/
       /yor + anai/   /yoQ + ta/

The past suffix is /da/ after /N/ and after an /i/ that alternates with /g/ (but not an /i/ that alternates with /k/), and it is /ta/ elsewhere (section 12.2.5.2). Bloch (1946a:9) handles this by marking the last phoneme of some stem allomorphs with a diacritic and stating the stem alternations as in [21]. In his words, "The superior v means that the stopped endings [i.e., the past and historically relates suffixes] appear after these bases with a voiced stop **d** instead of t."

[21] /t/ ~ /Q/   /g/ ~ /iᵛ/

/r/ ~ /Q/   /b/ ~ /Nᵛ/

/w/ ~ /Q/   /m/ ~ /Nᵛ/

/s/ ~ /ši/   /n/ ~ /Nᵛ/

/k/ ~ /i/

The alternations of /t r w/ with /Q/ can be described as AUTOMATIC in any of the senses that Wells (1949) considers. If we take the stem allomorphs ending in /t r w/ as basic, we can "predict" the alternants that appear before the past morpheme. The only basic forms in Japanese that end in consonants in a descriptivist morphophonemic treatment like Martin's (1952) are consonant verb stems. The only consonant-initial suffixes added to these stems in Bloch's account are the past and its relatives. Assuming that the basic forms of these suffixes begin with /t/, we can say that whenever a sequence /tt/, /rt/, or /wt/ arises, it is automatically replaced with /Qt/. The alternations of /s/ with /ši/ and /k/ with /i/ are also automatic. The only way the sequences /st/ and /kt/ can arise is if a verb stem is combined with the past or a related suffix, and these sequences will always be replaced with /šit/ and /it/.

The question of automaticity is a little more complicated in the remaining cases, but these alternations are also automatic under any of the definitions that Wells considers. Juxtaposing basic forms creates the phonotactically inadmissible sequences /gt/, /bt/, /mt/, and /nt/. The replacements in these four cases illustrate what Wells (1949:109) calls RECIPROCAL CONDITIONING, that is, the two morphemes in each case automatically condition each other. An /i/ replaces a /g/ and an /N/ replaces a /b/, /m/, or /n/ before /t/. At the same time, /d/ replaces /t/ after any one of /g b m n/. The only way any of these sequences can arise is if the past or a related suffix is added to a consonant verb stem, so the changes are all predictable.

12.3.5 The Continuative in Longer Formations

All the suffixes listed in [19] except the past have one allomorph after vowel verb stems and another after consonant verb stems. One might propose parallel allomorphy to account for formations such as those in [22]. These examples involve the vowel verb /taberu/ 'eat' and the consonant verb /yomu/ 'read'. In the traditional Japanese analysis, these forms contain invariant suffixes added to the conjunctional (1) stem (section 12.2.5.2). A descriptivist might analyze the suffixes as having the allomorphs /masu/, /tai/, and /nagara/ after vowel verb stems and /imasu/, /itai/, and /inagara/ after consonant verb stems. Bloch (1946b:41, n. 22, 1946c:111), however, analyzes the forms in [22] as containing invariant suffixes added to the continuative form. Thus, for example, /yomitai/ consists of the stem /yom/ plus the continuative suffix /i/ plus the desiderative suffix /tai/.

[22] Polite   /tabemasu/   /yomimasu/
     Desiderative /tabetai/   /yomitai/
     'while V-ing' /tabenagara/   /yominagara/

As noted in section 12.2.5.2, the conjunctional (1) stem (= continuative form) not only takes a variety of suffixes but also occurs as the first element in compound verbs like /yomi + owaru/ 'finish reading' (cf. /owaru/ 'finish'). If such compounds are treated on the model of /masu/~/imasu/, etc., every verb which can appear as the second element in a compound will have two allomorphs, one with an initial /i/ and one without. Since a very large number of verbs do in fact occur as second elements, the resulting analysis is certainly not as neat as Bloch's treatment.

Another problem arises in connection with the automaticity of the alternations in the past forms. If the desiderative suffix has the allomorphs /tai/ and /itai/, and we take /tai/ as basic, sequences like /mt/ will have two sources: the desiderative and the past (as in /yom/ + /ta/). Since the result is /Nd/ in the past and /mit/ in the desiderative, we could no longer describe the alternations in the past forms as automatic. If we take /itai/ as basic, the /tai/ allomorph after vowel stem verbs will not be predictable by Wells's (1949:102–103) criteria. The sequence /V + i/ arises frequently, and the /i/ is not generally deleted. For example, /kaki/ 'persimmon' and /iro/ 'color' combine to form /kaki + iro/ 'persimmon color', not */kaki + ro/.

In Bloch's treatment, the continuative suffix is ∅~/i/. It seems to me that if ∅ is basic, the alternation is automatic in any of Wells's (1949) senses. When added to a consonant verb stem, the basic form ∅ will produce an inadmissible cluster if a suffix follows and an inadmissible final consonant if no suffix follows. If there were another morpheme with the basic form ∅ and an allomorph other than /i/ in such environments, the appearance of /i/ would be unpredictable, but there does not appear to be any need for such a morpheme. In short, Bloch's treatment avoids the problems caused by the alternative suggested above.

The only difficulty I see with Bloch's account is a semantic one. It does not seem unreasonable to argue that the meaning of the first element in a compound verb is something like the meaning of the continuative form. Thus, the identification of the /i/ in /yomiowaru/ 'finish reading' with the continuative suffix is plausible. The case is not so clear for /yomimasu/, /yomitai/, and /yominagara/, but the formal identity of /yomi/ with the continuative probably seemed compelling. One way to avoid the semantic issue might be to treat the /i/ added to consonant verb stems as meaningless, that is, as what Hockett (1947:236) calls an

EMPTY MORPH. Since the continuative of a vowel verb is identical to the stem, this idea has some obvious appeal.

The notion of an empty morph might even be extended to the negative forms. The initial /a/ in /anai/ could also be treated as a meaningless EPENTHETIC VOWEL (Sloat, Taylor, and Hoard 1978:118–119), the insertion of which is conditioned by the addition of the negative suffix to a consonant verb stem. The negative suffix itself would then be invariant /nai/. The disadvantage of this extension is that the choice of epenthetic vowel (/i/ or /a/) would then have to depend on which suffix is added.

12.4 A GENERATIVE ANALYSIS

12.4.1 Background

It is clear from the discussion so far that Japanese verb forms involve a good deal of allomorphy. Generative phonology tries to handle as much allomorphy as possible by setting up what Linell (1979:10) calls "morpheme-invariant" underlying forms and deriving surface forms by rules. The description in this section is based on McCawley (1968), the standard generative treatment of Japanese. Although there are differences in minor details, I think I have preserved the spirit of McCawley's analysis.

12.4.2 Underlying Stems

McCawley (1968:93–94) divides regular verbs into the same two classes as Bloch (section 12.3.2), that is, into those with stems ending in vowels and those with stems ending in consonants. Aside from phonetic details, the underlying form of a vowel verb stem is identical to its surface form. For example, the underlying stems of /miru/ 'look at' and /taberu/ 'eat' are //mi// and //tabe//. (As in section 5.3, I will use double slants in this section to distinguish underlying forms from ordinary phonemic transcriptions.) Except for those consonant verbs whose citation forms end in /Vu/ (e.g., /kau/ 'buy'), the underlying stem of any consonant verb ends in the consonant that appears before most suffixes. For example, the underlying stem of /yomu/ 'read' is //yom//.

As noted in section 12.3.2, verbs like /kau/ have three stem allomorphs: /ka/, /kaw/, and /kaQ/. The underlying form that McCawley (1968:94) proposes is //kap//, and to understand the motivation for this proposal, we will have to consider some additional information.

First, as we saw in section 11.2.1, there are alternations between /p/ and /h/. For example, a morpheme meaning 'news' appears as /hoo/ in /hoo.koku/ 'report' and as /poo/ in /deN.poo/ 'telegram'. McCawley suggests underlying //poo// and a rule that converts underlying //p// into /h/ when it is word-initial or intervocalic. Recent borrowings (e.g., /opera/ 'opera') and mimetic adverbs (e.g., /paku + paku/ 'chomp-chomp') must be exempt from this rule, and there are some exceptions in the Sino-Japanese vocabulary as well (McCawley 1968: 77–78), but it will certainly work in verb forms.

Second, aside from recent borrowings, /h/ rarely occurs except immediately after a morpheme boundary. Ignoring a small set of exceptions (McCawley 1968:79–80), we can have a rule that converts /h/ to /w/ except at the beginning of a morpheme. We then need a further rule to eliminate /w/ except before /a/, since it does not occur before other vowels (section 4.6.1).

Third, if the underlying form of the stem of /kau/ is //kap//, we can derive the past /kaQta/ by a consonant assimilation rule (section 12.4.4) that we need anyway (McCawley 1968:94). See the sample derivations in [23].

[23]

	Negative	*Past*
Underlying form	//kap + anai//	//kap + ta//
$p \rightarrow h / \left\{ \begin{matrix} V \\ \# \end{matrix} \right\} - V$	kah + anai	—
h → w / except + —	kaw + anai	—
w → ∅ / except — a	—	—
Consonant assimilation	—	kat + ta

	Imperative
Underlying form	//kap + e//
$p \rightarrow h / \left\{ \begin{matrix} V \\ \# \end{matrix} \right\} - V$	kah + e
h → w / except + —	kaw + e
w → ∅ / except — a	ka + e
Consonant assimilation	—

12.4.3 Underlying Suffixes

Given the stems described in section 12.4.2, several verb suffixes have a consonant after a vowel verb stem that is absent after a consonant verb stem. I list these suffixes in [24].

[24]

	Vowel Verbs	*Consonant Verbs*
Causative	/saseru/	/aseru/
Volitional	/yoo/	/oo/
Nonpast	/ru/	/u/
Negative imperative	/runa/	/una/
Conditional	/reba/	/eba/
Passive	/rareru/	/areru/
Potential	/reru/	/eru/

The potential suffix forms listed in [24] require some comment. The passive form of any verb can express potential meaning, but all verbs have a specifically potential form as well. Prescriptive treatments like Nichieisha (1952:35) recognize this potential form of consonant verbs but regard the parallel form of vowel verbs as incorrect usage. The potential forms listed in [2]–[12] reflect this prescriptive judgment. Bloch (1946c:102) also gives a distinct potential form for consonant verbs but not does mention the possibility for vowel verbs. McCawley (1968:98) says that /reru/ potentials of vowel verbs are restricted to informal speech, and this is doubtless true for educated speakers.

McCawley (1968:95) adopts the forms that appear after vowel verb stems as the underlying forms of the suffixes in [24]. He then proposes a rule to delete //s y r// in the environment C + —. The derivations of the nonpast /kau/ and the causative /kawaseru/ proceed as in [25].

[25] Underlying form
s,y,r → Ø / C + —
p→ h / $\begin{cases} V \\ \# \end{cases}$ — V
h→ w / except + —
w → Ø / except — a

//kap + ru//
kap + u
kah + u

kaw + u
ka + u

//kap + saseru//
kap + aseru
kah + aseru

kaw + aseru
—

In the negative and continuative forms, the endings after consonant verb stems have a vowel not present after vowel verb stems, as in [26]. McCawley (1968:97–98) simply says that after a consonant verb stem, /a/ is inserted before the negative suffix, and /i/ is inserted in the continuative and in compounds. He treats the desiderative (suffix /tai/) and the polite (suffix /masu/) as compounds, and presumably other forms beginning with a sequence identical to the continuative (sections 12.2.5.2 and 12.3.5) should be handled in parallel fashion. McCawley's account thus treats the extra vowels after consonant verb stems as epenthetic and not as part of the underlying morphemes. The inserted vowel, of course, depends on which suffix is involved; it is not predictable in terms of the phonological environment. For example, the negative of /yomu/ 'read' is /yomanai/ (from //yom + nai//), but 'while reading' is /yominagara/ (from //yom + nagara//). Also, the desiderative is /yomitai/ (from //yom + tai//), but the past is /yoNda/ (from //yom + ta//; see section 12.4.4). This is the same problem we encountered in our consideration of the parallel proposal in the descriptivist framework (section 12.3.5).

[26]

	Vowel Verbs	*Consonant Verbs*
Negative	/nai/	/anai/
Continuative	Ø	/i/

An alternative generative analysis would be to take //anai// and //i// as the underlying forms of the negative and continuative suffixes. This analysis would require vowel deletion rule to apply to vowel verbs, and this rule could not be something general like V → Ø/V(+)—, since /V(+)V/ sequences abound in Japanese (section 12.3.5). The rule would have to apply only when the environment vowel is in a verb stem. This alternative seems simpler than the epenthesis described above at first glance, but it has the same drawback as the parallel proposal in the descriptivist analysis (section 12.3.5). It would require us to say that every verb that can appear as the second element in a compound has an initial //i// in its underlying form. This seems needlessly messy, and I therefore agree with McCawley's choice of insertion rather than deletion.

There are only two cases in verb morphology that a generative analysis cannot easily account for with invariant underlying suffixes. One is the imperative, which McCawley (1968:98) treats as involving SUPPLETION (Hyman 1975:13). He says the underlying suffix is //ro// after vowel verb stems and //e// after consonant verb stems, and I see no sensible alternative to this. The other problematical case is the negative volitional. Presumably, the underlying suffix is //rumai//, but it must have the alternative underlying form //mai// after vowel verb stems (section 12.3.3).

12.4.4 The Past

McCawley (1968:96) proposes the underlying form //ta// for the past tense suffix, and simply adding /ta/ to vowel verb stems gives the required forms. Consonant verbs whose stems have underlying forms ending in //g b m n// appear in the past with final /da/. McCawley accounts for this with an assimilation rule that voices a consonant immediately following a voiced obstruent or a nasal. The partial derivations in [27] show the effects of this rule.

[27]	*'sniff'*	*'call'*
Underlying form	//kag + ta//	//yob + ta//
Voicing assimilation	kag + da	yob + da
	'read'	*'die'*
Underlying form	//yom + ta//	//sin + ta//
Voicing assimilation	yom + da	sin + da

This assimilation rule cannot be completely general, of course, since there are many /NC/ sequences in Sino-Japanese words and recent borrowings where the /C/ is voiceless (e.g., /hoN.kaN/ 'main building').

Another problem in the past forms of consonant verbs is the appearance of /i/ when the underlying stem ends in //k//, //g//, or //s//. McCawley (1968:96) gives a sequence of two rules to handle this problem. The first (spirantization) converts stem-final //k// or //g// to /h/ when an obstruent follows. The second (epenthesis) inserts /i/ between a fricative and an obstruent. Any /h/ that the first rule produces will eventually disappear, because the h → w and w → ∅ rules (section 12.4.2) apply. The derivations in [28] provide illustrations.

[28]	*'write'*	*'sniff'*	*'lend'*
Underlying form	//kak + ta//	//kag + ta//	//kas + ta//
Voicing assimilation	—	kag + da	—
Spirantization	kah + ta	kah + da	—
Epenthesis	kah + ita	kah + ida	kas + ita

| h → w | kaw + ita | kaw + ida | — |
| w → ∅ | ka + ita | ka + ida | — |

The change of stem-final //b// to a nasal is accomplished in two steps. First, a general assimilation rule requires consonant clusters to be HOMORGANIC (Sloat, Taylor, and Hoard 1978:30). (This is the independently needed rule I mentioned in section 12.4.2 in connection with stem-final //p//.) This rule changes stem-final //p b m// to /t d n/ in the past forms. Second, another rule changes the first consonant in a cluster to a nasal if it is voiced. See the derivations in [29]. As we saw in section 5.3, the phonemes /Q/ and /N/ do not appear in a generative treatment.

[29]

	'buy'	*'call'*	*'read'*
Underlying form	//kap + ta//	//yob + ta//	//yom + ta//
Voicing assimilation	—	yob + da	yom + da
Place assimilation	kat + ta	yod + da	yon + da
Nasalization	—	yon + da	—

The only remaining problem is stem-final //r//. McCawley (1968:124) first converts //r// into an obstruent when it precedes an obstruent. Since there is no mention of a change in voicing, the result is presumably /d/. Since this rule follows the voicing assimilation rule involved in [27]–[29], the suffix remains /ta/. A later rule (McCawley 1968:125), needed for other reasons, assimilates the first consonant in a cluster to the second in voicing. The derivation in [30] illustrates these two additional rules.

[30]

	'approach'
Underlying form	//yor + ta//
r → obs / — obs	yod + ta
Voicing assimilation II	yot + ta

The rules in this section will account for the past forms of all regular verbs. The underlying forms of the suffixes historically related to the past (section 12.2.5.2) all begin with //t// and therefore trigger the same changes as the past suffix.

12.4.5 Recapitulating History

Generative phonology is a direct descendant of American descriptivist morphophonemic analysis. Distinctive features and a quasi-algebraic notation give generative descriptions a superficially very different look, but the analytical techniques have remained essentially unchanged.

The principal difference between the two approaches is the status attributed to the basic/underlying forms of morphemes. Lounsbury (1953:380) says the following: "[Morphophonemic representation] by-passes the problem of segmenting actual forms of a language of [the fusing] type. In effect it sets up a fictitious agglutinating analog such that a one-way transformation from the analog to the actual utterances is possible, and it segments that instead." Descriptivists have typically regarded the basic forms of morphemes as descriptively convenient fictions in this way.

Generative phonologists, on the other hand, have generally attributed some kind of psychological reality to their underlying forms. Of course, many generativists effectively insulate their psychological claims from empirical disconfirmation by invoking the notion of an "ideal speaker-hearer" (Lightner 1975:636). The generative approach has been criticized for a variety of reasons, and the interested reader can find detailed arguments and good bibliographies in Derwing (1973) and Linell (1979).

The purpose of this section is to consider the question of whether the rules in a morphophonemic/generative analysis simply mirror historical changes in the language under study. Lounsbury (1953:379) calls morphophonemic analysis "the method of internal reconstruction," because "whether the orientation be historical or avowedly synchronic, it is usually based on an operation which is similar to that of reconstruction from internal evidence." This does not mean, however, that the basic forms of morphemes are necessarily identical to the actual forms of some earlier stage of the language, or that the morphophonemic rules necessarily mirror actual phonological changes. As Lounsbury (1953:381) points out, "although strictly agglutinating languages have doubtless existed . . . there are no grounds for supposing that every language has descended from such a forbear simply because it is possible to construct an agglutinating morphophonemic analog to it." Nonetheless, Lounsbury agrees with Bloomfield (1939) that the basic forms often do resemble attested or reconstructed historical forms, and that the morphophonemic rules often correspond to documented or inferred phonological changes.

By the time Bloch did his work on Japanese, the morphophonemic approach had fallen out of favor to some extent. Bloch does not set up basic forms but segments actual forms and speaks in terms of morpheme alternants. Lounsbury (1953:381) says, "It may be argued that the method of morpheme alternants is the more realistic procedure since it deals with the segmentation of actual utterances rather than with constructs once removed from reality." The morphophonemic approach is, of course, central to generative phonology, and McCawley's treatment illustrates it very well.

Some critics have condemned generative phonological analysis as the pseudo-synchronic presentation of diachronic facts (Sampson 1980, ch. 8). Defenders have therefore tried to show that generative analyses do not recapitulate history exactly, even though there is a substantial overlap (Chomsky and Halle 1968:249–252). At the same time, some phonologists have argued that analyses which mirror historical changes are preferable to those which do not (Lass 1976:26–27). What is interesting about McCawley's analysis of Japanese in this connection is that it diverges from what we know about the history of Japanese in several respects.

The rules that obviously differ from known historical changes are those that account for the past forms. As we saw in sections 7.1 and 12.2.5.1, the onbin changes have altered the past forms, and this is why two conjunctional stems are required for each five-row (i.e., consonant) verb in the traditional Japanese analysis. The forms in [31] illustrate the changes.

[31]

	Older Form	Modern Form	
a.	/kaɸitari/	/kaQta/	'bought'
b.	/kakitari/	/kaita/	'wrote'
c.	/kagitari/	/kaida/	'sniffed'
d.	/kasitari/	/kašita/	'lent'
e.	/katitari/	/kaQta/	'won'
f.	/sinitari/	/šiNda/	'died'
g.	/yobitari/	/yoNda/	'called'
h.	/yomitari/	/yoNda/	'read'
i.	/yoritari/	/yoQta/	'approached'

The forms in [31] make it clear that the /i/ in the modern forms of 'wrote' [31b], 'sniffed' [31c], and 'lent' [31d] is historically not epenthetic. The older forms of all verbs had the vowel, and it was lost in most cases. Thus, the epenthesis rule involved in [28] does not recapitulate the historical change. There is also a related discrepancy involving the //k g// → /h/ spirantization rule that applies to produce forms like /kaita/ [31b] and /kaida/ [31c]. There is no evidence that the /k/ and /g/ in the older forms ever fell together with /h/.

The voicing assimilation rule illustrated in [27] seems plausible, assuming that /i/ simply disappeared from the older forms /kagitari/ [31c] and /yobitari/ [31g]. In fact, deChene and Anderson (1979:509) imply that /kagta/ and then /kagda/ preceded modern /kaida/. This is impossible, however, because consonant clusters such as /gt/ and /gd/ have never been admissible in Japanese. Thus, /kagita/ > /kagta/ > /kagda/ > /kaida/ and /yobita/ > /yobta/ > /yobda/ > /yoNda/ are historically impossible sequences. Although the actual series of events is not completely certain, McCawley's generative account certainly does not mirror the historical developments, since it begins with underlying sequences like //kag + ta// and //yob + ta// (section 12.4.4). It thus appears that McCawley's treatment is immune to some degree from the criticism that generative phonological analyses are mere recapitulations of history.

12.5 MORPHOLOGICAL ANALYSIS AND PHONOTACTICS

12.5.1 Phonotactic Admissibility

We saw in section 12.2.4 that the syllabic writing system constrains the segmentation of words into morphs in the traditional Japanese analysis; the morphs must consist of phonotactically admissible syllables. The descriptivist analysis is not constrained in this way, as the divisions in section 12.3.2 show. The generative account does not segment actual forms but morpheme-invariant underlying forms, and as the verb stems in section 12.4.2 show, these underlying forms are free to violate surface phonotactics. In this section I will briefly consider the role of phonotactics in phonology and morphology.

12.5.2 Conspiracies

In early generative phonology (Halle 1959), surface phonotactics have no independent status, but regularities in the underlying forms of morphemes play a major role. These regularities are expressed as MORPHEME STRUCTURE RULES (Hyman 1975:105–108), which fill in predictable feature values in the segments of underlying forms. The idea is that individual morphemes can then be left unspecified for these predictable values. This elimination of redundant information from underlying forms simplifies the overall description of a language. A single rule, stated once, can fill in redundant features in a large number of individual items.

Stanley (1967) argues that the economical statement of underlying forms is not the real reason for stating redundancies. He suggests that static MORPHEME STRUCTURE CONDITIONS (Hyman 1975:108–113) should replace the blank-filling morpheme structure rules. The role of these conditions is to express the constraints on the phonological makeup of underlying morphemes.

Stanley also addresses a question raised by Ferguson (1962) in his review of Halle (1959). Ferguson suggests that it is unfortunate to have to split phonological rules into two types, that is, into morpheme structure rules and (other) phonological rules. As Stanley makes clear, it is unfortunate because some rules seem to function both as morpheme structure rules and as phonological rules.

Russian, for example, requires that obstruent clusters be homogeneous in voicing (aside from some problems with labiodental fricatives; see Halle 1959:61). This requirement applies to underlying forms, and whatever the underlying forms of /stol/ 'table' and /zdan,ije/ 'building' might be, they will certainly start with //st// and //zd//. Given that //t// is voiceless, the fact that //s// is voiceless is clearly redundant, since the homogeneity requirement constrains underlying forms. Parallel remarks apply to //d// and //z//.

The same homogeneity requirement comes into play when morphemes are combined. Thus, the preposition //iz// 'from' appears as /is/ before a voiceless obstruent and as /iz/ elsewhere. The preposition //s// 'with' appears as /z/ before a voiced obstruent and as /s/ elsewhere. It thus appears that the same constraint on obstruent clusters is involved in the redundancy statements that apply to underlying forms and in the changes that apply when morphemes are combined.

Stanley (1967:406–408) proposes a convention to the effect that a morpheme structure condition applies automatically at any stage of a derivation when the output violates the constraint. This convention would obviate the need to state the same constraint as both a morpheme structure condition and a phonological rule. The problem with this proposal is that there are any number of different ways to bring an offending sequence into conformity. The notion of a phonological CONSPIRACY is a reflection of this problem. Kisseberth (1970), for example, analyzes Yawelmani (an Amerindian language of California) in such a way that no underlying forms contain three-consonant clusters. Whenever such a cluster arises in the course of a derivation, it is eliminated. Several different rules "conspire" to eliminate such clusters, and in some cases the notational conventions of generative phonology do not make it possible to collapse these functionally related rules. Vowel epenthesis and consonant deletion can both eliminate clusters, and Kisseberth's analysis involves both.

Shibatani (1973) contends that SURFACE PHONETIC CONSTRAINTS, rather than constraints on underlying forms, motivate conspiracies. In Kisseberth's analysis of Yawelmani, it happens that the constraint against three-consonant clusters also holds in underlying forms. Even if this were not true, however, the surface phonotactic pattern would still serve as the "target" for the conspiracy.

To illustrate this point, consider the generative analysis in section 12.4. The only possible syllable-final consonants in Japanese are /N/ and /Q/, but McCawley's underlying forms do not in general obey this constraint. Violations are eliminated in several ways, including epenthesis (e.g., //kas// + //ta//→ /kašita/) and deletion (e.g., //kas// + //ru// → /kasu/). Shibatani's conclusion is that surface phonetic constraints are necessary in addition to morpheme structure conditions.

Hooper (1975) goes a step further and argues that the morpheme is not an appropriate unit for phonotactic constraints at all. Her suggestion is that SYLLABLE STRUCTURE CONDITIONS can take care of surface phonotactics, and that there is no need for morpheme structure conditions in addition. Clayton (1976) also claims that surface phonotactic constraints alone are sufficient, and her article is a good review of the various roles suggested for phonotactics within generative phonology.

It should be clear at this point that given McCawley's underlying forms, many of the rules in the generative analysis in section 12.4 are motivated by the surface phonotactic pattern of Japanese. I will now consider the suggestion that underlying forms which violate the surface phonotactic pattern of a language should not be allowed.

12.5.3 Surface Phonotactics and Morphemic Segmentation

Hale (1973) presents evidence from Maori (the language of the native inhabitants of New Zealand) which suggests that speakers do not analyze words into morphs that violate the surface phonotactic pattern of the language. Since this example is widely known and has been repeated many times (Kiparsky 1978:38–40, Hyman 1975:184–185), I will illustrate the same point with data from a less frequently cited article.

Campbell (1974:269–270), in a phonological analysis of Kekchi (an Amerindian language of Guatemala), suggests a phonological rule of consonant-cluster simplification. In his words, "The final consonant of a word-final cluster is deleted unless it is k, q, s, or š (or in a recent Spanish loan)." The examples in [32] illustrate a few of the alternations that this rule accounts for. (The word for 'musical instrument' [32d] is apparently /kwax/ for some speakers and /kwaxb'/ for others.)

[32] a. /kab'/ 'house'
   /kab'lak/ 'to make a house'
b. /mol/ 'egg'
   /molb'ek/ 'to lay eggs'
c. /¢'ax/ 'dirty'
   /¢'axnok/ 'to get dirty'
d. /kwax(b')/ / 'musical instrument'
   /kwaxb'ak/ 'to play a musical instrument'

Each verb in [32] ends with /Vk/, and the consonant that precedes this /Vk/ is not predictable. It therefore seems reasonable to posit an underlying form for each stem that contains whatever consonant appears in the suffixed form. The consonant-cluster simplification rule is then necessary to delete the underlying final consonant when it ends up in word-final position.

Campbell (1974:278) says, "In Kekchi, with typically monosyllabic roots, vowel or consonant clusters arise normally only in polymorphemic forms." This restriction suggests that underlying forms such as //kab'l// or //¢'axn// are phonotactically anomalous, although Campbell does not say so explicitly. He does, however, provide evidence that speakers of Kekchi segment the suffixed forms in [32] so that the stem is identical to the unsuffixed form. This evidence comes from native speakers trained in morphological analysis. Campbell reports that these speakers were certain that the segmentation of the suffixed forms should be /kab' + lak/ [32a], /mol + b'ek/ [32b], /¢'ax + nok/ [32c], etc. In the case of /kwaxb'ak/ [32d], speakers who say /kwax/ segment it /kwax + b'ak/, and those who say /kwaxb'/ segment it /kwaxb' + ak/.

Campbell (1974:275) interprets these segmentations as evidence for Hale's (1973:419–420) suggestion that "there is a tendency in the acquisition of a language for linguistic forms to be analyzed in a way which minimizes the necessity to postulate underlying phonological representations of morphemes which violate the universal surface canonical patterns of the language." By "universal" Hale means "exceptionless within the language," and it is not clear whether Spanish loans violate the phonotactic patterns that apply to the native Kekchi words in Campbell's examples. This difficulty aside, however, the point should be clear.

It is important to note that in Kekchi (and in Maori as well), the phonotactically admissible stem is identical to an actual word form (ignoring allophonic details). Kekchi speakers analyze each suffixed form in [32] as consisting of the unsuffixed form plus some additional material. Linell (1979:81, 83) argues that, in general, "speakers . . . use concrete word forms, not abstract morphemes, as the operands of morphological operations," and that "these operations consist, if possible, in the mere addition of affixes." It is obvious that any actual word form is phonotactically admissible, but a phonotactically admissible sequence is not necessarily an actual word form. The requirement that a stem be identical to a concrete word form is therefore more stringent than the requirement that morphs be phonotactically admissible.

It is easy to analyze the forms of any Japanese vowel verb into an invariant stem plus suffixes. The traditional Japanese treatment does not do so for the reasons given in section 12.2.4, but the descriptivist treatment in section 12.3 and the generative treatment in section 12.4 both do. Not only is the descriptivist/generative stem of any vowel verb invariant, it is phonotactically admissible and identical to an actual word form, namely, the continuative.

Consonant verbs, on the other hand, do not allow such neat segmentation. The descriptivist analysis yields stems that are not invariant (e.g., /yob/~/yoN/), and few of these stems are either phonotactically admissible or identical to an actual word form. The generative analysis gives invariant stems, but all these underlying forms are phonotactically inadmissible and a fortiori not identical to any actual word form. The traditional Japanese analysis, on the other hand, has phonotactically admissible stems, and the analysis of each stem into an invariant root plus a stem-forming suffix (section 12.2.2) even gives us invariance of a sort. Several of the stem-forming suffixes are empty morphs, but this is not a very strong objection.

A much more serious problem is that in order to have roots that are both invariant and phonotactically admissible, the consonant in the stem-forming suffixes of each verb must be totally unpredictable. For example, both /yobu/ 'call' [10] and /yomu/ 'read' [11] have the verb root /yo/, and most of the stem-forming suffixes begin with /b/ in one case and with /m/ in the other. In spite of the clumsiness of this analysis, however, it is clearly in line with the analysis that Kekchi speakers make.

It thus appears that the traditional Japanese analysis may in fact be closer than the alternatives to what speakers of Japanese actually do with consonant verbs. It would certainly be a mistake to reject it without considering any additional evidence. The experiments described in the following section were designed to shed some light on this question.

12.6   EXPERIMENTAL EVIDENCE

12.6.1   Experimental Design

Akinaga (1966:45) makes the following remarks about Japanese verb forms (the translation is mine).

We conjugate verbs we have never used before without conscious thought, and we seldom make mistakes. This is because we have in our heads something like the grammatical rules for how the different groups of verbs conjugate, and we analogize from the verbs we know without conscious thought.

In designing the experiment described here, my intention was to test the claim that Japanese speakers can extrapolate from the verb forms they know and correctly conjugate verbs they have never heard before. I limited the experiment to consonant verbs, since such extrapolation is clearly much easier for vowel verbs.

The instrument was a simple questionnaire, and I give a translation of the instructions in [33].

> **[33]** All sorts of so-called student words are popular at Japanese colleges. The purpose of this survey is to study four verbs that are currently in use at X College.
>
> On each page there is one verb, its meaning, and an example of its use. There are also five example sentences containing blanks, and under each example sentence there are three forms of the verb on that page.
>
> Student words of this kind are slang, and there is no right or wrong, but supposing they were standard Japanese, choose the form that seems appropriate for each blank and circle it. A standard Japanese word corresponding to the form to be chosen for each blank is given in parentheses after each example sentence.

In fact, I simply made up the four words I identified as student slang verbs.

Following the instructions, on the same page, I provided an example of how to proceed involving the made-up verb /hacu/, which I identified as student slang and defined as /haǰimeru/, an actual vowel verb meaning 'begin'. This example had the same format as the actual test items, except that I had already circled the "correct" answers. I give this example in [34], with translated portions in brackets and the rest in phonemic transcription. The actual questionnaire, of course, was in ordinary Japanese orthography, with the made-up forms spelled in hiragana.

[34] [student slag verb] hacu [meaning] haǰimeru
[sample] sugu *hacu* N da Qte sa   (haǰimeru)

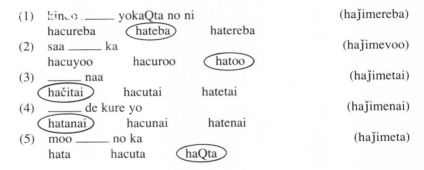

The sample sentence gives the nonpast (the citation form) of the made-up verb /hacu/ in a natural context, and the form in the following parentheses is the nonpast of /haǰimeru/, that is, the equivalent real word. The five sentence frames are natural contexts for five different forms of /hacu/: the conditional, the volitional, the desiderative, the negative, and the past. The parentheses after each sentence frame contain the appropriate form of /haǰimeru/, and the analogically correct form of /hacu/ is circled in each case.

In [35] I list the four made-up verbs involved in the actual test items, along with the real Japanese verbs I used to define them.

[35] *Made-up Verb*   *Real Verb*
    /homu/   /deru/ 'leave'
    /hoku/   /taberu/ 'eat'
    /yonu/   /neru/ 'sleep'
    /kapu/   /miru/ 'look'

The four made-up verbs differ with respect to the basis for extrapolation. There are many real consonant verbs with nonpast forms ending in /mu/ or /ku/, but the only real verb with a nonpast form ending in /nu/ is /šinu/ 'die'. There are no real verbs with nonpast forms ending in /pu/. I chose vowel verbs for all the real verbs in [35] so that the parenthesized forms after the sentence frames on the questionnaire would not show consonant-verb allomorphy.

In [36] I give the three choices provided for each test item on the questionnaire, using @ to mark the analogically correct forms.

Since there are no real verbs with nonpast forms ending in /pu/, the forms marked as analogically correct in [36d] are simply the obvious choices based on the patterns for consonant verbs that we have considered in this chapter. Because of a typographical error, the analogically correct volitional form /kapoo/ did not appear on the questionnaire, and I will ignore this item in reporting the results. I have marked two of the past forms in [36d] with @ because both /kaQta/, on the model of /kaQta/ 'won' (nonpast /kacu/), and /kapita/, on the model of /kašita/ 'lent' (nonpast /kasu/), are reasonable analogies.

I selected the "incorrect" forms in [36] from the responses I collected in a pilot study. The questionnaire for this pilot study had almost the same format as the one described here, but I required the subjects to fill in the blanks in the sentence frames rather than giving them three forms from which to choose.

The questionnaire described here was administered to fifty students in an advertising class at Sagami Women's College in Kanagawa Prefecture near Tokyo in the fall of 1984. All the students were second-year Japanese literature majors in the junior college division, and all were from Tokyo or Kanagawa.

[36] **a.** Made-up verb /homu/
        Conditional   /homureba/
                                    @/homeba/
                                    /homereba/

Volitional	/homuyoo/
	/homuroo/
	@/homoo/
Desiderative	@/homitai/
	/homutai/
	/hometai/
Negative	@/homanai/
	/homunai/
	/homenai/
Past	/hota/
	/homuta/
	@/hoNda/

b. Made-up verb /hoku/

Conditional	@/hokeba/
	/hokureba/
	/hokereba/
Volitional	@/hokoo/
	/hokuyoo/
	/hokeyoo/
Desiderative	/hotai/
	@/hokitai/
	/hokutai/
Negative	/honai/
	@/hokanai/
	/hokunai/
Past	@/hoita/
	/hokuQta/
	/hota/

c. Made-up verb /yonu/

Conditional	/yonureba/
	@/yoneba/
	/yonereba/
Volitional	@/yonoo/
	/yonuyoo/
	/yoneyoo/
Desiderative	@/yonitai/
	/yonutai/
	/yonetai/
Negative	/yonai/

	@/yonanai/
	/yonenai/
Past	/yota/
	@/yoNda/
	/yoneta/

d. Made-up verb /kapu/

Conditional	/kapureba/
	/kapereba/
	@/kapeba/
Volitional	/kapuyoo/
	/kapau/
	/kapuroo/
Desiderative	/kaputai/
	/kapetai/
	@/kapitai/
Negative	/kapunai/
	@/kapanai/
	/kapenai/
Past	@/kaQta/
	@/kapita/
	/kaputa/

12.6.2 Results

I give the results item by item in [37]–[40]. Here again I mark the analogically correct forms with @. The probability of twenty-three or more subjects choosing the "correct" answer for any item by random guessing is less than .05; in each case where twenty-three or more did in fact respond correctly, I give the number in boldface.

[37] /homu/

Conditional	@/homeba/	**34**
	/homureba/	16
	/homereba/	0
Volitional	@/homoo/	**31**
	/homuroo/	16
	/homuyoo/	3
Desiderative	/homutai/	22
	@/homitai/	21
	/hometai/	7

Negative	@/homanai/	**39**
	/homenai/	6
	/homunai/	5
Past	@/hoNda/	**24**
	/homuta/	14
	/hota/	12

Totals across items: 149 correct
101 incorrect

[38] /hoku/

Conditional	/hokureba/	27
	/hokereba/	14
	@/hokeba/	9
Volitional	@/hokoo/	**24**
	/hokeyoo/	14
	/hokuyoo/	12
Desiderative	@/hokitai/	**26**
	/hokutai/	19
	/hotai/	5
Negative	@/hokanai/	**33**
	/hokunai/	11
	/honai/	6
Past	@/hoita/	**31**
	/hokuQta/	16
	/hota/	3

Totals across items: 123 correct
127 incorrect

[39] /yonu/

Conditional	@/yoneba/	**29**
	/yonereba/	11
	/yonureba/	10
Volitional	@/yonoo/	**33**
	/yoneyoo/	11
	/yonuyoo/	6

Desiderative	/yonetai/	22
	@/yonitai/	15
	/yonutai/	13
Negative	/yonai/	22
	/yonenai/	17
	@/yonanai/	11
Past	@/yoNda/	20
	/yota/	15
	/yoneta/	15

Totals across items: 108 correct
142 incorrect

[40] /kapu/

Conditional	/kapureba/	26
	@/kapeba/	15
	/kapereba/	9
Desiderative	@/kapitai/	**23**
	/kaputai/	19
	/kapetai/	8
Negative	@/kapanai/	22
	/kapunai/	14
	/kapenai/	14
Past	@/kapita/	**30**
	/kaputa/	13
	@/kaQta/	7

To compare the results for /kapu/ with those for the other three made-up verbs, I consider only the conditional, desiderative, and negative forms. The past forms are not comparable, since there are two analogically correct answers for the past of /kapu/ (section 12.6.1). I give the totals across items in [41].

[41]

	Correct	*Incorrect*
/homu/	95	55
/hoku/	68	82
/yonu/	55	95
/kapu/	60	90

Only two of the fifty subjects chose all ten analogically correct forms for /homu/ and /hoku/. These two subjects both chose /yonai/ rather than /yonanai/

as the negative of /yonu/, but they chose all the analogically correct forms for /kapu/, including /kaQta/ for the past.

12.6.3 Discussion

The most obvious implication of the results in section 12.6.2 is that ordinary speakers have a great deal of difficulty conjugating verbs they have never heard before. The questionnaire simply required the subjects to recognize the analogically correct forms, not to produce them. In spite of the relative ease of this task, the responses for the forms of /homu/, /hoku/, and /yonu/ were only 51 percent (380 out of 750) correct.

As I mentioned in section 12.6.1, the only real verb with a nonpast form ending in /nu/ is /šinu/ 'die', and it was somewhat more difficult for the subjects to recognize the analogically correct forms of /yonu/ than to recognize those of /homu/ or /hoku/. The mean number of correct responses (out of 5.00) per subject was 2.98 for the forms of /homu/, 2.46 for the forms of /hoku/, and 2.16 for the forms of /yonu/. The results of Wilcoxon tests indicate that the difference between the means is statistically significant for /homu/ versus /yonu/ (p < .005) but not for /homu/ versus /hoku/ (p > .1) or /hoku/ versus /yonu/ (p > .2).

The difference in the number of correct responses for the forms of /homu/ and /hoku/ is due almost entirely to the fact that the conditional of /hoku/ proved surprisingly difficult. Only nine subjects chose analogically correct /hokeba/, while twenty-seven chose /hokureba/. By comparison, thirty-four chose analogically correct /homeba/, while only sixteen chose /homureba/. I have no explanation for this discrepancy.

The results in [41] indicate that speakers find a made-up verb with a nonpast ending in /pu/ about as difficult to conjugate as a made-up verb with a nonpast ending in a syllable that actually occurs in real verbs. Since there is no unambiguously correct past form for /kapu/ (section 12.6.1), I consider only the conditional, desiderative, and negative forms. The mean number of correct responses (out of 3.00) per subject was 1.90 for the forms of /homu/, 1.36 for the forms of /hoku/, 1.20 for the forms of /kapu/, and 1.10 for the forms of /yonu/. The results of Wilcoxon tests indicate that the difference between the means is statistically significant for /homu/ versus /kapu/ (p < .001) but not for /hoku/ versus /kapu/ (p > .4) or /yonu/ versus /kapu/ (p > .9).

The difficulty speakers have conjugating made-up verbs is consistent with a model of the kind Vennemann (1974:349) advocates.

> All paradigms are treated as lists in the lexicon. Differences in the regularities of paradigms are entirely captured by degrees of regularity of the rules, which function entirely as redundancy rules for forms already registered in the lexicon, and as generative rules only when unknown words are adapted to the lexicon, or new words are created by a speaker (where "new" can mean both 'new to the speaker' and 'new to the language as a whole').

As far as Japanese verb morphology is concerned, this proposal amounts to claiming that speakers memorize the forms of verbs they know and do not ordinarily use the regularities that exist as productive rules. When forced to use an unfamiliar form, as on the questionnaire, most speakers are not very good at extrapolating from the available patterns. As we saw in sections 12.1–12.4, the patterns in consonant verbs are fairly complex.

This raises the question of how the regularities in Japanese verb morphology are maintained if the patterns are not readily accessible to most native speakers. My suggestion is that even a small minority of speakers who can apply the regularities to novel forms is sufficient to keep the system fairly stable. It seems reasonable to assume that speakers who cannot use the regularities as productive rules have no strong feelings about what forms of an unfamiliar verb are correct. If speakers who can use the regularities this way do have strong feelings, their judgments will probably prevail (Vance 1980b:263–264). When insecure speakers coin irregular forms, confident speakers will generally reject them, and this rejection works to preserve the regularities.

I mentioned above that there was no dramatic difference in difficulty on the questionnaire between /kapu/ and the made-up verbs with nonpast forms ending in syllables that occur in real verbs. This fact suggests that the subjects handled /kapu/ in the same way as the other verbs. Further support for this conclusion comes from the fact that the two subjects who chose all the analogically correct forms for /homu/ and /hoku/ also chose all correct forms for /kapu/ (section 12.6.2). Thus, to the extent that speakers can correctly conjugate unfamiliar verbs at all, they seem to extrapolate the same way from nonpast forms ending in impossible syllables as from those ending in possible syllables.

This parallel extrapolation is evidence that speakers who can use the regularities in the system as productive rules segment words into phonotactically inadmissible consonant-final morphs. To illustrate why, we can compare the conditional of /homu/ with the conditional of /kapu/. Since there are real verbs like /yomu/ 'read' (conditional /yomeba/), it is possible to form the conditional of /homu/ analogically in terms of phonotactically admissible pieces, as in [42].

[42] /ho-mu/   /yo-mu/
       /ho-meba/   /yo-meba/

For the conditional of /kapu/, however, there are no real verb forms ending in /pu/ and /peba/ to serve as models. In other words, the analogy must be something like [43].

[43] /kap-u/   /...C-u/
                         (where C $\neq$ /p/)
       /kap-eba/   /...C-eba/

It thus appears that phonotactically inadmissible morphs cannot simply be ruled out in principle (section 12.5).

This conclusion does not necessarily mean that the American descriptivist morpheme divisions in section 12.3 are correct. It is also consistent with a modified version of the traditional Japanese six-stem system (section 12.2.2) in which vowel-initial stem-forming suffixes are added to consonant-final verb roots. This is essentially the analysis that Tsukishima (1964:117–118) proposes, and the forms of /yomu/ 'read' in [44] provide some illustrations.

[44] Negative   /yom + a + nai/
                     (indefinite stem + /nai/)
     Continuative   /yom + i/
                     (conjunctional stem)
     Nonpast   /yom + u/
                     (final stem)
     Conditional   /yom + e + ba/
                     (hypothetical stem + /ba/)

REFERENCES

Abercrombie, D. (1967) *Elements of General Phonetics*. Chicago: Aldine-Atherton.

Abercrombie, D., et al., eds. (1964) *In Honour of Daniel Jones*. London: Longman.

Abramson, A. S. (1962) *The Vowels and Tones of Standard Thai: Acoustical Measurements and Experiments*. Supplement to *International Journal of American Linguistics*.

Adams, D., et al., eds. (1971) *Papers from the Seventh Regional Meeting of the Chicago Linguistic Society*. Chicago: Chicago Linguistic Society.

Akinaga, K. (1966) Kyōtsūgo no Akusento. In Nihon Hōsō Kyōkai (1966: 45–90).

Anttila, R. (1972) *An Introduction to Historical and Comparative Linguistics*. New York: Macmillan.

Aoki, T. (1976) Kymograph ni Yoru Nichi-Ei Haretsuon no Hikaku Kenkyū. *Onsei no Kenkyū* 17, 197–209.

Arisaka, H. (1940) *On'inron*. Tokyo: Sanseidō. [References are to the 1959 expanded edition.]

Beckman, M. (1982) Segment Duration and the "Mora" in Japanese. *Phonetica* 39, 113–135.

Bell, A. (1975) If Speakers Can't Count Syllables, What Can They Do? [Distributed by the Indiana University Linguistics Club.]

Binnick, R. I., et al., eds. (1969) *Papers from the Fifth Regional Meeting of the Chicago Linguistic Society*. Chicago: Chicago Linguistic Society.

Bjarkman, P. C. (1975) Toward a Proper Conception of Processes in Natural Phonology. In Grossman, San, and Vance (1975:60–72).

Bloch, B. (1941) Phonemic Overlapping. *American Speech* 16, 278–284.

———. (1946a) Studies in Colloquial Japanese I: Inflection. *Journal of the American Oriental Society* 66, 97–109. [References are to the version in Miller (1970:1–24).]

———. (1946b) Studies in Colloquial Japanese II: Syntax. *Language* 22, 200–248. [References are to the version in Miller (1970:25–89).]

———. (1946c) Studies in Colloquial Japanese III: Derivation of Inflected Words. *Journal of the American Oriental Society* 66, 304–315. [References are to the version in Miller (1970:90–112).]

———. (1950) Studies in Colloquial Japanese IV: Phonemics. *Language* 26, 86–125. [References are to the version in Miller (1970:113–165).]

Bloomfield, L. (1933) *Language*. New York: Holt.

———. (1939) Menomini Morphophonemics. *Travaux du Cercle Linguistique de Prague* 8, 105–115.

Bruck, A.; Fox, R. A.; and LaGaly, M. W., eds. (1974) *Papers from the Parasession on Natural Phonology*. Chicago: Chicago Linguistic Society.

Bynon, T. (1977) *Historical Linguistics*. Cambridge: Cambridge University Press.

Campbell, L. (1974) Theoretical Implications of Kekchi Phonology. *International Journal of American Linguistics* 40, 269–278.

Catford, J. C. (1977) *Fundamental Problems in Phonetics*. Bloomington: Indiana University Press.

Chomsky, N.; and Halle, M. (1968) *The Sound Pattern of English*. New York: Harper and Row.

Clark, H. H.; and Clark, E. V. (1977) *Psychology and Language*. New York: Harcourt Brace Jovanovich.

Clayton, M. L. (1976) The Redundancy of Underlying Morpheme-Structure Conditions. *Language* 52,295–313.

Clyne, P. R.; Hanks, W. F.; and Hofbauer, C. L., eds. (1979) *Papers from the Fifteenth Regional Meeting of the Chicago Linguistic Society*. Chicago: Chicago Linguistic Society.

Darden, B. J. (1971) Diachronic Evidence for Phonemics. In Adams et al. (1971:323–331).

deChene, B.; and Anderson, S. R. (1979) Compensatory Lengthening. *Language* 55, 505–535.

Derwing, B. L. (1973) *Transformational Grammar as a Theory of Language Acquisition*. Cambridge: Cambridge University Press.

Dingwall, W. O., ed. (1978) *A Survey of Linguistic Science*. Stamford: Greylock.

Dinnsen, D. A., ed. (1979) *Current Approaches to Phonological Theory*. Bloomington: Indiana University Press.

Donegan, P. J.; and Stampe, D. (1979) The Study of Natural Phonology. In Dinnsen (1979:126–173).

Edwards, E. R. (1903) Étude phonologique de la langue japonaise. Sorbonne doctoral thesis. [References are to the Japanese translation by Y. Takamatsu (1969), *Nihongo no Onseigakuteki Kenkyū*, Tokyo, Kōseisha Kōseikaku.]

Elert, C.-C. (1964) *Phonologic Studies of Quantity in Swedish*. Stockholm: Almqvist and Wiksell.

Elimelech, B. (1976) A Tonal Grammar of Etsako. *UCLA Working Papers in Phonetics* 35.

Endō, K. (1966) Rendakugo no Yure. *Kokugo Kokubun* 35(5),68–77.

Endō, Y. (1955) Onbin. In Kokugo Gakkai (1955:119–120).

Ferguson, C. H. (1962) Review of Halle (1959). *Language* 38, 284–298.

Firth, J. R. (1948) Sounds and Prosodies. *Transactions of the Philological Society*, 127–152.

Fromkin, V. A. (1972) Discussion Paper on Speech Physiology. In Gilbert (1972:73–105).

————, ed. (1978) *Tone: A Linguistic Survey*. New York: Academic Press.

Fromkin, V. A.; and Rodman, R. (1983) *An Introduction to Language*, 3rd ed. New York: Holt, Rinehart and Winston.

Fujikawa, K., and Hio, A. (1974) *Uchū Senkan Yamato*, vol. 1. Tokyo: Asahi Sonorama.

Fujimoto, H.; and Abiko, S. (1974) *Doraemon*, vol. 1. Tokyo: Shōgakukan.

Fukushima, K. (1963) Renjō to Yomikuse. *Kokugogaku* 52, 28–36.

Furuta, T.; and Tsukishima, H. (1972) *Kokugogakushi*. Tokyo: Tōkyō Daigaku.

Gilbert, J. H., ed. (1972) *Speech and Cortical Functioning*. New York: Academic Press.

Goldsmith, J. (1976) Autosegmental Phonology. MIT doctoral dissertation. [Distributed by the Indiana University Linguistics Club.]

————. (1979) The Aims of Autosegmental Phonology. In Dinnsen (1979:202–222).

Grossman, R. E.; San, L. J.; and Vance, T. J., eds. (1975) *Papers from the Eleventh Regional Meeting of the Chicago Linguistic Society*. Chicago: Chicago Linguistic Society.

Habein, Y. S. (1984) *The History of the Japanese Written Language*. Tokyo: Tokyo University Press.

Hale, K. (1973) Deep-Surface Canonical Disparities in Relation to Analysis and Change: An Australian Example. In Sebeok (1973:401–458).

Halle, M. (1959) *The Sound Pattern of Russian*. The Hague: Mouton.

Hamada, A. (1952) Hatsuon to Dakuon to no Sōkansei no Mondai. *Kokugo Kokubun* 21(4), 18–32.

————. (1955a) Haneru On. In Kokugo Gakkai (1955:750–751).

————. (1955b) Kokugo On'in Taikei ni Okeru Chōon no Ichi: Toku ni O-dan Chōon no Mondai. *Kokugogaku* 22, 31–48.

————. (1955c) Tsumaru On. In Kokugo Gakkai (1955:655–656).

————. (1960) Rendaku to Renjō. *Kokugo Kokubun* 29(10),1–16.

Han, M. S. (1962a) The Feature of Duration in Japanese. *Onsei no Kenkyū* 10, 65–80.

————. (1962b) Unvoicing of Vowels in Japanese. *Onsei no Kenkyū* 10, 81–100.

Haraguchi, S. (1977) *The Tone Pattern of Japanese: An Autosegmental Theory of Tonology*. Tokyo: Kaitakusha.

Harris, Z. S. (1944) Simultaneous Components in Phonology. *Language* 20, 181–205.

Hasegawa, N. (1979) Casual Speech vs. Fast Speech. In Clyne, Hanks, and Hofbauer (1979:126–137).

Hashimoto, S. (1917) Kokugo Kanazukai Kenkyūshijō no Ichihakken. *Teikoku Bungaku* 23. [References are to the version in Hashimoto (1949:123–163).]

————. (1928) Ha-gyō Shiin no Henken ni Tsuite. *Okakura-sensei Kinen Ronbunshū*. [References are to the version in Hashimoto (1950a:29–45).]

————. (1932) Kokugo ni Okeru Biboin. *Hōgen* 2. [References are to the version in Hashimoto (1950a:1–9).]

————. (1937) Kokugo no Onsetsu Kōzō to Boin no Tokusei. *Kokugo to Kokubungaku* 19. [References are to the version in Hashimoto (1950a:201–228).]

————. (1938) Kokugo On'in no Hensen. *Kokugo to Kokubungaku* 15. [References are to the version in Hashimoto (1950a:51–103).]

————. (1942) *Kodai Kokugo no On'in ni Tsuite.* Tokyo: Meiseidō. [References are to the version in Hashimoto (1950a:105–199).]

————. (1948) Kokugo no Onsetsu Kōzō no Tokushitsu ni Tsuite. *Kokugogaku* 1. [References are to the version in Hashimoto (1950a:229–260).]

————. (1949) *Moji oyobi Kanazukai no Kenkyū.* Tokyo: Iwanami.

————. (1950a) *Kokugo On'in no Kenkyū.* Tokyo: Iwanami.

————. (1950b) Nihon Bungaku Daijiten Kaisetsu. In Hashimoto (1950a: 273–340). [Written ca. 1931.]

————. (1966a) *Kokugo On'inshi.* Tokyo: Iwanami.

————. (1966b) Kokugo Onseishi no Kenkyū (Shōwa Ninendo). In Hashimoto (1966a:1–186). [Based on 1927 lectures.]

Hattori, S. (1930) "N" ni Tsuite. *Onsei no Kenkyū* 3, 41–47.

————. (1939–40) Phoneme ni Tsuite. *Onseigaku Kyōkai Kaihō* 59/61. [References are to the version in Hattori (1960:229–239).]

————. (1950) Phone, Phoneme, and Compound Phone. *Gengo Kenkyū* 16. [References are to the version in Hattori (1960: 751–763).]

————. (1951) *Onseigaku.* Tokyo: Iwanami.

————. (1954) On'inron kara Mita Nihongo no Akusento. *Kokugo Kenkyū* 2. [References are to the version in Hattori (1960:240–272).]

————. (1955) On'inron (1). *Kokugogaku* 22. [References are to the version in Hattori (1960:279–301).]

————. (1956) On'inron (2). *Kokugogaku* 26. [References are to the version in Hattori (1960:302–322).]

————. (1957) On'inron (3). *Kokugogaku* 29. [References are to the version in Hattori (1960:323–352).]

————. (1958) Nihongo no On'in. In *Sekai Dai Hyakka Jiten*, vol. 22. [References are to the version in Hattori (1960:360–364).]

————. (1960) *Gengogaku no Hōhō.* Tokyo: Iwanami.

Hattori, S., et al. (1957) Nihongo no Boin. *Kobayashi Rigaku Kenkyūjo Hōkoku* 7. [References are to the version in Shibata, Kitamura, and Kindaichi (1980: 68–99).]

Hibiya, J. (to appear) Phonological Variation in Spoken Japanese in Tokyo. *Proceedings of the Thirteenth Annual Colloquium on New Ways of Analyzing Variation.* Georgetown University Press.

Higurashi, Y. (1983) *The Accent of Extended Word Structures in Tokyo Japanese.* Tokyo: Educa.

Hirayama, T., ed. (1960) *Zenkoku Akusento Jiten.* Tokyo: Tōkyōdō.

Hockett, C. F. (1947) Problems in Morphemic Analysis. *Language* 23, 321–343.

————. (1955) *Manual of Phonology.* Memoir 11, *International Journal of American Linguistics.*

————. (1958) *A Course in Modern Linguistics.* New York: Macmillan.

Homma, Y. (1973) An Acoustic Study of Japanese Vowels. *Onsei no Kenkyū* 16, 347–368.

————. (1980) Voice Onset Time in Japanese Stops. *Onsei Gakkai Kaihō* 163, 7–9.

————. (1981) Durational Relationships Between Japanese Stops and Vowels. *Journal of Phonetics* 9, 273–281.

Honikman, B. (1964) Articulatory Settings. In Abercrombie et al. (1964: 73–84).

Hooper, J. B. (1975) The Archi-segment in Natural Generative Phonology. *Language* 51:536–560.

Hughes, J. P. (1962) *The Science of Language*. New York: Random House.

Hyman, L. M. (1975) *Phonology: Theory and Analysis*. New York: Holt, Rinehart and Winston.

————, ed. (1977) *Studies in Stress and Accent (SCOPIL 4)*. Los Angeles: University of Southern California Department of Linguistics.

Iizuka Shoten Henshūbu, ed. (1977) *Nihon Shōka Dōyō Shū*. Tokyo: Iizuka.

Ikeda, T. (1975) *Classical Japanese Grammar Illustrated with Texts*. Tokyo: Tōhō Gakkai.

Inoue, A. (1977) Chōon. In Satō (1977:245–246).

Inoue, F. (1971) Ga-gyō Shiin no Bunpu to Rekishi. *Kokugogaku* 86, 26–41.

Inoue, F., et al. (1983) "Shinhōgen" to "Kotoba no Midare" ni Kansuru Shakai-gengogakuteki Kenkyū—Tōkyō Shutoken, Yamagata, Hokkaidō. Shōwa 57-nendo Kagaku Kenkyūhi, Hojokin (Sōgō Kenkyu A) Kenkyū Seika Hōkokusho.

Jakobson, R.; and Kawamoto, S., eds. (1970) *Studies in General and Oriental Linguistics*. Tokyo: TEC.

Jinbō, K. (1927) Kokugo no Onseijō no Tokushitsu. *Kokugo to Kokubungaku* 4. [References are to the version in Shibata, Kitamura, and Kindaichi (1980: 5–15).]

Johns, D. A. (1969) Phonemics and Generative Phonology. In Binnick et al. (1969: 374–381).

Jones, D. (1967) *The Phoneme: Its Nature and Use*. Cambridge: Cambridge University Press.

Jōo, H. (1977) Gendai Nihongo no On'in. In Ōno and Shibata (1977a:107–145).

Joos, M., ed. (1966) *Readings in Linguistics I*, 4th ed. Chicago: University of Chicago Press.

Kamei, T. (1954) *Chinese Borrowings in Prehistoric Japanese*. Tokyo: Yoshikawa Kōbunkan.

————. (1956) Ga-gyō no Kana. *Kokugo to Kokubungaku* 39(9), 1–14.

Kamei, T.; Yamada, T.; and Ōtō, T. (1963) *Nihongo no Rekishi 1: Minzoku no Kotoba no Tanjō*. Tokyo: Heibonsha.

Kaplan, H. M. (1971) *Anatomy and Physiology of Speech*, 2nd ed. New York: McGraw-Hill.

Karlgren, B. (1923) *Analytic Dictionary of Chinese and Sino-Japanese*. Paris: Librairie Orientaliste Paul Geuthner.

Kavanaugh, J. P.; and Mattingly, I. G., eds. (1972) *Language by Ear and by Eye: The Relationship Between Speech and Reading*. Cambridge: MIT Press.

Kawakami, S. (1962) Pitchi-guramu de Mita Nihongo no Akusento. *Onsei no Kenkyū* 10, 115–129.

————. (1977) *Nihongo Onsei Gaisetsu*. Tokyo: Ōfūsha.

Keating, P. A.; Mikoś, M. J.; and Ganong, W. F. (1981) A Cross-Language Study of

Range of Voice Onset Time in the Perception of Initial Stop Voicing. *Journal of the Acoustical Society of America* 70, 1261–1271.

Kindaichi, H. (1942) Ga-gyō Bionron. *Gendai Nihongo no Kenkyū*. [References are to the version in Kindaichi (1967b:168–197).]

———. (1950) "Satooya" to "Satōya": Hikionsetsu no Teishō. *Kokugo to Kokubungaku* 27. [References are to the version in Kindaichi (1967b:133–153).]

———. (1954) Haneru On, Tsumaru On. [References are to the version in Kindaichi (1967b:154–167).]

———. (1963) Hatsuon kara Mita Nihongo. *Nihongo Kyōiku* 3. [References are to the version in Kindaichi (1967b:113–132).]

———. (1965) On'inron Tan'i no Kō. *Gengo Kenkyū* 48. [References are to the version in Kindaichi (1967b:40–57).]

———. (1967a) Ga-gyō Bion ga Igi no Kubetsu ni Yakudatsu Rei. In Kindaichi (1967b: 430).

———. (1967b) *Nihongo On'in no Kenkyū*. Tokyo: Tōkyōdō.

———. (1967c) Onsetsu, Mōra oyobi Haku. In Kindaichi (1967b:58–77).

———. (1976) Rendaku no Kai. *Sophia Linguistica* 2, 1–22.

Kindaichi, K. (1938) *Kokugo On'inron*. Tokyo: Tōe.

Kiparsky, P. (1978) Historical Linguistics. In Dingwall (1978:33–61).

Kisseberth, C. W. (1970) On the Functional Unity of Phonological Rules. *Linguistic Inquiry* 1, 291–306.

Koizumi, T. (1971) Yōroppa no On'inron. In *Eigogaku Taikei 1: On'inron I*, 1–210. Tokyo:Taishūkan.

Kokugo Gakkai, ed. (1955) *Kokugogaku Jiten*. Tokyo: Tōkyōdō.

Komatsu, S. (1978) *Amerika no Kabe*. Tokyo: Bungei Shunjū.

Kuno, S. (1973) *The Structure of the Japanese Language*. Cambridge: MIT Press.

Kuroda, S.-Y. (1965) Generative Grammatical Studies in the Japanese Language. MIT doctoral dissertation. [References are to the 1979 version, New York, Garland.]

Labov, W. (1972) *Sociolinguistic Patterns*. Philadelphia: University of Pennsylvania Press.

Ladefoged, P. (1967) *Three Areas of Experimental Phonetics*. London: Oxford University Press.

———. (1971) *Preliminaries to Linguistic Phonetics*. Chicago: University of Chicago Press.

———. (1982) *A Course in Phonetics*, 2nd ed. New York: Harcourt Brace Jovanovich.

Lange, R. A. (1973) *The Phonology of Eighth-Century Japanese*. Tokyo: Sophia University.

Lass, R. (1976) *English Phonology and Phonological Theory: Synchronic and Diachronic Studies*. Cambridge: Cambridge University Press.

Laver, J. (1978) The Concept of Articulatory Settings: An Historical Survey. *Historiographia Linguistica* 5, 1–14.

———. (1980) *The Phonetic Description of Voice Quality*. Cambridge: Cambridge University Press.

Leben, W. R. (1978) The Representation of Tone. In Fromkin (1978:177–219).

Lehiste, I. (1970) *Suprasegmentals*. Cambridge: MIT Press.

Lehmann, W. P. (1962) *Historical Linguistics: An Introduction*. New York: Holt, Rinehart and Winston.

———. (1983) *Language: An Introduction*. New York: Random House.

Lieberman, P. (1967) *Intonation, Perception, and Language.* Cambridge: MIT Press.

Lightner, T. M. (1975) The Role of Derivational Morphology in Generative Grammar. *Language* 51, 617–638.

Linell, P. (1979) *Psychological Reality in Phonology: A Theoretical Study.* Cambridge: Cambridge University Press.

Lisker, L.; and Abramson, A. S. (1964) A Cross-Language Study of Voicing in Initial Stops: Acoustical Measurements. *Word* 20, 384–422.

———. (1967) Some Effects of Context on Voice Onset Time in English Stops. *Language and Speech* 10,1–28.

———. (1971) Distinctive Features and Laryngeal Control. *Language* 47, 767–785.

Lounsbury, F. G. (1953) The Method of Descriptive Morphology. [From *Oneida Verb Morphology, Yale University Publications in Anthropology* No. 48; references are to the version in Joos (1966:379–385).]

Lyman, B. S. (1894) *Change from Surd to Sonant in Japanese Compounds.* Philadelphia: Oriental Club of Philadelphia.

Lyons, J. (1968) *Introduction to Theoretical Linguistics.* Cambridge: Cambridge University Press.

———. (1977) *Semantics*, vol. 1. Cambridge: Cambridge University Press.

McCawley, J. D. (1968) *The Phonological Component of a Grammar of Japanese.* The Hague: Mouton.

———. (1977) Accent in Japanese. In Hyman (1977:261–302).

———. (1978) What Is a Tone Language? In Fromkin (1978:113–131).

———. (1984) Today the World, Tomorrow Phonology. *Southern Illinois Working Papers in Linguistics* 12, 88–102.

McClain, Y. M. (1981) *A Handbook of Modern Japanese Grammar.* Tokyo: Hokuseidō.

Maeda, M. (1971) *Kokugo On'inron no Kōsō.* Tokyo: Keibundō.

Maeda, T. (1977a) Bidakuon. In Satō (1977:67–68).

———. (1977b) Rendaku. In Satō (1977:68).

Manaster-Ramer, A. (1981) How Abstruse in Phonology? University of Chicago doctoral dissertation.

Marchand, J. W. (1956) Internal Reconstruction of Phonemic Split. *Language* 32, 245–253.

Martin, S. E. (1952) *Morphophonemics of Standard Colloquial Japanese.* Supplement to *Language, Language Dissertation No. 47.*

———. (1967) On the Accent of Japanese Adjectives. *Language* 43, 246–277.

———. (1968) On the Forms of Japanese Adjectives. *Glossa* 2, 46–69.

———. (1970) Junctural Cues to Ellipsis in Japanese. In Jakobson and Kawamoto (1970:429–446).

———. (1972) Nonalphabetic Writing Systems: Some Observations. In Kavanaugh and Mattingly (1972:81–102).

———. (1975) *Reference Grammar of Japanese.* New Haven: Yale University Press.

Masuda, K., ed. (1974) *Kenkyusha's New Japanese-English Dictionary*, 4th ed. Tokyo: Kenkyūsha.

Matsumoto, H. (1970) Renjō Genshō no Taikeisei o Meguru Gimon. *Kokugogaku Kenkyū* 10, 11–18.

———. (1977a) Ha-gyō Tenkōon. In Satō (1977:248–249).

———. (1977b) Renjō. In Satō (1977:246–247).

———. (1977c) Wa-gyō On. In Satō (1977:239).

Matthews, P. H. (1972) *Inflectional Morphology*. Cambridge: Cambridge University Press.

————. (1974) *Morphology: An Introduction to the Theory of Word Structure*. Cambridge: Cambridge University Press.

Miller, D. G. (1975) All Rules Precede All Syntagmatic Natural Processes? *Linguistic Inquiry* 6, 171–177.

Miller, R. A. (1967) *The Japanese Language*. Chicago: University of Chicago Press.

————, ed. (1970) *Bernard Bloch on Japanese*. New Haven: Yale University Press.

Miyake, T. (1932) Dakuonkō. *Onsei no Kenkyū* 5, 135–190.

Mizutani, O. (1981) *Japanese: The Spoken Language in Daily Life*. Tokyo: Japan Times.

Morohashi, T., ed. (1957-60) *Dai Kanwa Jiten*. Tokyo: Taishūkan.

Naitō, K. (1961) On Some Japanese Peculiar Consonant Phonemes. *Onsei no Kenkyū* 9, 117–125.

Nakagawa, Y. (1966) Rendaku, Rensei (Kashō) no Keifu. *Kokugo Kokubun* 35(6), 302–314.

Nakamura, M.; and Kindaichi, H. (1955) Tōkyōgo. In Kokugo Gakkai (1955: 697–680).

Nakano, K. (1969) A Phonetic Basis for the Syllabic Nasal in Japanese. *Onsei no Kenkyū* 14, 215–228.

Nakata, N., ed. (1972a) *Kōza Nihongoshi 2: On'inshi, Mojishi*. Tokyo: Taishūkan.

————. (1972b) Sōsetsu. In Nakata (1972a:3–61).

Nakata, N.; and Tsukishima, H. (1955) Dakuten. In Kokugo Gakkai (1955: 622–623).

Nakazawa, M. (1955) Ga-gyō Bion. In Kokugo Gakkai (1955:142).

Nichieisha, ed. (1952) *Kokubunpō Yōkō*. Tokyo: Nichieisha.

Nihon Hōsō Kyōkai, ed. (1966) *Nihongo Hatsuon Akusento Jiten*. Tokyo: Nihon Hōsō.

Nihon Onsei Gakkai, ed. (1976) *Onseigaku Daijiten*. Tokyo: Sanshūsha.

O'Connor, J. D.; and Trim, J. L. M. (1953) Vowel, Consonant, and Syllable — A Phonological Definition. *Word* 2, 103–122.

Ohala, J. J. (1974) Phonetic Explanation in Phonology. In Bruck, Fox, and LaGaly (1974:251–274).

Okuda, K. (1970) Review of McCawley (1968). *Language* 46, 736–753.

————. (1971) Accentual Systems in the Japanese Dialects. UCLA doctoral dissertation.

Okumura, M. (1952) Jion no Rendaku ni Tsuite. *Kokugo Kokubun* 21(6), 8–22.

————. (1955) Rendaku. In Kokugo Gakkai (1955:961–962).

————. (1972) Kodai no On'in. In Nakata (1972a:63–171).

Ōno, S.; and Shibata, T., eds. (1977a) *Iwanami Kōza Nihongo 5: On'in*. Tokyo: Iwanami.

————, eds. (1977b) *Ianami Kōza Nihongo 7: Moji*. Tokyo: Iwanami.

Ōtsu, Y. (1980) Some Aspects of *Rendaku* in Japanese and Related Problems. In Ōtsu and Farmer (1980:207–227).

Ōtsu, Y.; and Farmer, A., eds. (1980) *Theoretical Issues in Japanese Linguistics. MIT Working Papers in Linguistics* 2.

Pike, K. L. (1947) Grammatical Prerequisites to Phonemic Analysis. *Word* 3, 155–172.

————. (1948) *Tone Languages*. Ann Arbor: University of Michigan Press.

Pye, M. (1971) *The Study of Kanji*. Tokyo: Hokuseidō.

Sakuma, K. (1929) *Nihon Onseigaku*. [References are to the 1963 reprint. Tokyo: Kazama Shobō.]

————. (1973) *Hyōjun Nihongo no Hatsuon, Akusento*, expanded ed. Tokyo: Kōseisha Kōseikaku.

Sakurai, S. (1966) Kyōtsūgo no Hatsuon de Chūi Subeki Kotogara. In Nihon Hōsō Kyōkai (1966:31–43).

————. (1972) Heian Insei Jidai ni Okeru Wago no Rendaku ni Tsuite. *Kokugo Kokubun* 41(6), 1–19.

Sampson, G. (1980) *Schools of Linguistics*. Stanford: Stanford University Press.

Sapir, E. (1921) *Language*. New York: Harcourt Brace.

Satō, K., ed. (1977) *Kokugogaku Kenkyū Jiten*. Tokyo: Meiji.

Schane, S. A. (1971) The Phoneme Revisited. *Language* 47, 503–521.

Sebeok, T. A., ed. (1973) *Current Trends in Linguistics*, vol. 11. The Hague: Mouton.

Shand, W. J. S., ed. (1907) *Japanese Self-Taught*, 3rd ed. London: E. Marlborough.

Shibata, T. (1955) Gōyōon. In Kokugo Gakkai (1955:375).

————. (1980) Akusento. In Shibata, Kitamura, and Kindaichi (1980:630–639).

Shibata, T.; Kitamura, H.; and Kindaichi, H., eds. (1980) *Nihongo no Gengogaku 2: On'in*. Tokyo: Taishūkan.

Shibatani, M. (1972) The Non-Cyclic Nature of Japanese Accentuation. *Language* 48, 584–595.

————. (1973) The Role of Surface Phonetic Constraints in Generative Phonology. *Language* 49,87–106.

Shinmura, I., ed. (1969) *Kōjien*, 2nd ed. Tokyo: Iwanami.

Sloat, C.; Taylor, S. H.; and Hoard, J. E. (1978) *Introduction to Phonology*. Englewood Cliffs: Prentice-Hall.

Smith, N. V. (1973) *The Acquisition of Phonology: A Case Study*. Cambridge: Cambridge University Press.

Someda, T. (1966) Ei, Futsugo to no Hikaku ni Okeru Nihongo no Chōon no Ippanteki Haikei ni Tsuite. *Onsei no Kenkyū* 12, 327–346.

Sommerstein, A. H. (1977) *Modern Phonology*. Baltimore: University Park Press.

Stampe, D. (1973) A Dissertation on Natural Phonology. University of Chicago doctoral dissertation.

Stanley, R. (1967) Redundancy Rules and Phonology. *Language* 43, 393–436.

Stetson, R. H. (1951) *Motor Phonetics*, 2nd ed. Amsterdam: North Holland.

Suzuki, S., et al., eds. (1975) *Kadokawa Saishin Kanwa Jiten*. Tokyo: Kadokawa.

Tagashira, Y. (1979) Two Kinds of Emphasis in Japanese. Presented at the Sixteenth Regional Meeting of the Chicago Linguistic Society, Chicago, April 18.

Takahashi, R. (1982) *Mezon Ikkoku*, vol. 2. Tokyo: Shōgakukan.

Tōdō, A. (1977) Kanji Gaisetsu. In Ōno and Shibata (1977b:61–157).

Toyama, E. (1972) Kindai no On'in. In Nakata (1972a:173–268).

Trubetzkoy, N. S. (1969) *Principles of Phonology*. Berkeley: University of California Press.

Tsukishima, H. (1964) *Kokugogaku*. Tokyo: Tōkyō Daigaku.

Ueda, M. (1982) *Matsuo Bashō*. Tokyo: Kōdansha.

Umegaki, M. (1963) *Nihon Gairaigo no Kenkyū*. Tokyo: Kenkyūsha.

————, ed. (1966) *Gairaigo Jiten*. Tokyo: Tōkyōdō.

Unger, J. M. (1975) Studies in Early Japanese Morphophonemics. Yale University doctoral dissertation. [Distributed by the Indiana University Linguistics Club.]

Uwano, Z. (1977) Nihongo no Akusento. In Ōno and Shibata (1977a:281–321).

Vance, T. J. (1979) Nonsense-Word Experiments in Phonology and Their Application to *Rendaku* in Japanese. University of Chicago doctoral dissertation.

———. (1980a) Comments on Ōtsu (1980). In Ōtsu and Farmer (1980:229–236).

———. (1980b) The Psychological Status of a Constraint on Japanese Consonant Alternation. *Linguistics* 18, 245–267.

———. (1982) On the Origin of Voicing Alternation in Japanese Consonants. *Journal of the American Oriental Society* 102, 333–341.

Vennemann, T. (1972) Rule Inversion. *Lingua* 29,209–242.

———. (1974) Words and Syllables in Natural Generative Grammar. In Bruck, Fox, and LaGaly (1974:346–374).

Weitzman, R. (1969) Word Accent in Japanese. University of Southern California doctoral dissertation.

Wells, R. S. (1949) Automatic Alternation. *Language* 25, 99–116.

Welmers, W. E. (1973) *African Language Structures*. Berkeley: University of California Press.

Yoshioka, H. (1981) Laryngeal Adjustments in the Production of the Fricative Consonants and Devoiced Vowels in Japanese. *Phonetica* 38, 236–251.

INDEX

Issues:
Is there a "mora cons"?
Is there PIP for V-devoicing, or
a variable rule referring to a
strength scale?